Praise for Laptop Dancing and the Nanny Goat Mambo

"…a brilliant read from one of the acknowledged best sports journalists in Ireland, or anywhere else for that matter…"

Books Ireland

"…impossible to put down… I heartily recommend this book as a present for sports fans everywhere – and also for fans of great writing."

Michael McLoughlin, *Sunday Business Post*

"…a book rich in background, observation, insight and humour…compulsive reading."
"Humphries is sometimes the reluctant observer…but he brings what all good sportswriters must bring us, the smell of the dressing-room and the crunch of the tackle."

Bill O'Herlihy, *The Irish Times*

"Even if you don't know your Roy from your Robbie, grab yourself a copy of Tom Humphries' *Laptop Dancing and the Nanny Goat Mambo*… Nobody does hangdog underdog quite as well as Humphries, and his tales of traipsing round the world's top sporting events are richly comic, gossipy, and literary in equal measure."

Louise East, *IMAGE*

"…brilliantly surreal…a gentle, humourous, melancholic account of a sportswriter's year."

The Dubliner

"…high-calibre sports journalism…episodes from many sports – from curling to hurling – are retold with insight, humour and self-deprecation…recommended."

Irish Independent

"…an exceptional writer… Just about every word and sentence here is beautifully chosen and flawlessly executed. It's a book that takes no time whatsoever to read, so gently rhythmic is the flow of the words. After a while, you realise that it doesn't matter how little interest anyone has in the life of a sportswriter – if Humphries was a librarian, you know he'd produce just as brilliant and funny a read."

Sunday Tribune

"The coolest memoir around this summer has to be Tom Humphries' hilarious, unputdownable *Laptop Dancing and the Nanny Goat Mambo: A Sportswriter's Year*. Sport be damned: this is reminiscent of Bill Shankly's comment about life and death and football being far more important than either/both."

The Irish Times

"…hugely entertaining…a damn good read. Grab it for the next long journey."

The Times

"In nearly 400 pages, Humphries does his best to refute the claim, familiar to all those who write about sport, that it is the best job in the world. Unfortunately, he writes so engagingly that nobody will believe him."

Dion Fanning, *Sunday Independent*

"At his best, Humphries can strip bare a subject or issue with his literary and languid prose, bringing his readers into the inner realms of sport with a dispassionate style that is laced with wit and pathos."

Phoenix

"…a spellbinding read…"

Modern Woman

"…the funniest book of sportswriting ever published in Ireland. His account of some of the goings-on in Saipan is grim, grippingly written, sad, and hilarious."

Joseph O'Connor, *Sunday Independent*

"Paranoid about being out-scooped or out-written, forced to fawn to fools to get a quote, driven by a craving for recognition as 'a real writer', this is the sportswriter as a nervous wreck."

Sunday Times

Tom Humphries

BOOKED!

(v. carefully)
Selected Writings

FOREWORD PAUL KIMMAGE

TOWN
HOUSE
DUBLIN

First published in 2004 by

TownHouse, Dublin
THCH Ltd
Trinity House
Charleston Road
Ranelagh
Dublin 6
Ireland

www.townhouse.ie

1 2 3 4 5 6 7 8 9 10

ISBN: 1-86059-212-0

Cover design by Anú Design, Tara
Text design and typeset by Typeform
Printed and bound in Great Britain by
Cox & Wyman Ltd, Reading, Berkshire

Tom Humphries is a sportswriter and regular columnist with *The Irish Times*. He lives in Dublin with his partner and two children. His critically acclaimed book, *Laptop Dancing and the Nanny Goat Mambo*, was published by PocketBooks/TownHouse in 2003.

Malachy Logan made the selection for this book. He is the Sports Editor of *The Irish Times*.

Paul Kimmage is a sportswriter with *The Sunday Times*. A former sports journalist of the year, his first book, *Rough Ride* (Yellow Jersey Press, 2001), won the William Hill Sports Book of the Year in 1990. In 2001, he was shortlisted for the same award with *Full Time: The Secret Life of Tony Cascarino* (Scribner/TownHouse, 2001). He lives in north County Dublin with his wife Ann and children Evelyn, Eoin and Luke.

Amnesty International is a worldwide activist movement working for the impartial promotion and protection of all the human rights enshrined in the Universal Declaration of Human Rights. Amnesty is independent of any government, political persuasion or religious creed. Please join us. For more information, see www.amnesty.ie.

For all the sportspeople who talked

and to Mary, Molly and Caitlín with love as always.

I ♡ my mom she is
the smartest most
prettiest girl in the
world she cares so much
about me and Daniel
I feel like crying
my eyes out but
i know in my heart
and soul shes an →

Acknowledgements

It's usual at this point in journalistic collections to enter a caveat for the reader who has just haplessly shelled out some good money. Generally we point out early on that the pieces which have been exhumed and pressed into service between these covers were never meant to have a life beyond wrapping cod and chips the day after they were published.

Secretly of course we all wonder if our collected works mightn't break all rules and become far more than the sum of their hastily written parts. In moments of quiet fancy we imagine that we have an oeuvre, a canon, which might stand as a towering testimony to our hitherto unsuspected genius. We just need somebody to suggest a collection in the first place.

Thanks then to Sean Love of Amnesty International for the suggestion of a collection. Sean and his work have opened my eyes to lots of things and even if these pieces are judged not to have been worthy of rescue from the counter of my local chipper, the experience has been a good one for me. So there!

Thanks to everyone at TownHouse for their patience and care. Even these acknowledgements are being delivered way beyond deadline, yet there have been no tantrums other than my own.

Speaking of deadlines, thanks to Paul Kimmage for the foreword. At time of writing, I have yet to read the foreword and suspect Paul has yet to write the foreword, but I have no worries. Over the many dinners Paul has bought for me on working trips abroad, I have dropped more than enough hints regarding the things I need to be said about me in these circumstances. Also I have stolen and borrowed so much from Paul's work that he should view large parts of this book as homage.

Thanks to *The Irish Times* for keeping me and putting up with my dislike of rugby. I don't think either party thought the relationship would last but we've been through quite a bit together now and the years have slipped by quickly. Thanks also to Jim Herre of *Sports Illustrated* who commissioned the Bobby Locke piece included here, as well as several other pieces which have been a pleasure to work on.

Finally, huge thanks to my editor and friend, Malachy Logan, who not only conceived of and commissioned most of the pieces here, but who also sifted through roughly 2,500 other bits and pieces which didn't make the cut.

Malachy smuggled me into the real world when he gave me my first and only full-time job in journalism and as such shoulders at least half the blame for the havoc which has ensued. It's a testimony either to Mal's cunning or my remarkable maturity that I can't remember the last time we had a good argument.

Contents

Foreword

envy, v. – syn. grudge, begrudge, covet, lust after, regard with envy, resent, have hard feelings towards, desire inordinately, crave, be envious of, feel resentful towards, hunger after, thirst after, desire, long for, yearn for, hanker after, be green with envy.

One of the all-time great opening scenes from the movies begins with a priest trudging through the snow-filled streets of Vienna on a winter's morning in the early-nineteenth century. His journey takes him to a well-furnished room in the city's mental asylum where an old man is sitting in a wheelchair playing the piano. Antonio Salieri, once court composer to the Emperor Joseph, has been admitted to the asylum after slashing his own throat with a knife.

The priest removes his cloak and pulls up a chair.

'Leave me alone,' the old man groans.

'I cannot leave alone a soul in pain,' his visitor replies, piously.

Salieri stops playing and fixes him with a stare: 'Do you know who I am?'

'That makes no difference. All men are equal in God's eyes.'

'Are they?' Salieri spits, his voice laden with contempt.

'Offer me your confession. I can offer you God's forgiveness,' the priest insists.

A flash of mischief flickers in the old man's eyes.

'How well are you trained in music?' he asks.

'I know a little,' the priest replies. 'I studied it in my youth.'

'Where?'

'Here in Vienna.'

'Ahh! Then you must know this.'

Salieri wheels round and runs his fingers over the keys, but the priest is at a loss. 'I can't say that I do. What is it?'

'It was a very popular tune in its day,' Salieri enthuses. 'I wrote it.'

An awkward pause ensues.

'How about this?' he asks. 'This one brought the house down when they played it first.' He plays another melody and his spirits visibly soar as he is carried back in time to a packed opera house and a standing ovation. The priest gazes at him vacuously. 'I regret it is not too familiar,' he says.

Salieri is crestfallen. 'Can you recall no melody of mine?' he pleads. 'I was the most famous composer in Europe! I wrote forty operas alone!'

But the priest shifts uneasily.

'Here! What about this one?'

The third offering is the opening melody of *Eine Kleine Nachtmusik*. Suddenly the priest's face lights up and he begins to hum along: 'Bam, bam-bam, bam-bam, bam-bam, bam-bam . . . Yes, I know that!' he beams. 'I'm sorry, I didn't know you wrote that.'

But the old man stares back as if a dagger has just been thrust into his chest. 'I didn't,' he mourns. 'That was Mozart... Wolfgang Amadeus Mozart.'

Has there ever been a finer portrayal of envy than F. Murray Abraham's Oscar-winning performance as Salieri in *Amadeus*? Not in this writer's book.

Consider for one moment the misery of the Italian composer's life: rewarded with a gift for music after taking a pledge of celibacy as a boy, he is acclaimed all over Europe until 1776, when he discovers that the god-like musical gifts he so desires have been bestowed on someone else. A genius. Mozart redefines music. His work is the voice of God. Salieri cannot compete with such a monumental talent. The realisation is crushing.

'All I ever wanted was to sing to God,' he mourns. 'He gave me that longing and then made me mute. Why? Tell me that. If he didn't want me to praise him with music why implant the desire like a lust in my body and then deny me the talent?'

Salieri's voice returned to me immediately when the request came from the publisher to pen these words. His envy and rage and pain seemed somehow appropriate, because, if you'd shared a press box with Tom Humphries for the last fourteen years, you'd know exactly how that feels.

I first noticed his by-line in the spring of 1990, a few months after Vincent Browne had invited me to join the staff of *The Sunday Tribune* as a features writer. Tom had also just started with the paper but was a long way down the order, writing obscure match reports of 150 words for pay that would hardly have covered his expenses. I came across a couple a few weeks ago whilst trawling through the archives for an interview I had written. It was like gazing at an old Ronald Reagan film; you would never have believed he would go on to be President. But I digress. The moment I noticed his first by-line? That would have been a half-page feature (I was obviously on holiday that week) on the remarkable Brendan Ingle, the Ringsend-born Dubliner who was building an empire in Sheffield as a world-class boxing trainer. The interview was good. It was very good. But even a blind squirrel will find an acorn from time to time and I dismissed it immediately, packing my laptop for Italia '90 while Tom spent the summer in the miscellaneous columns writing amateur golf reports. But you were never going to keep a talent like that under wraps.

He didn't stay long with *The Sunday Tribune*. There was more opportunity freelancing for a daily paper, and over the next two years he began to establish himself at *The Irish Times*. He was still a fringe player, still playing second fiddle to the David Walshes and Eamon Dunphys and Con Houlihans and Peter Byrnes and Dermot Gilleeses and Vincent Hogans. The marquee names! The kings! But he was writing some really fine pieces and progressing steadily.

And then, in May 1994, a month before the World Cup finals, he wrote a major feature on Jack Charlton. I remember picking it up that morning with my usual jaundiced eye, ready to pick holes and discard it. But from the opening paragraph it was spellbinding. Jack was telling a story about an afternoon he had spent with his ageing mother, Sissy, and her friend Nora, by the sea. Except it didn't read like he was telling a story; it read like we were with them, smelling the salt air, feeling the stiff breeze. And the affection between mother and son was a side of the manager we had never seen before:

So he drives onwards to a pub he knows. Nice lunches. Homely. He's taking Sissy out of the car and has her by the wrist as he leans to shut the door. Suddenly, a jet flies overhead. 'Whooooshaw,' he says, conveying the surprise, his flattened hand describing the arc of its flight. Sissy looks skywards and, still being held by the wrist, her body takes off in a perfect circle, swivelling out of her son like an acrobat in an old lady's coat. 'Oooooheeee,' she cries, pointing skywards, 'ooooooheeeeee.'

Shaken, he pulls his giggling mother to attention.

'You silly old buggah,' he roars, pushing her towards the pub, 'why can't yeh be bloody sensible instead of being so bloody stupid. Yeh could have broke your bloody neck there. Silly, stupid…'

Through the pub door and Sissy is laughing and Nora is laughing. Laughing their old heads off. Exasperated, he gets Sissy to a seat and deposits her gruffly. The whole pub knows her and the whole pub knows him. She's flopped there in a big high-back seat and she's laughing and laughing. Hee hee hee. And Big Jack is glowering and embarrassed and at last she looks around the pub.

'Ooooh,' she says finally to her rapt audience. 'Our Jack's a bad-tempered buggah, yeh neh. Eee's one bad-tempered buggah.'

The writing was astonishing. I remember putting it down and feeling almost physically sick. How could I compete with that? How could anyone compete with that? What word power! What awe-inspiring talent! A talent you have to witness to believe. There are times when I truly despise him for how easy he makes it seem, for writing has always been childbirth for me. I don't write, I chisel, an affliction best summed up by my colleague Hugh McIllvanney: 'Even leaving a note for the milkman can be hell.' Making deadlines on the Saturdays of football or rugby internationals (I've always worked for Sunday papers) has always been a nightmare. It takes me at least three hours to write 1,000 words on a game, which is roughly three times slower than the norm. Tom works on a different level entirely. Tom is a machine under the cosh. I've seen him cover a championship game at Croke Park and write a front-page lead, a colour piece from the dressing room, a comment on the game and sometimes even a 'Locker Room' column for the paper next morning. And none of it dross!

Atlanta was his first Olympics, in 1996. We were staying together in one of those cheap, soulless hotels near the airport. A year before, Sonia O'Sullivan had won the 5,000 metre at the World Championships in Gothenburg and she would dominate our lives when she arrived to compete in the second week. The first week promised to be much more leisurely: a little boxing, a little rowing, and a Saturday night at the pool to check on the progress of the rapidly improving Michelle Smith de Bruin. She won a gold medal that night and did it again two days later. The country went crazy.

Michelle Smith de Bruin had to be the greatest Irish sports story of all time. There was just one problem; her sport didn't believe in her. The experts were sceptical. The whispers were deafening. How had the swimmer achieved all this so late in her career with a coach who had experience in just two fields – discus throwing and doping? A week later, in his first major piece on the controversy, Tom filed a response Ireland didn't want to hear.

If we are to be journalists and not cheerleaders with typewriters, we must pause to listen to the questions. If we are to be lovers of sport and not mere worshippers of success, we must ask for answers. If we are to cherish Michelle Smith as a true hero, we mustn't do her the injustice of demeaning her by means of whispered innuendo. Her achievements have been of such a magnitude these past seven days that they almost defy comprehension. The further you delve into the science of swimming, the more unusual all that gold seems. It was right that the questions should have been amplified and not whispered.

He did his best work as a journalist in the two years that followed. It would have been easy for him to move on and coast on his phenomenal writing ability, but he rolled up his sleeves, examining the questions being raised about de Bruin with forensic zeal. It wasn't popular work and it almost cost him his job and there were times when the public backlash really got to him.

But if we are to be journalists and not cheerleaders, to quote his words, then there is always a price to be paid, and often for no reward. This time, his work was vindicated: de Bruin was duly exposed as a cheat and banned.

If de Bruin remains his best work, then the story that has made his name is the Roy Keane interview from Saipan. Here he displayed the most valued attribute in the profession, not the ability to write well or to investigate, but to deliver the big one when the chips are down.

And, in the summer of 2002, they didn't come much bigger than Roy Keane's explosive exit from the World Cup. But the interview was only the start of it and over the next four weeks Tom's daily bulletins from Korea and Japan were compulsive reading.

Booked is an anthology of his finest feature writing (if you'd read his Chris Eubank interview on the morning of the Steve Collins fight in Millstreet, you'd have been cheering for the Brit). It is also a collection of 'Locker Room', the column he has been writing each Monday since 1993. I like 'Locker Room' and usually save it for eleven to savour with my morning coffee, but, if there is one weakness in his game, 'Locker Room' is it. Too many of them (and, surprisingly, a number have been reproduced here) are too clever and self-indulgent by far, but then, even Mozart would struggle to write a symphony each week for eleven years. And even on the bad weeks you'll always find a couple of brilliant lines. He wrote one recently on the UCD camogie team. Now I'm not sure how you feel about college camogie, but it wouldn't make my list. In fact, you'd have to chain me to a chair and force the strips of paper into my mouth before I'd take it in. The opening paragraph was classic Humphries:

Davey Billings calls. He says the Ashbourne Cup is on out in UCD soon, so be sure to give it an old mention. This is the Billings Method. Enthusiasm. It is better for you to be disappointed in Billings than it is for Billings to be disappointed in you. You make a mental note. Circle in red. Camogie. Ashbourne Cup. UCD. Must do.

And he does. He does it for 1,500 words! Jaysus! 1,500 words about the UCD camogie team! Can't say I stayed with it (sorry, Tom, life's too short), but it was a noble effort. Indeed, if my daughter played camogie for UCD I'd probably have thought it was the best thing he'd ever written. But that one didn't quite do it for me and some are even worse. Some weeks, when he's jerking off about his sports editor's cigars or trying to be clever, I'll fling the paper across the room and take delight in shouting 'THAT WAS CRAP!' But some weeks are worth the price of a year's subscription alone.

Check out 'Stick on Freddie, Mick, and mellow out' on page 387. I disagreed with practically everything Tom wrote about Mick McCarthy after the fallout from Saipan, but this column, written shortly before McCarthy's resignation, was truly outstanding.

It opens with a great story about the singer Freddie White and just gets better with every paragraph. Note how humorously and seamlessly he makes the link between the introduction and the subject matter:

To hear Freddie White brings me right back to the summer when myself and Sean K. were so flat broke that we shoplifted tins of sardines and packets of sausages for two months just to live. I hear Freddie White and I'm belching John West.

Few things in life have that redolence. For some people it is scents. Or places. For me it is voices. I hear Mick McCarthy's voice and I think of 1990.

Not just that mad summer, but the innocent build-up which preceded it, the impossibly dull friendlies of that spring. What was the sound that you could hear all over Lansdowne Road? Mick McCarthy's voice. Foghorn Leghorn at the back. That bluntness, a second blade of it behind Charlton's, it seemed indicative of our proud defiance.

Brilliant.

A few months ago, I sat down for a coffee one afternoon with Tom's publisher (and mine), Treasa Coady. She had an idea for a book in mind, a collaboration with Tom. Her idea was that we would both take a subject, an old football legend or a year in the life of a team, and present it to the reader like a double-sided jacket, with Tom's version on one side of the book and mine on the other. Now I've been offered some pretty hilarious books in my time, but this had me falling off my chair. 'Treasa,' I said, 'I can't think of anyone in the world, with the exception of Mary [Tom's partner], who would be prepared to share covers with Tom Humphries. I'd need at least a five-year start if we were to deliver at the same time.' But Treasa, being Treasa, always finds a way and, when she offered me the chance to write this introduction, I couldn't resist. The introduction, you see, comes FIRST! Readers would open my pages BEFORE they got to his! Yes, that was a much more palatable proposition. Enjoy the read. It gets better from here.

Antonio Salieri
April 2004

Ah, but doesn't it feel just fine, just fine

22 March 1993

Alive-alive-O

Alive-alive-O

Can that long, grinding run of defeats really have sucked the marrow from the bone to the extent that an Irish team had to plead with their countryfolk to sing and shout and provide encouragement? It seemed so. There was Pat O'Hara, at one moment a mauling, rucking demon, at the next a lonely Georg Solti. Rabble-rousing has never had such reward. The old roar returned, 'Molly Malone' got a dusting down, the hairs on the back of the neck stood to tingling attention.

And in the press box, decorum was abandoned as Mick Galwey ran in that try, which, with a massive flourish of the quill, put a full stop to the game. Pens and notebooks were dropped as clenched fists punched the air. Good-natured English colleagues smiled indulgently and prepared to write the obituary for their national team.

Whether Saturday was an Irish rebirth only time will tell. Irish rugby history is littered with green oases which become enshrined in song and story during the lean time.

Whatever Saturday meant, it felt fine. Just fine to see an Irish side camped resolutely in opposition territory, fine to see an outhalf of international class blossom in the green jersey, fine to see Irish tactics work so well in set pieces. We played with passion and wisdom and had the pleasure of hammering the last nail into the pine lid of this English team that has stomped all over us in recent years. Ah.

That whistling sound. That's the sound of Will Carling falling a long way to earth. Thud! There goes the Lions' captaincy. When England were back-pedalling, Will was missing in action. Will Carling, who has been eulogised ad nauseam as a Churchill for our times, didn't have the stomach for it all on Saturday.

England found themselves drained of resolve, happy to get out alive and into the beckoning pastures of retirement and after-dinner speaking. Jeremy Guscott was marked absent. Stuart Barnes was marked for life. Brian Moore found it physically impossible to throw the ball over the head of big Bayfield and, time after time, Barnes was set up for an Irish hit.

The Irish heroes were many and the naming of names would be invidious. This was an afternoon of collective ferocity. Eighty minutes of frenzied plunder underpinned somewhere by practised method. Passion at last was matched by technique. The Welsh game provided a transfusion of self-confidence and England, lucky England, were the hapless victims. Ireland were as unstoppable as a storm.

In the aftermath, as the olés rang out around the old ground, an anti-climactic press conference took place in the corner of the ground. There can hardly have been a member of the press corps present who could place hand on heart and say that the faith never waned during the bad years. Yet Noel Murphy and Gerry Murphy and Michael Bradley declined to extract their pound of flesh, recognising by their manner that the criticism of the team has been born of shared frustration, not malice. They were dignified and eschewed triumphalism.

The English contingent that followed them in carried themselves well also. Will Carling looked battered and crestfallen and more than a little bewildered, and was treated gently. Geoff Cooke admitted that the Lions' selection process would take a little longer than expected.

It was a day for gutswelling partisanship. An afternoon when we got to the core of what Irish sport is about. As we wended our way out under the still trembling stands, we passed the roomful of alickadoos supping free drink from their hosts, Digital. 'Where's their f***ing pride?' we wondered. But even that sight couldn't spoil a wonderful day.

We're going to America

Oh America! A night of dangled nerves and jumbled memories. Love and hate and much between. Songs. Chants. Shocked silences. And in the end? Lo, it came to pass. Happy days are here again. Sing it. In an arena where charity and the assisting wind of passionate support were always absent, the Republic of Ireland soccer team drew on the deepest wells of passion and commitment and prevailed.

It was a Belfast night not to be forgotten, the last stage of a painful footballing passage to America. Nails were chewed to the quick and beyond and, when the long whistle finally sounded, the dream was reality. Just think of it.

For some long heavy minutes, the golden thread seemed broken. A long visceral howl of spite rent the northern skies as one, Jimmy Quinn, rustled the Republic's net with a sweet volley as the game lay three-quarters dead. 'The Sash My Father Wore' rang around the ground. Nobody, it seemed, was going anywhere but home next summer.

'Always Look on the Bright Side of Life' came the teasing tune from the stands in the triumphalist aftermath of Quinn's goal. Always look on the bright side of life. It was hard, it was hard. Life

seemed drained briefly of its colour. What the national soccer team
have come to mean to a bedraggled nation was suddenly shockingly
clear. The air was hissing out of the national morale. Back among the
also-rans we were. And then BOOM!

Alan McLoughlin, scarcely long enough on the pitch to have
broken a sweat, gave the kiss of life to a fatalistic race. One apiece
and all the news from Seville was good news. Southern fists silently
punctured the air. Out of hiding came the faithful, eyes fixed greedily
on America.

Yes. After weeks of worry and poison, in the end it was mostly
about football last night. The Windsor Park crowd huffed and puffed
with the ersatz menace of a mob without a foe.

'God Save the Queen' was punctuated with sharp cries of 'No
Surrender'. Orange scarves bore the legend 'For God and Ulster'.
The Union Jack hung from most railings. 'The Sash' got an
obligatory airing every few minutes.

In all, though, it didn't amount to very much intimidation for
professional football. It was a football night, a night not suited to
insularity. Football grounds throughout Europe bristled with news of
each other. San Marino winning, then losing. Wales trailing, then
clawing for air. Holland ahead, hee hee. And, critically early on, an
expulsion, but no goal, in Seville. The football itself was a largely
unpretty tangle of two stolid teams.

Northern Ireland were all short passes and cutery, their southern
neighbours more direct and passionate. Hopes that this meant
nothing to the North were banished a full three-quarters of an hour
before the kickoff when Billy Bingham, that silvery fox of Northern
football, taking charge of his team for the last time, took the field to
prolonged and lusty applause, which he milked shamelessly until it
was amplified tenfold.

Half-time and hearts were heavy. The bulletins dripping in from

Seville brought no news of goals. Jack Charlton evidently spent the fifteen minutes profitably and his side swirled passionately around the northern goal after the break. The gods, it seemed, were conspiring amenably. The wires from Seville brought news of a Spanish goal and that, together with the resurgence of Charlton's team, seemed to suck the last spark out of the home support, until, that is, Quinn set the evening alight again. After that, the happy story is already well thumbed.

Jack Charlton, mobbed briefly at the finish, declared his feelings in predictable terms. 'Wonderful,' he croaked, his voice hoarse from overuse. 'It's been a long, hard trip for us up here and in the end it wasn't a great performance, but we got the goal and we got the news that Spain had done us a favour. I hadn't expected that. I don't know what was wrong with us, the spirit was willing, but the football wasn't good, but our heart saw us through. I think I'm getting the flu, you know.'

With that, he was gone, seeking out his adversary, Billy Bingham, for some words of reconciliation. 'I won't enjoy my pint tonight if I feel like this all through.' As for Alan McLoughlin, the saviour of the hour, the emotions welled more freely. 'It's the first goal I have ever scored for Ireland. I am thrilled, so thrilled. I did it for my wife and family back home, for everybody. It's a great night for us. I am thrilled.'

And with that the curtain of heavy but discreet northern security fell again and the victorious squad went about their business until that magic moment one minute before midnight when a boisterous plane left northern soil and all thoughts turned briefly to happy journeys to come. A familiar chant echoed.

'Here we go, here we go.'

The fall guy

Monday 26 February 1994

'Good luck,' says Linda, the burly information assistant, and, in a strangely British gesture, she gives *The Irish Times* an encouraging punch on the arm.

'Good luck,' she says again, biting her lip and looking like Trevor Howard sending a man out to die.

The Winter Olympics are being staged in Lillehammer and *The Irish Times* has found budget accommodation near the North Pole. At the media centre, they are shocked and impressed by the derring-do of *The Irish Times*. Handing over the shiny accreditation that makes *The Irish Times* a member of the Olympic Family, albeit the one the family doesn't talk about, they eye *The Irish Times* up, thinking to kill him for his oily blubber. Then, waving at the snowy yonder, they begin spooling out their directions. 'Out, out past the middle of nowhere. On and on through the back of beyond, across the Fjord of the Frozen Foreigners and over the Mountains where Goats Fear to Tread, and then across the Land that Time Forgot…'

Many hours later, it is dark and Torvill and Dean have wasted their sweetness. The Official Irish Times Winter Olympics Mountain Lodge hoves into view somewhere in the lunar blankness. Why had the words 'winter' and 'mountain' not set alarm bells ringing before this?

Mysteriously, a pub brimming with revellers sits at the bottom of Irish Times mountain. The faces of Torvill and Dean, whose tragedy is as nought when set against that of *The Irish Times* (who, sickeningly, will now never see T&D in the flesh), blare out from half a dozen television screens.

Unleashing a howl of undiluted misery, *The Irish Times* trails his drooping hands in the banked powdery snow and sets his face towards his monastic lodging above.

It is difficult to be up before the crack of dawn in Norway, but *The Irish Times* manages it simply by arriving at his bedside at that precise instant and doing an about-turn. The Troll at reception offers a fish for breakfast, but, wisely, *The Irish Times* stows it away for company in the evenings. Trekking down the mountain next morning in search of Lillehammer, *The Irish Times* notes bitterly that the snow outside the pub is jaundiced with cold, yellow stains.

Never, ever trail your drooping hands in the banked powdery snow outside the Laven pub in Sjusjoen.

Tuesday

On the main drag in Lillehammer, there is a thriving trade in Olympic pins. People come up to *The Irish Times*, stare at the accreditation which distinguishes him as a member of the Olympic Family, and inquire: 'You got pins?' Until you get used to the Norwegian accent, this is a difficult question. You can't buy Sarajevo Olympic pins for love nor money in Lillehammer, but the promise of Dublin Olympics pins sends a *frisson* through the market.

The Irish Times has no pins, but he has plenty of aches. Every four or five yards he does his fat-man-on-a-banana skin routine for the locals. The Americans, who are finding the going equally rough, have a joke about Norwegian humour. 'You say: "It's damn cold today," and they say: "No, it's very warm. Ha, ha."' The sight of an army of journalists bouncing around Lillehammer certainly has the locals in kinks. 'You fall on your butt, ja?' they call heartily in their singsong voices as they slide up ice-lagged hills, impervious to gravity.

The British press contingent is a little sore this morning for different reasons. Torvill and Dean, the skating thirty-somethings, are no more. T&D, as they are knowingly called in the press centre and on the cramped pistes where headline writers apply their art, have left the faithful scribes without a story. Five days of slipping and sliding left, and the bronze token awarded the two has-beens from Nottingham looks like being the only British medal.

The hacks bunch together and reminisce about Sarajevo. 'At least back then we got the week out of the romantic angle. Do they, don't they; will they, won't they. That's gone now as well. Bah.'

The tabloid tendency is sure that Torvill and Dean have been the victims of some dastardly foreign larceny. It's an odd spin to put on the fact that the British judge awarded T&D the highest marks throughout the competition, but it's what people want to hear.

Feelings about Torvill and Dean, and indeed about Nancy and Tonya, are mixed among the sports hack pack. Most concede that skating is artistic, often beautiful, but it isn't sport. There was pronounced disgruntlement in the restless media ranks when Surya Bonaly, the French champion, was officially barred from doing her thrilling back flip in practice because it 'bothers and intimidates the other skaters'. Not as much as a swinging crowbar, one suspects. The back flip, weighted as it is with the awful possibility that Surya's beautiful skull might make violent contact with the rink ice, takes the breath away and is a thousand times more thrilling than anything else on offer.

At the Nancy and Tonya practice sessions, the most exciting thing is the schoolboyish nudging and smirking that goes on when either of the ice warriors hits the deck unexpectedly. 'Careful of that tush, Nancy!' 'Careful of that rink, Tonya!' There is a vague recognition among the lay hacks that a triple salchow gone wrong might be more painful than being hit on the knee with a crowbar by somebody from Portland, but there is no doubt about which makes the better copy.

The practice session for Nancy and Tonya takes place at lunchtime with a reprise performance in the evenings at teatime. Depending on your deadline, you go to the early or the late show. Tonya doesn't skate much but uses her inhaler all the time and coughs and sneezes a lot. The hack pack has become resigned to the fact that there isn't going to be a fist fight or any scratching or eye-gouging at the practice sessions, so everyone sits and makes jokes about Nancy and Tonya. Because of Nancy's vigorous virtuousness and Tonya's height, these jokes all have a Snow White/Seven Dwarfs theme to them. Who did Tonya hire to get Snow White? Dopey, Sneezy and Grumpy, of course. How will the marking go tomorrow for Tonya? 5.5, 5.6, 5.7, 5.8, 5.4 and five to 10 for good behaviour.

Once again Tonya fails to finish her practice session, but she looks more impressive than Nancy while she is on the ice. Nancy's teeth score straight sixes for technical merit, however, and, in a sport where what the judges think is all that matters, shiny teeth are probably more useful than being friends with Dopey, Sneezy and Grumpy.

Wednesday

Today is the day. *The Irish Times* rises with the sun, gives The Troll a cheery kiss as he skates out the door, throws yellow snowballs at passers-by near the pub and skis straight into Lillehammer singing lightly as he goes.

It's Tonya and Nancy day. Rejoice. All day the excitement mounts. *The Irish Times* scouts the town and, finding tickets retailing for $500 a time, falls to his knees and kisses his shiny Olympic Family accreditation badge. 'Is very warm. Ha, ha,' he tells a group of gaping Norwegians.

In the afternoon at the Finland vs US hockey game, his head swirls. Tonya's theme, Much Ado About Nothing, thrums in his brain. He finds himself hoping that the padded goalkeepers will suddenly find their lives devoid of artistic impression and, in a spontaneous tribute to the ice queens, perform a triple lutz–double toe loop combination leading in to a death drop and back to a spiral sequence and a layback spin, finishing up perhaps with a delayed double flip and a flying camel. Hockey players lack imagination though. Tick. Tick. Tick.

The buses fly in fleets towards Hamar. The gossip is Tonya and Nancy-oriented. You can probably tell which way an American votes by gleaning his or her attitude to Tonya and Nancy. The guys in the sports jackets, who have rented homes in Lillehammer, are virulently in favour of sending Tonya to the electric chair and wish their damn daughters could be a little more Nancyesque.

The Irish Times, and other journalists billeted in distant mountain lodges overlooking slum fjords, make heartfelt pleas in Tonya's defence. 'Maybe it was all just a silly mix up,' we say. In Hamar, Nancy fans and Tonya fans alike are somewhat taken aback to discover that there are twenty-seven other skaters on the programme.

Tonya, bless her little cotton socks, warms up in the second group of skaters. In this cheerleaders-on-ice setting, she looks more dangerous than ever. She is an enthusiastic smoker and, out on the ice, she looks as if she needs a fag in her mouth to finish the look.

When her turn comes to skate, *The Irish Times* realises how perfect his ignorance of ice dancing is. 'Oooooh,' says everyone as the red snapdragon whizzes past, 'critical hesitation.' To *The Irish Times*, it looks as if the only way Tonya could hesitate was if she hit the wall. Afterwards, with her moderate marks delivered like a sentence, Tonya faces us. 'Get outta my face,' she bellows. Five hundred of us obey.

The Irish Times patiently helps translate the quote for mystified foreign journalists. Suddenly *The Irish Times* suffers a terrible flash of *déjà vu*. Jack Ruby shooting Lee Harvey Oswald in that crowded corridor. 'Look out,' shouts *The Irish Times*. 'Get down; she's got a gun.' She puts the gun in her mouth and inhales.

Nancy Kerrigan, who has gone to the trouble of ironing her outfit and her hair, skates second last. Like the movie queen she is about to become, she does it perfectly on the first take and goes into gold medal position. We all crane our heads to see how Tonya is taking it.

She is in tenth place and deep in thought. Two days, nine kneecappings, wish Jeff was here…

Thursday

The Irish Times has been exposed to Nancy and Tonya for too long.

He yearns for those events where anonymous, hooded people travel at speed, to the delight of hearty Norwegian hordes. He heads early morning for Hiinderfossen. Perhaps there will be a media luge competition he can enter.

Instead there is the strange world of the bobsleigh practices. Groups of four men jumping into giant suppositories and sliding away. '*Ar nós na gaoithe,*' comments *The Irish Times* approvingly.

The bobsleigh takes all sorts. The Jamaicans are here for the third time but, as they get better at bobsleighing, so the interest in them declines. The Bosnians are the story. They shouldn't be here at all, and when their bright green sled trundles to the finish and they clamber out, etiolated but smiling, we approach them cautiously. None of the rough-housing that we subject those skating girls to. Zoran Sokolovic is of another branch of the Olympic Family to that which gave us Nancy and Tonya. He escaped from Bosnia two weeks ago, with the help of a UN official, to come here and steer the bob for Bosnia. It seems a trite thing to do in the midst of massacre, yet, for Zoran, it is an assertion of normality. 'I was nine when the Olympics came to Sarajevo. I watched them open with my father and have dreamed of the Olympics since then. Now, in Sarajevo, there is nothing of the Olympic Games that I remember. Nothing.'

Indeed. The bobsled track is a fortified Serb position. The ice rink is a UN headquarters. The stadium used for the opening and closing ceremonies is pockmarked with shells and bullets. The Olympic Village lies ruined in the death corridor from the airport to the city. In Lillehammer this week, the IOC has been collecting money and talking bravely about repairing all the damage when the war is over. Another assertion of normality.

Until Zoran got here he didn't know if he would have enough team-mates to form a team. Everybody made their own way. The team is light and weak compared to their rivals. The sled has been borrowed from the Dutch, the first real sled they've seen since their own were destroyed during the war. Zoran is a Serb, two of his team are Muslims and the other is a Croat. The first thing they do with everybody they meet is announce the ethnic breakdown of their team. People mightn't ask, otherwise. 'We want to show people at home. If you can live together in a bob, you can live together anywhere.'

Zoran talks about the marketplace massacre, about the difficulty of getting food and exercise in Sarajevo, about his plans for the future. There are three journalists standing as he sits on the nosecone of his sled – *The Irish Times* and two Americans. When Zoran's voice trails off, nobody can think of anything to say or ask. Here in the pristine snow, it all has an air of unreality.

Zoran won't be going home when these games finish; he hopes to get himself into a home and stay away from Sarajevo until he can face it again. Maybe he can do a little sledding. Maybe a little study. If he goes home, he faces a refugee camp. Maybe a friend can put him up till he finds his feet, he says. The Olympics have made him many friends.

Nobody says anything. One of the Americans is embarrassed and ashamed straight off, but he blurts out a question about Tonya and Nancy. Zoran shakes his head. He knows nothing of Tonya and Nancy. We each shake his hand in turn and we shuffle off. Good luck, we say to him, smiling. All the best. He is nineteen years old.

Friday

The Irish Times is an old snow hand by now. No more Monsieur Hulot on ice routines for the natives. No sir. *The Irish Times* carries a large bag of gravel around, spreading it before him as he goes.

They sell Olympic pin badges on the streets in Lillehammer. The same guys travel from Olympic event to Olympic event, hawking their trayfuls of pins to members of the Olympic Family. Practices are sharp and you need to know the exchange rates before you delve in the market. The most valuable goods they sell, however, aren't pins at all. For $150 or so, you can buy an athlete's Olympic participation medal. These aren't on display, but they are hauled out of pockets and rucksacks if a dollar-backed inquiry is made.

Trade is brisk. The medals are set in a tidy presentation box and glitter like gold, although that's not what they are. Eastern Europeans sell them. They will give you a little history of each participation medal for sale. This one is from a Romanian skier, this was an

Armenian's and so on. Everybody wants an Olympic athlete's participation medal. In lounges and living rooms and saloon bars, the medals will make fine conversation pieces.

The Irish Times lays down his gravel and wonders how much a hawker would pay for a gold medal winner's participation medal – Bonnie Blair's or Dan Jansen's, say.

The question takes Bob Bradley, from Colorado, by surprise. 'How would I prove to people that it was a famous person's participation medal? They all look the same. People buy these and they know they don't belong to nobody famous. These are losers' medals. They belonged to losers. That's by definition.

It has been a fortnight of winners and losers, of paths crossing in the snow. The Olympic Family, with all its ready commercialism, is easily and rightly derided at times. Yet the message of friendship is sold so relentlessly that it flavours the proceedings in a positive way. In the little Olympic Village, those athletes who have chosen to stay there trade their pins and their embraces.

Nancy and Tonya, Torvill and Dean and the mechanised masses from CBS are less of the real world than they are. Nancy goes for gold tonight, yet a loser's participation medal is more poignant and interesting than anything in her Disneyworld life.

The Irish Times passes on. Just a 40-kilometre trip to collect those bags and say goodbye to The Troll. Participation medals. There's an idea The Troll might take it up for the benefit of his guests.

Northern exposure – Jack Charlton

May 1994

He can tell a story. Roll it around in his mind and unspool it sparingly. He comes from that age. The Ashington of his childhood had just the wireless to link it to the outside world. You learned to tell a story.

He is talking about his mother. The matriarch. Sissy.

He laughs to himself, teasing you with what is about to come. Sissy has had open-heart surgery, you see. She's over it now and she's in a residential home in Newbiggin-by-the-Sea. He spools away, describes the sweep of the view from her room, the beach, the grey water, the sky. She's happy there.

He pushes the pace a little. Paints the character for you, crushing the vowels, Geordie-style.

'She's an independent buggah, too, yeh neh. Aye. Sissy Charlton. If she can do something herself she'll do it, or she'll attempt to do it. She has one of those frames, but she won't use it. Only if they are looking at her.'

He laughs some more, shaking his head.

Anyway, he phoned her the other day and, brimful of innocent mischief, she inveigled a day out for herself and her friend Nora.

He collected the pair of them the next day, bundling them into his car out of a soft drizzle. He had an idea. Fish and chips. Up the grey coast to Amble. The best in the northeast. Old time stuff.

He drives them and when they arrive Sissy announces that herself and Nora have enjoyed fish and chips just the previous evening. 'Ya daft buggah,' he tells her chidingly, 'why didn't ya tell me before now?'

So he drives onwards to a pub he knows. Nice lunches. Homely. He's taking Sissy out of the car and has her by the wrist as he leans to shut the door. Suddenly, a jet flies overhead. 'Whooooshaw,' he says, conveying the surprise, his flattened hand describing the arc of its flight. Sissy looks skywards and, still being held by the wrist, her body takes off in a perfect circle, swivelling out of her son like an acrobat in an old lady's coat. 'Oooooheeeeee,' she cries, pointing skywards, 'ooooooheeeeee.'

Shaken, he pulls his giggling mother to attention.

'You silly old buggah,' he roars, pushing her towards the pub, 'why can't yeh be bloody sensible instead of being so bloody stupid. Yeh could have broke your bloody neck there. Silly, stupid...'

Through the pub door and Sissy is laughing and Nora is laughing. Laughing their old heads off. Exasperated, he gets Sissy to a seat and deposits her gruffly. The whole pub knows her and the whole pub knows him. She's flopped there in a big high-back seat and she's laughing and laughing. Hee hee hee. And Big Jack is glowering and embarrassed and at last she looks around the pub.

'Ooooh,' she says finally to her rapt audience. 'Our Jack's a bad-tempered buggah, yeh neh. Eee's one bad-tempered buggah.'

The telling is done and his long face dissolves to laughter. The unlikely line of his mouth turns cartoonish, pegged up high at the edges as his grin spreads. The eyes of North Sea blue disappear almost behind wrinkled lids. Bad-tempered buggah. She's a one...

Bobby, our kid, might have been closer to Sissy than Jack ever was, but her role in the bloodlines cannot be discounted. As long as there has been professional football, Milburns or Charltons have played it. An inherited craziness.

Sissy's father was a noted goalkeeper. Tanner Milburn. Tanner's father before him, who Jack never met, was a professional around the northeast. 'He was known,' says Jack, proudly, 'as the old war horse.'

Sissy's four brothers played. Jackie Milburn, Jimmy Milburn, George Milburn and Stan Milburn. Sissy herself could dribble around most men with a ball at her feet if she'd a mind to. Later she would coach Bobby, easing out his immense potential on long evenings in a field she would mark out herself. First, though, when she brought Jack – newborn and her eldest – back home to the long straight row of terraced houses in Ashington, Northumberland, a neighbour asked after the baby.

'Eee,' said Sissy, ' the bairn's lovely and his feet are fine too.'

He's a football man then, from the era of hated Saturday crowds and capstans and Walnut plugs and brilliantined outside rights. He's more than that, too. He is Ashington and Geordie and northeast England. Worn and proud.

The bairn's grown now, an old war horse himself. He stands on the cusp of another World Cup final. Since 1966 he's been a part of these football celebrations, either playing for England, or managing Ireland, or doing television for money.

He hunches over his breakfast, waiting for the next question. Interviews go against his knotty grain. Question, answer; question, answer; and so on. He likes to chew the fat over a pint, looks forward to a quiet pub argument, but this question and answer business, bah.

Football management is a strange job. On the whole a football manager should be a good communicator, should tolerate fools easily – indeed, a football manager should cultivate fools for their usefulness. Jack Charlton, though, well he's a bad-tempered bugger. He learned the trade in pre-Ron Atkinson days, at the feet of stern men – Major Frank Buckley, the legendary Raich Carter, Don Revie... Football men back then didn't suffer fools gladly. Jack bears the maker's mark.

In a curiously old-fashioned way, he is an island. One of those stiff-necked men born to the pre-war years who have never bent or wavered. He walks tall and straight and in Ireland is everywhere besieged by admirers and hangers-on. It is strange to see him in the lobby of a hotel, his distinctive beak protruding above a milling crowd as he works out the next move towards his destination. With ordinary people, he never forgets his manners or his origins. Occasionally, with the press milling around, he'll play the bad-tempered bugger, stringing the curses together like a miner in peril. 'Dunt know why I'm talking to yows. Yow'll print this. Bastads.'

An island? You wouldn't think so to see him with half a nation dragging out of him at any one time, yet he seems locked into his own private world. During the great moments of the last eight years, he has always stood to one side smiling that bent smile. One indelible image is of him standing grinning in Stuttgart in 1988, rubbing the scalp he has just bumped badly as Ray Houghton headed his goal. He was part of it, yet curiously aside from it.

He was the same always, he thinks, always off on his own somehow or other. Life in Ashington provided nothing if not variety. To the south was thriving, grimy Newcastle, to the east was the sea, and to the north and northwest was the land. Rivers, streams, ponds, forests. As babies, Sissy would bring Bobby and Jack to Ashington's games together in a pram. As they grew they would travel further, to Blythe or Whitley Bay or beyond to see the local boys play. 'We'd go,' says Jack, 'to those other towns for a reason, but you didn't need a reason to go to the sea or the forests. It was because they were there. I never needed a reason.'

He taught himself to fish. His father never fished so he taught himself, painstakingly, by trial and error. He remembers long skites off on his own learning the art. Fields, rivers, streams, forests. He'd wander then. 'Miles, you could go, and never meet a soul, yet just to the south of you were those crowded towns stretching forever.' When he was small, older pals would bring him along. When he was older, he would go alone looking for peace and quiet and the satisfaction of solitude. He loved the sea and he loved exploring the dense Northumberland landscape. He hunted after a fashion, whippets being a popular breed locally. 'I never went south if it wasn't for a reason. I knew every street for eight or ten miles to the south of us, but I only went for a reason. On me own I headed for the open spaces, always went north or east.'

He misses it all now, town and country. He lives there still. It's not the same country, though. Television, he thinks, has made it all a bit more bland. Nobody talks real Geordie anymore. 'Anyway,' he says smiling, 'you don't talk Geordie, you tekk Geordie.'

He regrets its passing. Something in him was stung by the crazed de-industrialising rape of his country in the 1980s. By reflex he supported the miners' strike. In the long, terraced rows peopled by hard-working folk, he had formed the basis of his blunt, straightforward philosophy, which a lifetime of travel and money hasn't altered.

He's still a Geordie and proud of it. But he won't be sentimental. He would be forgiven this morning if over breakfast in this fine hotel he played up his life as a miner a little bit, stretched the facts until he emerges in the imagination blackened, with a lamp shining from his forehead. How close did he come to a life in the pits?

Well. He doesn't play the romantic. With his pedigree he had football clubs willing to sign him when he was fifteen, yet some spiky sense of his own place made him keen to see the inside of the pits. He went off and trained and enjoyed the training, the weeks in college, the variety of work. He can remember the day it finished when they showed him what they intended him to do for the rest of his life.

'Hanging on and knocking off, it was called. That was my job, hanging on and knocking off. Forty-three years later I can picture the scene, I can tell you exactly where everything was.'

The breakfast room becomes a pit top. He is animated. He points around the place. 'The tubs would come out of the pit on a wire and the wire would pass over big, grimy Jack Charlton. The tubs, you see, were hung by a lever which snapped onto the wire and tightened with the pressure. As long as the wire moved and the pressure was on, the tub would move forwards. Still following, are yeh? The trick was to take the pressure off sufficiently so that the tubs could be knocked off. The line of tubs had to be kept moving always. Another rope disappeared away into another hole and that rope had to be pulled down and tubs hung on it. All day long. Hanging on and knocking off.

'You had to jump pretty quick to get out of the way before the rope took the tension again. The rope and the tub would go flying up. If you got into trouble with it all, there was a bell you had to ring. We pulled the ropes and knocked the tubs with something called a handboden. I had a good look at it all and I said no.'

It was a big decision for a fifteen-year-old son of a miner reared in a mining town, but he'd wanted a look, he'd had a look, and he'd decided he didn't like it. The boy lives on in the man. For all his doughty pragmatism, Jack Charlton doesn't do what he doesn't like to do. He abandoned a succession of management jobs at Middlesboro, Sheffield Wednesday and Newcastle when they ceased to absorb him. In at least one case, Newcastle, he jumped before he was pushed, but in doing so he retained his integrity. He turned a side teeming with promise into a primitive version of the Jack Charlton trademark team. He was credited with driving Chris Waddle away, but Charlton left town unrepentant. He didn't like or need coal-mining and he didn't like or need clubs where he wasn't wanted. Anyway, Jack has always had something to fall back on.

The habits of a lifetime. When he went to Leeds he was fifteen, approaching sixteen. Every club in England wanted his younger brother's signature, but Jack, who could only stop others playing, headed for Leeds. He worked hard. He lived half an hour's walk from Leeds city centre and visited it once in his first two years as an apprentice. Life was simple. Maths was simple. He earned £4 a week. Spent £2.50 on digs. Sent a pound home and had the rest to himself.

'I would do anything to earn money,' he says now, explaining a habit rather than renouncing a vice. 'Back then I used to go with the third team to their Yorkshire league matches, because more often than not one of the linesmen wouldn't turn up, and if that happened you got ten bob for running the line. It was a regular event that all three officials wouldn't turn up. I always went along. Anything to earn a few quid. I stuck at it a few years, worked very hard really.' He was a ground-staff boy in the days when the ground staff consisted almost exclusively of such boys. He cleaned boots and he swept terraces and he cleaned toilets and did all the jobs necessary to the existence of a small, dowdy Yorkshire football club.

Coaching football wasn't a priority at football clubs then. You learned what you could by looking around you. During the summer, the apprentices would play football all day long in the lee of the main stand; in season, the routine for training never varied. Run the long side of the pitch, jog the short side, run the long side, jog the short side. When the first team players would have a game on the cinder car park, the rest would scrabble around in a corner, great packs of young fellows hungry for a kick.

Charlton played for the first team at seventeen, a big ungainly centre back who could get his head or his toe to most things. His career was interrupted by a spell in the Royal Horse Guard in the early 1950s, a spell away from the game which cost him the chance to work with a legend of the northeast, Raich Carter. He outlasted the reigns of a couple more managers after Carter and before Revie. One of them, Jack Taylor, he remembers as a pioneer of coaching at the club. Here's how to learn the art of kicking a football.

'He would lay down two bricks and put the ball between them and ask you to take a run up and hit it full on. Aye, you would be tentative at first, but you soon learned to keep your eye on the ball.'

He learned from Taylor and he learned from those around him. John Charles was a legend. He'd show Jack things. Revelations. How to head the football with your eyes open. How to kill it on the chest. How to take it on the thigh and turn it in the direction you wanted it. How to sell a dummy to a centre forward before he sells one to you. 'When he's running at you, go forward as if you are coming to tackle him, but don't tackle him, check back and go the way he's running so you match his run. He's pushed it when he's seen you come and you've got a yard or two start anyway. You'll get him.'

He explains it all with a hint of pride, the trade explained by one who has lived it. That thrill is still there. He can't take a training session without having a couple of pegs at the ball. 'Boom. Take it out, Packie, take it out. Again. I'll double or quits you, Packie, double or quits. Boom.'

From 1953 to 1973 he wore the white of Leeds in 629 league games. He watched the club pass from era to era. In the early days when he broke through to the first team – he debuted in a scrappy draw at Doncaster Rovers – and had begun making his way in the world, Ashington was still home. Bobby and he would arrange their time off to coincide and they would travel by train together home to Ashington. When Bobby prospered and bought a car, he would drive to Leeds and pick up Jack and his new wife, Pat, and together they would head for Northumberland.

He was close to Bobby then. Time has wedged them apart and, while he doesn't encourage prying, he speaks of his brother in tones freighted with regret. It's a private business, this absence. In all the years that Jack has been an Irish landmark, his brother has never even been a dot on the landscape, has never been photographed with him, or appeared suddenly in an Irish dressing room. There is no bone of contention between them, nothing Jack can get his teeth into, just the distance that different paths have created. Munich has been suggested as a turning point. He is keen to tell you, for starters, that never was there any hint of jealousy between them.

'I knew it from when he was little that he would be a soccer player. Ashington knew it. There couldn't be any jealousy between us because that was the way he was and we were close. I never saw him as other than a great footballer. I was just a lad that could stop others playing. It was always like that. Always. You couldn't be jealous of our kid for his football because that was what he was. I was with him when he learned he was selected for England at twenty years of age, he'd just bought a paper in Manchester and there we were in the street celebrating. I was delighted for him, I really was. Delighted. It was a happy time.'

Success came slower for Jack than for his younger brother. He was twenty before he won his first England cap, a reward for a steady plod of a career that progressed in tandem with Leeds United Football Club. Protected by a select midfield, Jack found international soccer easier to cope with than club soccer. He soon learned the eagle's art of watching and watching until his blood told him to swoop.

By 1966, and all that, he was a professional in the prime of life. The idiosyncracies that have marked him as a manager marked him as a player. He was long and toothless. Prematurely bald. He carried a little black book containing the names of players who needed sorting in the future. For corners he stood on the opposition goal-line, his long Lowryesque frame blocking the opposing goalkeeper's view. When England won the World Cup, Jack wandered dry-eyed around the pitch, had a quiet night and the next day was on the road back to Pat, who was expecting their youngest son.

That day, and his speedy flight from the delirium of it, typifies him. In the trade, when the job needs to be done, he is immersed and wrapped up in football. Away from it, when the long whistle sounds, he detaches himself.

'I never needed that, the celebration, the people everywhere. I can enjoy it, but I don't need it, I think. Not the way some players need it. You know, in here,' He taps his temple. 'What you have done and how you have done it.'

He is keen on this notion of an internal level of expectation. Something deep inside prevents him from deluding himself. He is dogmatic about football and tactics and putting them under pressure because he likes to think that effort and work is a good benchmark of honesty. If good players are honest on the pitch, they will do well. He feels he shares that internal clock with the Irish people, that in Ireland he has come upon a race who won't fool themselves.

'People in England, and I am an Englishman, people in England have expectations based on many things, like the past and the size of the country and other achievements. They don't know a good result in terms of their own team. In Ireland people deep down know what to expect. If the team performs honestly and achieves what the Irish people expect, deep down then they are happy. I like that. If you want to know about the relationship with people, I think it is down to that. Irish people are realistic and so am I. We don't fool ourselves or each other. The Irish people know that our team give an honest effort. They can measure that. They are realists and I am a realist.'

He's a realist, but, like the Irish, he has his quirks. Superstition. Romance. In his days at Leeds, wild horses wouldn't drag him from the dressing room unless he had headed the ball ten times to Norman Hunter. Talk of the 1966 World Cup and the subsequent birth of a son reminds him of another tale.

'For the birth of me first son, our John, I was away playing at Leicester. When I got home, Pat had been taken in and had the baby. There was no question then, not a thought of not playing, or being there to hold her hand, or see your kid born. It wan't done, man. No way. Nobody did that. When Debbie was born, I was in Lilleshall at a coaching course. Away again. When Peter was born, I sent the two kids to me mother's. I was working and couldn't look after them. Anyway, I was never at home for any of the kids being born. For the third one I went away and left town. I hadn't been there for the first ones, so it was lucky for us. Silly really, but…'

Then he remembers himself, and, lest you get the wrong idea, he adds, 'I came back like… I came back to see the kid an' all.'

There's a streak in him that's cussed and contrary and makes him suspicious of anything that the masses clamour for. Something there, too, that makes him prickly about criticism. He's not made for public consumption. It is a pity that his problems with the press became polarised so quickly and so bitterly into a feud with Eamon Dunphy. The ferocity of that engagement has quietened most critics. It would have been interesting to see Charlton operate in an environment of healthy and vigorous debate. As it is, the press is cowed and he's not complaining.

One morning last year, as the team made its way successfully through the Baltics and onwards to qualification, Charlton arrived to a press conference in uncharacteristically chipper mood. 'What's the team then?' he was asked. 'You tell me,' he replied gamely. There followed a long and embarrassing silence until the woman from *The Guardian* eventually ventured the name Bonner and the ice was broken. Eight years of travelling with Charlton and nobody felt confident enough of his humour to risk his wrath by getting an answer wrong.

He concedes the point that he is, well, a bad-tempered bugger really. He's mellowing, though. He says he finds the right time now when he needs to issue a bollocking. He is a man who grew up in hard times in the shadow of the world's greatest footballer, though, and he doesn't consult psychology handbooks before he tackles players. Sending home Gary Waddock in 1990? 'That was a decision. Hard. But my job is decisions. That's what I'm paid for.'

He looks back over those World Cups he attended as a television analyst, a man on the other side of the media fence. Turning up at training grounds every morning to find the security barring them, the camera crew would stick Big Jack out front and he would attempt to catch the eye of a superstar. 'Hey, Dino, over here. Oye, Franz.' It worked every time.

'We're all in the same business, they'd always come over to me. I used to wonder then what it would be like to be on the inside like that with me own team. I know now. The security. It keeps people out, but it locks you in as well. You have to give people a little slack. Everyone is under pressure. Everyone is doing their job. It's nothing now, you know, for the phone to ring at three or four in the morning and there to be a journalist from Japan or China on the line looking to do an interview. Sometimes I even talk to them. I'm getting better. The one thing with me, you can fart about with me all you bloody like, but don't fart about with me if you've got a football at your feet.'

He is dogmatic, but if you don't present a question wrapped around an opinion but just let something float across his consciousness, he'll entertain it. He's worrying now about the heat in Orlando, but he's taken good advice on that, he thinks, and he's tinkering with formations in his head. 4-4-2. 4-5-1. 4-4-1-1. The defeat to Spain was a crushing disappointment, a result that came in under the internal level of expectation and he finds it hard to build up an enthusiasm for 4-5-1. But Tilburg, against the Dutch, created such clamour, all those young players fidgeting about waiting for action. Think. Think. Think.

He dreads the summers now. He says they have become long for him, the working end of them, that is. There is football and there is a holiday and then football again. No time to get away and really think. No escape. He misses his grandchildren too. Away all that time, with everyone wanting a piece of him. He misses them.

He knows what will happen when he, Maurice, Charlie and Mick arrive in America. They'll hunt out a remote pub somewhere around Orlando. In the evenings they'll take a taxi, have a few pints, talk about football and home and America.

'Aye, we'll chew the fat a bit. We're not looking for night clubs, or girlie bars, or nowt. We're looking for a bit of quiet. I'll enjoy that and I'll enjoy a bit of crack with the lads. But you know what I'll be looking forward to? A few days fishing meself on a weir in Galway, getting down to that water and taking a little stock of it all.'

Fishing. It's the great Jack Charlton cliché. He'd rather be fishing. Truth is, he'd rather be far from the madding crowd.

He has always headed that way. Away from the streets to the

fields and the rivers. A solitary man in a team game. There's something very Irish in that, isn't there?

'Might be,' he says, 'just might be.' He stands up, ready to go, the last practitioner of the old family trade.

No sleep till dawn as Irish fans bawl and balladeer

20 June 1994

We danced all night on Broadway. Twisting and turning beneath the neon lights, our feet hardly touching the ground.

New York was awash with green and echoing with song till the early hours. Down in Little Italy, the losing nation was left to its sorrow. Elsewhere, the Irish bawled and balladeered. No sleep till dawn. No sleep till dawn.

Saturday was the longest day. The greatest day too. From early morning the great thoroughfares of New York bristled with Irish fans. Some alchemy had been worked, 4,000 tickets had turned into 40,000.

The Port Authority building from where the buses to Giants Stadium across the broad Hudson departed almost buckled under the pressure.

From ten o'clock onwards, the Irish bars threw the drink out with abandon.

Bertie Ahern hunched over breakfast in the East Side Irish bar between 3rd Avenue and Lexington as the TV screens all around blasted out the live coverage of the Dublin and Kildare match.

From lunchtime the great concrete sea of parking space that the ground is set in was covered by the battalions. Saturday was the day that the Irish reclaimed New York. Everybody was Irish.

Blacks, Asians and Hispanics were seen wandering through the cars and stalls, wearing Irish jerseys and being photographed for posterity.

Even the weather smiled benignly on the fair-skinned Paddies. It was hot, but the sun was masked by cloud and the humidity was down on previous days. As the day wore on, the conviction grew that Ireland would win. To enter the stadium was to become a believer.

Three tiers, the highest stretching high towards the sky. Empty on Friday, the ground had looked commendably compact from ground level. Full and electric on Saturday, Giants Stadium looked massive and daunting.

In the arteries that circulated people to their seats, familiar songs wafted through the general din. The great dirge of fun and limited ambition. 'You'll never beat the Irish, you'll never beat the Irish,' and then a blast of 'We are green, we are white, we are f***ing dynamite, tra la la la la la.'

The anticipation grew exponentially through the tedium of the pre-game show.

The banners carried familiar messages from home. Davy Keogh saluted the world as usual, his travel agent getting in on the act with a neighbouring banner declaring itself the carrier of the nation's most famous fan.

The national anthem was mangled by the Marine Band, emerging as a dog's dinner trapped between foxtrot and samba. So the people took control and sang regardless, belting out the old grisly tune as the band did its own thing. About twelve minutes later the crowd was hugging itself. Mr Cianluca Pagliuca bent his back to pick the ball out of the Italian net. In the press box there was hugging and clapping and some tears before the notebooks were scribbled in.

The next seventy-eight minutes of football were head in hands, knuckles in mouth, knee-shaking drama. What we would have been happy with on Friday night – a draw – suddenly became the symbol of moral defeat. The heroes were familiar and plentiful. Bonner's save. McGrath's sorcery. Coyne's running. Townsend's streaky confidence. Houghton's engine. McAteer's outright cheek, slipping the ball through Italian legs and running into places he had no right to go. The long final whistle came late and after much longing.

The cacophony was shaking the ground to its core. The police manhandled the odd Irish fan who trespassed deliriously onto the pitch and Irish players wandered about pleading for clemency on the fans' behalf. Otherwise they were welded to each other in hugs and embraces, mirroring the scenes throughout the stands.

Saturday night was different from the other great days of recent years played out in soccer grounds all over the world. Saturday owed nothing to luck, or desperation, or heroic individual performances. Saturday represented control and maturity, an arrival on the world stage for Jack Charlton's team.

No more patronising words praising the effort and the sweat. No more damnation by faint praise. Saturday was the consummation of long-promised potential and patient planning. In the tunnel afterwards we watched Albert Reynolds and Jack Charlton embrace, the politician thanking the sportsman for doing what no politician can do, lifting a nation's morale and self-image.

As the fans drifted back towards the glistening spires of Manhattan, the news from Co. Down drained the joy from the faces. Six local Catholic men had been shot dead in a UVF attack on O'Toole's Bar in Loughinisland. There was silence, sadness, then bitter words and, then, anger. The realisation grew that just such a sapping, such a sandbagging of the spirit was what the perpetrators wanted. Those who died were remembered, those who killed them were cursed, but the spirit burned on and song seemed like the only antidote, the only reassertion of what is good and positive in our lives.

It was a day when to be Irish was to clench the fist and bolster the heart and tell the enemy that they'll never win. Never.

The whiff of an obsession

6 August 1994

When I was very young and knew no better, I fell in love with a man
called Sniffer. He was a footballer: Sniffer was my sun, my moon
and my stars. When his groin was strained, I felt sympathetic tweaks
myself. When his hamstring was hamstrung, I walked the schoolyard
with a gallant limp. When *Shoot* magazine informed me that Sniffer
stroked the ball as if it were bone china, I took to performing
dangerous and lewd acts with my mother's gravy boat.

Sniffer played with Leeds United. I presume, because he never
found time for me, that he had a wife and family somewhere. If they
existed, they hardly knew him as Sniffer. His real name was Allan
Clarke and, in all likelihood, they addressed him by some variant of
that rather conventional English sobriquet. Mrs Clarke would hardly
kiss her husband's pale forehead and fondly declare her love for him
in football fan terms. 'I love you, Sniffer, I do. Oh yes, Sniffer, I love
you.'

Back then, though, I imagined all things were possible in Sniffer's
life.

Sniffer wasn't the most manly of nicknames, but a boy who
answered to 'Humpy' could feel a certain empathy there. 'Here
comes Humpy' weren't words to chill childish hearts.

Then, as now, Africa was in trouble. Our class was dragooned into an unlikely scheme by which each of us would adopt an African child or a 'black baby', as the generic term was then. One new penny a week would be collected from each pupil and this would be forwarded to Africa (where exactly? The nun said she had an address) to ensure the upkeep of each adopted child. Naturally I argued against this smug, First World paternalism, setting the paltry drip of our charity against the monstrous crimes of England's colonial past. I proceeded to rage against the half-heartedness of western efforts to adjust the balance of trade or to encourage indigenous industry and self-sufficiency...

My ideas later formed the basis of the Brandt Report, but, shamefully, back then I was bought over by the more novel aspect of the nun's wheeze. Each of us penny donors was to conjure up a name for our African adoptee. The nuns, with their well-documented connections in the christening business, would make the moniker stick.

Such an opportunity doesn't often fall the way of a seven year old. So today, somewhere on the African continent, unless those pennies were sadly wasted, is an Allan 'Sniffer' Clarke. Christened such by Humpy, a confused Leeds fan living in Chelsea territory. Humpy did well actually. Allan S. Clarke was the only one of his community not to have been named Peter Osgood.

The memory of the penny-a-week scheme is all jumbled up with childish needs to emulate footballers and the pressing need to shed the name Humpy before girls became discerning.

An advertisement in a soccer magazine brought it all back this week. After a month of sweating in the oppressive heat of Orlando, the Irish soccer team has launched 'Team Spirit for Men – The Fragrance for Champions', an official licensed product of the FAI, yours for £7.95, including a classy little football-shaped bottle.

Now, I longed once to have a half respectable nickname like Sniffer. I wore a white replica shirt with a number eight on the back and when I scored a goal I would raise my right arm and walk slowly away from the scene of my heroic deed, just like Sniffer. I even heaped all manner of confusion and stigma on a child in Africa by naming him after a centre forward. Never though (I say nevah!) did I yearn to smell like Sniffer. Or any other footballer.

I have been in dressing rooms (my calling demands that I hang out with naked sweating men from time to time) and I have sniffed the potions which soccer players apply to themselves. My throat has been rendered dry but fragrant by the smell of Wild Forest, for hours on end having inhaled too deeply half an ozone layer's worth of body spray as it hits rippling pecs. Then comes the underarm treatment and the bucket of hair gel. Finally, and most critically, there is the serious slap-it-on-all-over business. Eau de Lad. Parfum de Disco. Chanel Big Number Eleven.

Why does Team Spirit exist? What exactly is the fragrance of champions? Does it really cost £7.95 to capture that fragrance in a bottle? Do champions not smell like the rest of us? Can soccer scouts literally sniff out new talent?

The cult of the fan is entering a dangerous era. A long-running soccer debate hinges on the fact that English teams (and the Irish international side) change the design of their jerseys every first Friday in order to reap a profit from those for whom the wearing of replica shirts is an act of worship. 'It's very hard on parents with young children,' runs the pious mantra.

In this parish, sympathy and body massages are always on offer to parents with tyrannical children, but in the matter of replica jerseys the little tykes are the least alarming aspect of the whole business. Grown men and grown women feel compelled to invest heavily in identifying with their heroes.

When yet another new Irish jersey is launched next month, not many adult fans will decline to invest, on the basis that it is the same shade of green as all the other jerseys they have bought. Wearing the new jersey is a mark of piety and devotion. It isn't uncommon on Irish soccer trips to meet fans whose entire travelling wardrobe consists of soccer jerseys. For a lengthy trip they might bring along three Irish jerseys (the white away strip for evening wear) plus, in many cases, the jersey of their favourite English club and that of their county GAA team.

There is something strangely out of kilter about all this, as if being a fan of a certain assembly of professional footballers is the only way in which another swathe of society can define itself.

In Ireland we are obsessed with the quality of our fandom. Identification with our team transforms us into something more significant than a bedraggled island nation on the fringes of Europe. Sport in general, and soccer in particular, acts as a mass hallucinogenic for marginalised communities. We don't just trail after the boys in green, we are the boys in green. That's why Team Spirit, the fragrance of champions, exists.

Sniffer and I were different though.

So haunt me fella – sport is sport, see

24 September 1994

Yeah. It was one of those slow drag Friday afternoons, rain rapping on the cracked window, persistent like a debt collector I know. Nowhere to call home but the inside of a bottle of ten-buck malt. Yeah. Sadder than a beautiful dame with a wart on her lip.

Poured a glass. Thought better of it. Drank straight from the bottle instead.

Cockroach walking across the remains of yesterday's pastrami-on-rye sandwich. No fear. Gotta like him for that. Roaches know a loser when they see one. I've been around enough to know that much. Losers' motel. They check in, but they can't check out. I laughed like a drain. Dribbled all over my cheap suit.

It was near folding-up time when the big schlep knocked on my door. I saw his shoulders and his huge head through the frosted glass and reached for my fake Luger. Painted cardboard.

'Locker Room', it said on the glass. 'Private'. People said 'Locker Room' was a dumb name. Bad for business. 'Blame Ma,' I told them. The guy was giving the frosted glass a good once over. 'Locker Room'. Sports Hack. Yeah.

He came in and the lights went out. He stuck a dime in the meter and spilled out his story. Same old story. New angle. Good talker.

Those shoulders were padded. The big head was a gridiron helmet. Hey. Don't think I cared. I know two things about sport. When the Sox fixed the series in 1919, it wasn't broken. After Clay got done fixing Liston, he was broken. Daddy told me those things the day I left home. Never forgot them. Never will.

Things were bad. Guy was hurting. The boys from forensics were all over the scene like bounty hunters. The chief had the DA's office on his back. Nobody said anything about that though.

I still had no name for the schlep. I tried to get a look at his back.

Pretended to be chasing a butterfly around the room. These gridiron lugs wear their names on their backs just so they'll know each other going through a revolving door. Smarter than the average bear though. Rumbled my little number.

He swivelled on his chair as I passed. Never did see his back.

The big schlep introduced himself finally. My little lecture on trust broke him down. Used it on dames a million times. He'd a voice smoother than a velvet tongue in my ear. Not that I'd know. But I've been around. Don't think that I haven't. He called himself The Juice. Something like that. O.J. I knew the guy from way back. He thought I was a friend. Something nice I once wrote. Jeez.

Haunt me.

He was taking the rap for the filleting of a dishwater blonde broad that used be his wife. Her, and a waiter too. I know angles better than I know basic geometry. This was a good one. I asked if he'd sung to anyone else before coming here. 'The *Sunday Indo*,' he said. 'But no newspapers,' I said. 'Nope.'

I needed to keep the schlep under raps. He'd pulled a dumb panicky stunt in a white bronco car and thought one or two saps out there might have gotten the gist. Slapped him around a bit just to show him who was boss. Then he hit me with his idea.

The haymaker of ideas. Blindside. Out of left field. OJ was a bigger schlep than I thought. He wanted me to take the rap for the wife and waiter job. He reckoned it was my fault. People like me.

'Guys like you,' he said, like he was talking to some bozo he'd just bounced out of a bar.

'Guys like me,' I said real fast, 'don't get into jams like what you're in, fella. Watch your mouth or I'll slug ya again.'

He didn't get the message. Wouldn't have got it if it had been in flashing neon two feet from his kisser.

'Guys like you,' he said, 'build a guy up from the time his voice breaks. Gotta be the best. Gotta be the most aggressive. Gotta hit them where it hurts. Gotta be a winner. Gotta be a man.'

He was giving me bellyache. Him or the soda in the fifteenth malt the night before. Bellyache just the same.

'Anyone ever tell ya to go out and get into a mess like this one? Any sports hack in this town ever tell ya that?'

He gave me the patter. Since he was a kid nothing worked. Only aggression.

Guys like me wrote him up good for it.

When he packed in the football racket, he couldn't make real life. People like me never called him up no more. Nobody cheered no more. He settled down with the dishwater blonde. She was from a different planet. He was the only kinda guy he knew how to be.

Beat her. Cops called. It was smoothed over. I wrote that he was too good a guy to have done something like that to such a pretty little filly. He liked that. Remembered it. I didn't.

He was shouting. So loud that you couldn't hear the rain no more.

I told him that his case would make great TV, this was comeback stuff. He wouldn't listen. We'd prized his aggression. We'd made him what we wanted him to be. We'd used him all up and we'd left him there. Started using someone else up.

Told him that this was a man's world.

I began making with the home truths. Sport is sport fella. Serious damn business. Same for dames as it is for guys. Everyone gets the same twist from the hacks on my beat. You kill your lollapalooza, you face a stretch. Don't come mouthing to me about how tough it's been. Take it like a man.

He smiled. Narrow smile. Thin as a blade.

'Ya goin' to the big camogie game tomorrow?' he asked.

I laughed like a drain.

'Them broads don't hit. You know that. Not the real thing.'

Lonesome refrain of the Real Fan

8 October 1994

There was a man on the radio this week who was concerned about the plight of that most endangered of species, the Real Fan. ''Tis a scandal and a national shame and a blight on our very nationhood that the Real Fan is being treated so poorly by the powers that be,' said the man. 'The Real Fan can never get a ticket,' said the man.

Now, I am a Real Fan myself. On soccer afternoons my waistband dips provocatively at the back revealing just the right amount of buttock cleavage.

Around front, my belly sways like an untended udder beneath the stressed fabrics of my replica jersey. I like nothing better than to lean forward slightly, letting my behind stick out and my belly sag, and then to sway from side to side, can of beer in one hand, cigarette in the other, deliriously singing 'Here we go, here we go, here we go.' I'm faithful to ancient traditions. I wear a crêpe paper hat wherever I go. I'll be buried in that oul' hat. I carry a big whirring rattle and my lapel is naked if it hasn't got a handsome rosette pinned on.

I'm one of the thousands of Real Fans who packed grounds out when it was neither profitable nor popular. I was there before Jack Charlton. Oh yeah. I was one of the 8,100 lusty-throated fans who terrified the Poles when they played here in 1984. They'd never seen a crowd like it. Frenzy. I remember 5,100 of us turned out for the Mexico game later that summer. Then 3,000 of us packed Dalymount the following spring for the game against Israel and in early summer there were 15,000 of us jammed to the rafters in Lansdowne Road when Ireland played their crucial World Cup qualifier against Norway. Ah, the magic of the World Cup. And 17,300 of us squeezed in somehow for the Swiss game and we had a little bit more breathing room when just 15,154 managed to get into the place for the final game with Denmark.

We were the Real Fans. Thick and thin and all that. We were packing out the greatest stadiums in the world when Big Jack was still down the pit. Ah, the rare oul' times. We'd go to a soccer game in England of a Saturday and then take the overnighter back and, sure as eggs were eggs, we'd all be at a League of Ireland match the following day. Same songs, different colours. Get up the yard.

Thank God for the man on the radio, someone who wants to preserve the Real Fan and his natural environment. The Preservation Society looks after us very well. They want the old terrace preserved for us. Ah, we loved the terrace.

Many is the rainy afternoon I've spent standing like a sodden heron watching my favourites struggle on the field. I'd gaze over at the dry folk with the excellent view of the pitch, them sitting in their seats in the stands eating sandwiches and reading the programme, and, no kidding now, I'd pity them suckers.

They didn't know what they were missing. I loved the rain and the lovely scent of all the manly bodies pressed against me. I loved not being able to see what was happening at the other end of the ground.

Exciting days. By half-time I'd be jigging up and down, the need to urinate having beset me like a St Vitus's dance. Pressed in with the masses there was only one thing for it – the Anfield baptism, as it's called, after its Liverpudlian inventors. Give yourself a nice steamy 'hot leg'. Then there was the terrace wit. That's gone too. 'Who's your father, referee?' somebody would shout. I always waited for that, suppressing the giggles till someone said it.

'Who's your father?' Ho, ho, ho. Stop the lights. That would be the beginning of a whole chain of witty barbs. 'Get yourself a pair of glasses, Ref!' 'Is that a guide dog or is it your wife, Ref?' I tell you, your trousers would soon dry out, you'd be slapping your thighs so heartily. Yes, winning streak, losing streak, League of Ireland or World Cup, we Real Fans never let the lads down. Can we get tickets? Bah!

I'm a Real Rugby Fan too, of course. When I venture out to a rugby game with my cronies, Real Fans to a man, I toss the sheepskin jacket on to top off the look with the old school scarf, a tweed fishing hat and a hip-flask. I don't attend any away games involving the roughnecks down in Munster. I believe the traffic is dreadful afterwards, but I never miss a home match and I often wander out of the pavilion and have a look at the Firsts close up. There is no greater sight in rugby surely than an All-Ireland League game between two Dublin clubs, being played out in hallowed Lansdowne. Two hundred, maybe three hundred, of us bringing the roof down and eating hot roast-beef sandwiches as the boys set about each other on the sacred sward. The spectacle, man – the spectacle. We'll have a drink together afterwards, maybe we'll even give it a lash if the little woman is doing the driving. Can I get a ticket come the big day out? Of course not.

Ah, still and all. I love the oul' soccer and I love the oul' rugby and of course don't I love the oul' Gah. The Preservation of the Real Fan Society is very perplexed about the fate of us old Gah fans. We're the ones in the black coats and the flat caps.

We stand behind goalposts at club games talking to the goalkeeper and the fullback. 'If you'd a few pints less of the porter last night you might have got to that one,' we'll say to the fullback if a goal has just gone in. 'A farmer would make a good living off the amount of land you need to turn on,' we'll tell him as he flails after some nippy forward.

The fans of the oul' Gah are ever-faithful, of course. Isn't it ourselves who have kept the Railway Cup going all these years? Isn't it the Real Fans who make the National League Division Three games in deepest winter such a heartening sight for Gaels everywhere? Wasn't it the Real Fans who packed Croke Park time and time again for all those dreary All-Ireland semifinals through the 1970s and 1980s?

Now what do the Gah crowd want to do? They want to let the corporate brigade into Croker. 'C'mon, you guys in Blue' shall ring out when me jewel and darlin' Dubs are disporting themselves. They want to increase the capacity. They want to do away with the terraces. They want to put in restaurants and shops and give everyone a good view of the game.

It's a sellout, that's what it is. The man on the radio got it in one. Bloody sellout. Nobody gives a tuppenny damn about the plight of the Real Fan.

Nobody cares about the lore of the terrace, about us being there through thick and thin, through rain and shine.

We are Real Fans. We demand to be treated as such. Give us back our crêpe hats and our rackety rattles and our terraces and our funny taunts and our lovely ditties. Stop treating us like, well, I'll say it because nobody else will, like consumers. Like bloody paying customers.

We won't have it. Me and mother is very humble, see?

Reds left for dead

5 November 1994

The 'Carlow Reds' are unfurling their colours. Somehow they lack the menace of an LA street gang as they lift the corners of their large tricolour outside Casa Bailen. 'Glory Glory Man United' they sing with the curiously English accent which Irish soccer fans adopt on such occasions. 'Carlow Reds' says the banner. A young Catalan strolls past and, smiling hugely, gives the little knot of supporters the thumbs down. Carlow Reds don't have a mean bone in their bodies. They wave back. All smiles.

It is 5.30 in the afternoon. The sun is rapidly withdrawing. On the bus to the stadium somebody tries to spark a little life into the Manchester United fans with a croaky rendition of 'Blue Moon', the anthem for which the other half of Manchester stands to attention. Nothing doing, however. Outside, Barcelona is streaking by like a dream world.

The Nou Camp Stadium swings into view and there is a collective intake of breath. The Nou Camp stretches upwards forever.

'Makes Old Trafford look like a toilet, lads,' roars one excited blasphemer.

Inside the bus, the observation is greeted with quiet good humour. 'Jaysus, look at it.'

This is perhaps the biggest soccer game since the World Cup. Both sides carry baggage stuffed with desperation into the Nou Camp tonight. Both have made only moderate starts to their European challenge. The proceedings are being broadcast live around the world. In the US, 60 million homes will receive this game. A Louth man, Tommy Smith, will provide the commentary.

Manchester United and FC Barcelona are names that haunt the imagination. Their clash takes additional spin from the fact that, when the sides met in Manchester two weeks ago, they produced a football classic, a game bursting with passion and skill. Outside the window of the bus, there is the depressing reality of modern soccer. A couple of thousand Manchester United fans have been herded together on a stretch of waste ground 500 yards from the stadium. Eight mounted policemen are keeping the herd in check, but the herd has discovered that rhythmic clapping and chanting disturbs the horses.

Nobody knows for sure whether a panicked horse might just plough into the crowd. The sight of the policemen riding rodeo is enough to keep the herd amused, however. In the dim orange light, the sense of tension and malice is palpable, yet when the United fans manage to break off from the herd it is to exchange shirts and scarves with their Catalan rivals. Which came first, the malice or the dehumanising herding routine?

Tonight two football cultures collide. Manchester United produce the same blind passion in people that FC Barcelona do, yet the English club are very much the inferior planet this evening. Something about these two clubs symbolises the opposing strains of modern Europe.

Big football clubs often like to boast that they are something more than that. More than a club. Barcelona have made those words their motto. More than a club. And nowhere is the claim more justified.

When Robert Hughes unleashed his impressive urban history of Barcelona two years ago, he contrived tragically to miss the point. FC Barcelona are mentioned just once in Hughes's hefty text as the Australian unfolds a world which revolves around the politics of Catalan separatism and the artistic imaginations of Gaudí, Miró, Montaner, et al.

At the heart of the city, though, is its football club, founded in 1899 and home to 110,000 members or socios today. Among that 110,000 are the Pope, the current president of the International Olympic Committee and just about anybody with pretensions to political or commercial influence in Catalonia.

Three weekly television programmes devote themselves exclusively to the proceedings at FC Barcelona. Every newspaper has at least one reporter whose daily beat consists of nothing more than news from the Nou Camp.

During the long and bitterly resented decades of Falangist oppression which stemmed from Madrid, ordinary Catalans expressed themselves through the football of FC Barcelona. The rival club in Barcelona, the reviled Espanol, made the mistake at the outset of choosing a name which means simply 'Spanish'. Though attitudes have softened as Barcelona has grown in affluence, Spanish is the one thing which Catalans have always refused to be.

Outside the Nou Camp stadium on the northeast side of the city, they sell long scarves in the Barcelona colours. They don't bear the club's name but the more potent legend 'Antimadridistas'.

Real Madrid, or, in English, Royal Madrid, the white-kitted side from the capital, served for decades as the symbol of all that Catalonia feared and hated. Franco was a devoted follower, able to name team line-ups stretching back decades. In Barcelona they suspect that the Nou Camp and its heroes were allowed to prosper only because Franco needed worthy and passionate opponents for his team. The language, the culture and the flag of Catalonia were banned, but, in a football stadium, one could display all three against the team of the dictator for ninety minutes at the weekend.

That is the legacy of FC Barcelona. More than a club. Since the death of Franco and the liberalisation of Spain, Barcelona has progressed beyond the traditional kneejerk reactions to everything Spanish. The city has asserted its independence by flexing its muscles and its imagination. Barcelona has reconstructed itself as a beautiful modern city, culturally vibrant and commercially thriving. The novels of Eduardo Mendoza, the designs of Javier Mariscal, the enlightened mayoralty of Pasqual Maragall, have all been part of a movement which has transformed Barcelona into one of the key centres of European culture.

Catalan politics now accommodates a political philosophy which suggests that Spain should redraw itself as a federal state and create two capitals – one in Madrid the other in Barcelona – although the notion of separatism does not sit easily with Catalonia's vision of its role in the new Europe.

The city's relationship with its football club has developed too. FC Barcelona are a celebration of their own city now. They are expected to entertain, to play beautiful football. They became the champions of Europe two years ago and have been Spanish champions for the last four years, a spell of unprecedented affluence which matches the rise in the city's fortunes.

Barcelona once struggled against the notion that Africa began at the Pyrenees. Today, the city is consummately modern and European. Manchester, by contrast – once the centre of the old industrial revolution, once a great vibrant industrial city – has little left of its tattered pride but good intentions and a good football team.

And Manchester has tried long and hard to win those things which Barcelona won in 1992. The club yearns to bring the European championship back to Lancashire. The city longs to hold the Olympic Games, which had their most memorable celebration to date in Barcelona two years ago.

Yet the shared aspirations serve only to illustrate the differences. Franco died in 1975 and the nineteen years since then have marked a period of exciting growth and regeneration for Barcelona. In Britain, four years after the death of Franco, Margaret Thatcher swept to power. Since then, the north of England has been in steady decline.

When Manchester first went looking for the Olympic Games, Thatcher was studiously indifferent, which dented their credibility. The city has never really caught up. Second time round, John Major threw his inconsiderable weight and wallet behind Manchester's bid, but the impressions of that disastrous first run still remain.

Then there are the problems of Manchester itself. The urban decay, the industrial graveyard, the grinding weather, the official neglect. The city has struggled on as best it can, but Manchester remains a marginalised place in a country with its face set against modern Europe.

On the days when they uncork their most flowing football, Manchester United do so less as a celebration and more as an act of defiance. 'What's it like to have no job?' sing the London supporters when they visit. They need something to distract them from the football.

Outside the Nou Camp, Manchester fans in their great herd display an aggressive fervour which is lacking in their Barcelona counterparts. In a gesture of scary unison, they stab their fingers in the air, jabbing aggressively at the chest of some imaginary foe. Football in Manchester still represents one of the principal boundaries to the working-class imagination. You can live through your team, you can use your team as an outlet for belligerent chauvinism.

In Barcelona, the need to do those things has long since vanished. You live to enjoy your team, amongst many other things.

Inside the Nou Camp, on the sheer cliff faces that surround the pitch, the Manchester fans are herded to the fifth and highest tier. Up there in the night sky, they sit as living exhibitions of their own plight.

The Manchester United contingent stretches across the top of the stand, a great swathe of red. At least four out of every five fans wear the club jersey.

'Glory, Glory, Man United,' they sing pluckily.

When the Barcelona team emerges from the tunnel minutes before kickoff, though, the Nou Camp vibrates with excitement. A huge yellow, red and blue banner materialises in the stand behind one goal stretching gloriously right across the width of the pitch.

The Barcelona hymn is sung, ending in a crescendo with 110,000 voices roaring 'Barca! Barca! Barca!' Nothing but the popping of flashbulbs emanates from the Manchester United contingent.

The Nou Camp represents the future of football. Tribalism has vanished. The socios don't arrive potbellied and beer-breathed and kitted out like players.

They arrive in suits and sweaters and jeans and dresses and they arrive expecting to be entertained. They buy cushions to sit on and drinks to swig and deign to surrender their individualism only when that which they have paid to see merits the garland of a collective chant.

As the game unfolds, Johan Cruyff, Barcelona's Dutch manager, strolls up and down the sidelines, the epitome of European chic, one hand resting casually inside the pocket of his rich blue suit, his world-weary face bobbing above the collar of his yellow polo neck.

On the press box monitor, the Manchester United manager's face suddenly fills the screen. Alex Ferguson's face is a mess of broken capillaries. His red Manchester United tie clashes with his complexion.

His club blazer is too severe. He looks like Taggart. He is biting his nails.

Not long after the start, Hristo Stoitchkov, the Barcelona number eight, essays a shot. The ball takes freakish flight as it deflects off a flailing Manchester United boot and loops in a curious arc past the waving arms of the goalkeeper. The ball hits the back of the net and the ripple spreads across the rigging like a shock wave of dark implications. 1-0 to Barcelona.

It hurts. Manchester United has come here tonight desperately needing some sort of result. The European Cup is all about money. The club has spent hugely on its ambition to bring that trophy and the prestige and money that goes with it back to Old Trafford.

Last year, they were knocked out of the competition by a little-known Turkish club. This year, some tampering with the rules by UEFA permitted Manchester United (but not Galatassary, their conquerors last year) to advance automatically to the league play-offs' stage of the competition. Manchester United, resonant of a glorious, tragedy-tinged past, is the sort of name that sells a competition to television companies, so the English club was lifted like a baby over the first hurdle.

If they can hold the score to 1–0, perhaps they can sneak something from this occasion. That's what they are telling themselves as half-time approaches; probably still telling themselves as a high treacherous spinning ball lands on Romario, drops dead at his feet and is poked past the sturdy plodding figure of Gary Pallister and whipped into the net.

The Nou Camp, one of Manchester United players had

commented, 'just looks like a big building outside, but inside it's hard to play football.' The truth of that is ringing in their ears now.

Barcelona is conjuring up neat little ten-yard passes, stabbing epigrams which cut through United's more boisterous arguments. The United fans perched up in the clouds are wasting their passionate imprecations on the bats who fly jauntily around the floodlights.

Barcelona finish the affair by adding another two goals, swift picador-jabs to the bleeding body of the victim that is Manchester United. Behind one goal the younger Barcelona fans are whirling their scarves above their heads. At one stage, a tidal version of the Mexican wave engulfs every section of the stadium, apart from the surly, red-shirted contingent up top. 'Barca! Barca! Barca!'

When Barcelona score their final goal, it comes after a spell of two or three minutes when, to the delight of the socios, Barcelona have denied their visitors so much as one kick of the ball.

English passion and defiance have wilted before the death-by-a-thousand-cuts torture that the truly creative players of Barcelona have conjured up. No bludgeoning football tonight.

Afterwards, as the Catalan crowd cheerily evaporates and the English followers wait to be herded away, the press makes its way down to the dungeons where the post-match conferences are held. Everywhere there are commemorations of Barcelona's past, the faces of past captains peering in monochrome posterity from the walls; sepia newspaper pages carrying news of past championships; names of players in great, long lists like war dead; a pictorial history of the growth of the Nou Camp. Glum-faced and stricken, Alex Ferguson sits and faces the questions. It's a bizarre little tableau vivant. The journalists are all eating large ice-pops doled out by a sponsor at the entrance to the press room. 'We were slaughtered,' says Ferguson.

'Humiliated.' His honesty is bracing. The European Cup is a long way from his grasp now.

Behind him, the backdrop lists more names. Not those of footballers, but those of 'football's partners', Reebok and Ford, Canon and Mastercard, Phillips and Aguila beer.

Johan Cruyff, multilingual, handsome and suave, glides in when Ferguson vacates his seat. His victorious team exist because of the city around them, a product of local culture. The club he manages are a symbol of football's possibilities…

Ferguson's side exists despite their surroundings. Manchester United loom out of the rubble that is northern England. Cruyff speaks about rhythm where Ferguson spoke about tackles.

Outside, many policemen are herding the Manchester United fans towards their coaches. They will be driven straight to the airport.

When they sing, the Manchester United fans unleash a great belch of beery breath into the still night air. 'Always Look on the Bright Side of Life', they sing. 'Always Look on the Bright Side of Life.'

Setting out own manifesto in new locale

5 December 1994

High time for this column, having moved to a new locale, to set out
its stall, to draw a line in the sand, to publish its own manifesto. Here
we stand, that sort of thing.

For instance, this column subscribes to the view that Jack
Charlton is God. An Old Testament version of God who doth smite
the unworthy and drink stout and catch fish, but God nonetheless.
God is always on the record. We sports journalists are the
handmaidens of the Lord.

Charlton may be God, but it is Gay Mitchell who shall be called
the Creator. 'Locker Room' believes that verily there shall be three
spanking new national stadiums in Dublin by the turn of the century.
These stadiums shall be full to capacity day in and day out. Probably
with greyhound fans. People shall promise to build casinos in the
public service just as a device for getting planning permission to
build stadiums. Dublin shall host the 2004 Olympics. In Cape Town
there shall be gnashing of teeth as Gay Mitchell lights the Olympic
Flame. The Games shall be the Gay Olympics. Not long after,

playing in the Olympic Stadium, the RUC shall win the All-Ireland club hurling championship. No ugly handpassing either.

This column believes that the National Lottery is a fine thing and that the funds extracted by this tax on the adventurous has indeed been used in the manner intended. Golf clubs are fitting recipients of such funds, particularly if they lie in the constituency of a government minister.

Nothing more embarrassing than a shabby golf club. This column doesn't see the need for swimmers to swim fifty metres in a straight line. Aren't we an island, don't they have the sea if they want that sort of thing.

This column has been to the mountaintop. The news from there is that Northern Irish soccer fans mean no harm. We straight-laced southerners need to start digging their rich vein of black humour. For that reason Cliftonville probably prefer playing all their games with Linfield away from home.

Furthermore Glasgow Rangers FC are our friends. Lastly, League of Ireland soccer is a top-class product. Only football people know that. I am a football person.

I loved Drums. I am a northsider. I played a bit for Home Farm. I was going to League of Ireland when it was neither profitable nor popular.

While we're talking hard facts about popular institutions, let it be said that RTÉ do a fine job covering minority sports and that Jackie Fullerton on the BBC is the finest Gaelic-games presenter this island has known, that Formula One motor racing makes splendid tele-vision, that our heart never sinks when *Sportsnight* is replaced by the Northern Ireland version of the same programme featuring Linfield's never-ending European first round game with Odense. 'Three goals needed away from home, a hard task surely, but not all over for the Blues.'

This column believes that there was never a dirty blow thrown during any of the Dublin–Kerry games of the 1970s. That the GAA's experimental rules are a resounding success and should be evolved further so that handling the ball is eliminated altogether. The British Army shall get out of Ulster before Cavan shall.

Now that we are making a clean breast of things, let it be said that rugby players move from club to club because some clubhouses have a better atmosphere than others and in a wholly amateur game ambience is important. Rugby hasn't been given due credit for ending apartheid in South Africa; why, shucks, some of our guys even played multiracial teams over there.

This column cannot go along with the popular view that professional golfers look like flamboyant refugees from the world of pimping. Certainly Ronan Rafferty may yet be a chaperone at next year's Rose of Tralee. As may John Daly.

With the help of EEC structural funds, this country will one day consist of nothing but golf courses and motorways. Nothing worse than being stuck behind a ladies' four-ball, is there?

In this world, where much is shallow and counterfeit and where marketers force us to consume dangerous things as unwittingly as a British athlete taking steroids for his asthma, this column shall be your guide. We believe that TV wrestling is for real, that Andre Agassi is for real, that Mick O'Dwyer's Kerry side was an elaborate hoax which accidentally won eight lucky All Irelands (well look what he did in Kildare), that Sky Sport has educational (and possibly nutritional) value, that Andy Gray would make a fine attorney general.

White men can jump, so can horses. Arsenal play total football. George Foreman has nothing to fear when Mike Tyson gets out of prison. Neither does the female population of this earth. Don King is much misunderstood. Being misunderstood is a flimsy legal defence.

Dixon of Dock Green keeps goal for Southampton these days. You are never too young to start on the professional tennis circuit. Members of the IOC only get presents at Christmas. Even if it means bringing down the whole house of cards, those IOC folks will remove drugs from sport.

It's always Christmas somewhere. Hares enjoy being coursed, foxes like being chased, GAA officials like being questioned by the media. During the National League in the winter, many people attend games merely to enjoy the spectacle of the half-time show.

By and large this column subscribes to the view that folk preferred standing groin to buttock with complete strangers in the pouring rain rather than sitting in seats at sporting events. That was a pleasure many of them were willing to die for. Terrace wit was often Wildean. Ra Ra Ree, kick him in the knee, Ra Ra Rollox, kick him in the other knee. Gets you every time. You don't hear stuff like that in your executive boxes. This column doesn't believe it is possible for one man in a press box to get a Mexican wave going at a major sporting event. This column has tried.

This column believes too that, despite the dubious evidence offered by stopwatches and statisticians, all sport was better when this column was young. Better and fairer. Those nancy boys today wouldn't have lasted five minutes with some of the players our fathers brought us to see.

These things 'Locker Room' believes. This be The Word. 'Locker Room' has no answers for any of sport's sorrowful mysteries. What happens to all the good minors? How did Nigel Mansell win BBC Sports Personality of the Year? Is the runner-up still with us? Where's Shergar? Where are The Floaters, for that matter? And Fat Larry's Band? 'Locker Room' has no answers, but he is searching.

'Locker Room' shall not rest until these things are known. You lot can rest easy in your beds now.

Rugby's exclusivity results in rugby's loss

23 January 1995

On a couple of afternoons every winter, just as *The Irish Times* is bracing itself for a blizzard of letters carrying strident claims regarding the sighting of the year's first cuckoo, those of us who live in the ghetto of the fourth floor brace ourselves for a blizzard of a different kind. Phone calls regarding the composition of the Irish rugby team.

For hours on end the phones hop. Men on their office phones demanding news of the team. Men on their car phones demanding information on the team. There is a well-etched mutual understanding submerged in the light banter of these calls.

The customer never asks for news pertaining to the Irish rugby team, just for the team.

Often on the GAA desk we might begin the recital thus: O'Leary, Walsh, Deasy, Moran and, before we get to poor Keith Barr, we are talking to nothing but a dial tone. Sometimes our callers are so knowing, they need only ask darkly if there are any changes. Just that. You pick up the phone and the deep burr of a confident southside accent says, 'Hello. Any changes?'

No other sport gives rise to this sort of phenomenon. No other sport has a constituency as clearly defined and as self-confident as that which follows rugby in Dublin. They are a breed as distinct and separate as the Jewish race.

Apart from watching the Irish team play, they have no real race history of suffering, of course, but they cling together in their communities and schools and clubs nevertheless and those of us who don't understand them are reared to fear them.

They have their own timeworn rituals and their own music. (Anyone know all the verses to 'Bestiality is Best, Boys'?) On the northside we are pure terrified of them. The aberrant presence of Clontarf Rugby Club in our territory does nothing to assuage our fears. Castle Avenue is a small corner of a northside field that shall be forever southside.

It is of course a small task to perform each year, chanting the team selection out to the faithful over the phone. Not much to ask.

Sportswriting is one of those blessedly trivial pursuits which offers up an eternal variety of events and an endless stream of new starts to those of us who lack the concentration or ability to do real jobs.

Write a bad piece today and there is another piece waiting to be tackled tomorrow.

See a dull match this week and there will be a veritable thriller around the corner next week. So taking the phone calls of the faithful merely provides a little seasonal flavour when the frost is on the ground.

Yet, dark shameful fears go coursing through the idle brain. Things we learnt on our mothers' laps. Little resentments. Another rugby weekend has just slipped past into the record books and this sporting heart hasn't missed a beat, hasn't quickened one jot. Why does rugby leave so many of us out in the cold?

Well. Here's my nightmare.

When the great nuclear winter comes and there aren't enough tins of food to cater for all the survivors, we all know that some bright spark is going to suggest that the greater good will be served by driving people of limited usefulness out from the shelters.

Those who will be of most value in rebuilding society will remain underground, warm and well fed. We sports journalists will certainly be left to wander the desolate face of the earth with nobody for company except disc jockeys, chat-show hosts and politicians.

(Decades later, when the engineers and the doctors and the lawyers who pretended to be doctors emerge from their bunkers, they shall be surprised to see great herds of mutants wandering the valleys and the plains, speaking a long-lost version of English which consists of nothing but clichés and sound bites. The politicians will have formed themselves into a primitive hierarchy, the disc jockeys and the chat-show hosts will have learned to keep out of each other's way. All the sports journalists will be dead, having mistaken the untended saloon bars of the earth for one last freebie.)

I always think fretfully of that grim post-nuclear future when I go to Lansdowne Road for a rugby international. I know that, when the worst comes to the worst, the first voice to propose ejecting the fat and the indolent out of the nuclear shelter will have the modulated tones of the southside Dublin rugby worshipper who doesn't want to make the same mistakes vis-à-vis the welfare state, etc., in the next world as were made in this.

The same voice that needs to know the composition of the team before the evening newspapers appear will now propose the culling. He'll be a hip-flask and gold-card chap, a fifth-generation graduate who recovered from the disappointment of never having made the senior cup team in school by going on to start his own business and giving jobs to a few of the boys with medals and bad Leaving Certs. Sees himself as a self-made man. Worships his creator.

On the afternoons of rugby internationals, he brims over with bonhomie, having had a fine lunch and a few jolly scoops at the club.

His booming voice issues like a clarion from the West Upper. The language is distinct. He never mutters 'Ah Jaysus, Mullin.' No. He bellows 'C'mon Brendy! Cut out the shitinology!'

To drift towards Lansdowne Road on the day of an international is to be a gentile in a great sea of the chosen people. Rugby isn't one of those sports which reaches out and embraces you. Not in Dublin anyway. You are born within the caste or outside it.

Limerick apparently produces scary rugby-playing specimens drawn from every swathe of society. In Dublin, however, looking in from the outside there exists a series of barriers which stifle one's concern for the fortunes of the Irish rugby team.

Occasionally there are of course refugees from the more demonic world of Gaelic games who make the cut in the rugby world.

Having infiltrated the world of rugby, their names appear in match programmes in that bewilderingly pompous style of rugby team sheets, P.V.C. Studs, P.D. Voter, I.T. Reader, and we forget them entirely. They are soon holders of the masonic secrets of front-row folklore, a messy cut-throat world into which we outsiders have no right to pry.

That culture of hair-pulling, flesh-biting, stud-raking, testicle-squeezing and head-butting is a closed one, where you take your punishment and buy the perpetrator a drink afterwards.

As individuals, rugby people are generally splendid and warm company. As a tribe, though, they tend to the onlooker to expand menacingly into the outsize dimensions of the rugger stereotype. That sense of exclusivity which the rugby fraternity almost unconsciously radiates means that the pubs won't be full to bursting when Ireland play in South Africa this summer; it also means that Ireland won't achieve as much as they might at the World Cup.

The great sadness is that the gulf of understanding and, let's face it, gulf in class and wealth, that separates many of us on the outside from many of those on the inside, will eventually cost Irish rugby dearly. With a small playing population, manufactured in essentially the same schools and clubs decade in and decade out, there is little room for expansion and little prospect of improvement.

You look sometimes at a man like Anthony Tohill, with soccer and GAA pulling at him for his attention, and think that in all probability he would excel most as a rugby wing forward. You look at the speed of a youngster like Jason Sherlock, torn between the blue of UCD soccer club and the blue of Dublin, and think what an astonishing scrum half he might have made.

Then you think of the chosen people and all the barriers that surround and cosset them, and think that it could never be, and that knowledge feeds the indifference so many of us feel.

Around our place, kids have favourites in everything: favourite GAA players, soccer teams, US basketball teams, wrestlers, gridiron teams, but no favourite rugby teams or players. Rugby doesn't exist for them. The indifference is mutual, just as it was when I was growing up. Rugby is the loser.

Muzzling the dogs – a game of splitting hares

6 February 1995

Here on the sports desk, where we are perpetually busy about the business of retailing what Marshall McLuhan called 'pickled Gods and archetypes', we seldom stop to examine the claims we make on behalf of our subjects. Indeed, we live in a sort of twilight zone where, although confronted daily with first-hand evidence that sporting giants have feet of clay, we find ourselves unable to express that fact through the nibs of our pens. The ombudsman could busy himself for a year in this locality.

For instance, it is only within the loving bosom of his self-help group that this columnist can find the strength to declare openly that he doesn't think much of Howard Wilkinson's talent for playing the transfer market. Then, of course, once the dam has been breached, it all comes pouring out in a spiteful but cathartic rage.

Ah for just one evening of poker with somebody who passes on Cantona, Batty and Rocastle but who busts the bank for Brian Deane and Carlton Palmer. Soon I am standing on my chair shouting the odds: 'Tony Yeboah might well be the saviour, but were I spending £3.4 million (or any fraction thereof) on a saviour I would at least

like to have glimpsed a miracle being performed in the flesh. Wilko
has only seen him on video. Never give a sucker an even break,
that's what I say.'

Those evenings always end in tears, sobbing on the shoulder of
the man who believed in Graham Souness. I have three sessions left
before we start deconstructing my fantasy world built around the
stark monastic existence of the Dublin football team.

There are others among us whose delusions are equally affecting.
There is that raging figure of a man who believes that all sport was
better in the old days. Whatever match is currently unfolding before
his eyes is always dismissed as the worst exhibition of its sort ever to
have been staged.

Then there are those poor divils who believe that certain styles of
hurling are deviant abominations not to be permitted in the presence
of civilised people (hurling people from Cork, that is). In the years
when neither Cork nor Tipperary reach the Munster hurling final,
some explanatory footnote should be appended to the record books.

There are too those long-suffering folk who believe that being
proud to play for Ireland is sufficient tactical and physical
preparation to secure the verdict in any international contest.

Lately the ranks of the deluded have been swelled by a new and
exciting breed. There are among us those who believe that some
sports are now graced by players and creatures who can operate
comfortably in the sixth dimension. The most celebrated instance
came at Selhurst Park just a fortnight ago.

This column bows to no man when it comes to frowning upon the
froth-mouthed antics of certain members of the English soccer-fan
tribe. Nevertheless, it is straining credibility to be asked to believe
that Eric Cantona somehow knew that the victim of his two-footed
attack was in fact a man most worthy of being on the wrong end of
such an assault.

We are asked to believe that, out of the great English array of common-or-garden anti-frog bigots, Eric had the psychic powers to choose the one with the National Front tendencies and the criminal record which involves performing a Buddy Rich drum roll with nothing but a spanner and a man's head. It is no use pointing out to these people that the list of Eric's victims is so long by now that, by the law of averages, he must have pandered to most people's prejudices at some time or other.

Anyway we come not to bury Cantona nor to praise him but to further examine this phenomenon of life in the sixth dimension. Cantona may indeed be the first footballer to be able to sense the presence of evil in one individual amidst a large crowd and, if so, his feat is one large step for mankind but a very small step for hares.

Down in Clonmel last week, the folks in the flat caps and waxed jackets were enjoying the All Ireland of coursing, the Grand National of hare chasing, indeed the very Wimbledon of doggie deeds. This column had occasion to visit the national coursing championships a few years ago and still has bad dreams about the appalling squealing which a hare emits as he is being dismembered by two salivating greyhounds. It was a bumper year that year for kills and squeals.

Indeed 'Locker Room' and his colleague looked set to do a little squealing themselves when an inspection of the conditions the hares were held in after the course was ended quite abruptly by a herd of heavies with itchy fists. (Incidentally, we say 'he' when referring to the hare, but it was alleged to us afterwards in confidence by a coursing person that, given the soft winter we had enjoyed that year, the number of kills was up at Clonmel because many of the hares being coursed were in fact pregnant at the time.)

Since then, coursing folk have, after years of resistance, grudgingly muzzled their dogs. Unwittingly, however, by removing the spectacular gore from their 'sport' they have moved us closer to the very nub of the argument. The ethical cleanliness of a coursing meeting or a hunt can't be measured by the number of kills completed or the number of near misses totted up. That misses the whole point about the sporting spectacle involved in setting animals on each other.

Yet the ranks of the deluded are swollen. There are always some facts which are too plain for the fanatic to see.

So, in the brave new world of muzzled coursing, the super sensory powers of the hare are a tremendous accessory. Some people think that a hare that has been captured and trained to run from the passage at one end of a field to the slip at the other end of the field cares not a whit when it discovers that the two big greyhounds pursuing it are muzzled.

Those bleeding-heart liberals have it wrong, apparently. Hares have been coming out of the fields and giving themselves up in droves. They have been seen squabbling in undignified fashion over their place in the queue and many freely admit that the benefits of being coursed are so great now that the days of the amateur hare are numbered. Full-time professional hares with agents and managers are the inevitable next step.

In Clonmel last week, punters were shocked by the sight of several hares unfolding parasols and promenading across the field on their hind legs whistling old show tunes, all safe in the knowledge that the worst that could happen to them was that they might be driven into the ground and killed by the sheer weight and power of their pursuers. Yes. By the simple deed of muzzling the dogs, the world of coursing has freed itself of all moral complications and liberated the simple hare to enjoy the thrill of the chase and possibly improve its lot by having a wager on the side like the rest of us.

A hare used think he had a one in five chance of being killed, but, now that he has a one in twenty chance of being killed, deep down the hare enjoys coursing four times as much as it used to and is wont to reassure onlookers that nineteen times out of twenty there is nothing at all for the hare to worry about.

Hares and foxes have apparently been boning up on the laws of probability and exploring the outer edges of the sixth dimension. If Cantona can sense the presence of evil at a sporting occasion, our little furry friends can detect a sense of the sporting in that which their ancestors have traditionally regarded as evil. Of course, their sense of society's demographic nuances and tensions is sufficiently sophisticated that they realise too that those who demur are in reality just trying to stir up trouble between rural folk and city folk.

Hares and foxes are soon to join with their one-time persecutors in a joint campaign to secure more sponsorship and increased TV coverage of the much misunderstood worlds of coursing and hunting. The animals will wear little jackets bearing sponsors' logos and TV will run preview programmes in the days before a big event focusing on the background and ambitions and record of the hare or fox in question.

Furthermore, Howard Wilkinson will sign at least two really useful midfielders and Leeds will win the championship fighting off the challenge of Graham Souness's new crazy gang. Their vast pride in the colour green will entitle teams from this island to a hefty head start in all sports and, lastly, The Meek and Contemplative Order of Dublin Footballers shall inherit the earth.

Good man cometh

11 March 1995

He knows. He knows that you hate him. All of you out there. And that's OK. Chris Eubank has been nourished by the thought, so this fine morning he takes his seat and he gives you the hard stare. He knows.

He knows the texture and the dimensions of your hate. Knows its heat. Knows its root. Your hate is an inversion. You don't hate Mr Eubank for being the champ. You hate yourself for being a work-a-day loser.

'Little children on the street call me wanker,' says the champ with sudden and startling candour. You gasp? Save it. The champ has equipped himself with enough tortuous locutions to expose the literal and figurative error in their cruel, childish jibes.

'I have a wife,' he explains. 'I have no need to masturbate. I am not a man who says he will do things and subsequently does not do them. Therefore, I am not that which they say I am. I am the receptacle of their resentments and those of their fathers. For men it is always hunter vs hunter. I am that which they are too inhibited ever to be. If you resent my big car and my house, you are wrong, you are evil. You are mal.'

Christopher Livingston Eubank is not that which little children say he is.

Furthermore, and he can't stress this quite often enough, he is not a bad man.

He is a good man.

He will tell you, too, that he is the mystique, the enigma, a great man, the lionheart, a rude boy, an inspiration, the voice, a proper man, the great romantic, paragon of what he does. Most of all, though, he tells you (twelve times in two hours) that he is a good man. Not a bad man. Yes, he is a good man, a righteous man, and truly the path of the righteous man is beset on all sides by the inequities of the selfish and the tyranny of evil men.

The righteous champ has just been doing the dusting. Meticulously. The fragrant mist of Mr Sheen lingers in the drawing room. The fussy, gold carriage clock gleams after a once over. So do the four telephones, including the two mobiles.

The champ has lingered meaningfully over the portrait photographs of himself, bare-chested and leather-trousered, holding up his two angelic sons. Tenderly, he has flicked the duster over the mottled blue cover of his beloved and gigantic *Webster's Dictionary*. Finally, he has switched off the television and settled down to deal with this prickly hate question.

'I speak that which is on my mind,' he explains. 'In this world you are not to do that. My father, you take my father. He talks to himself. I say: "Why do you talk to yourself, Dad?" He says: "That way I don't get into trouble, son. Talk to people and you get into trouble." Maybe he is right.'

Eubank is wearing grey shorts and a grey tracksuit top. White trainers. The working clothes of a boxer. All brand new and straight from the cellophane. You see, one of the champ's little luxuries is new training gear every morning.

When he leaves this well-appointed, mock-Tudor compound in sedate, suburban Hove and drives into bustling Brighton in one of his two Range Rovers, or in his soft-topped Aston Martin, he will, of course, have metamorphosed into Versace man.

He likes Versace a little too much, perhaps, for a guy with his pronounced lisp, but he'll spend £100 on a fashionable pair of underpants if needs be. The champ believes in doing things correctly. The champ believes that good taste is the mark of a good man. For work, though, fresh tracksuits must suffice.

The loss of ostentation is a sacrifice a champ must make.

Next weekend, Chris Eubank steps into a ring at alien Millstreet and lays his World Boxing Organisation (WBO) super middleweight title on the line. Strangers in their thousands will bay coarsely for his noble blood. Dublin's Steve Collins is the latest bruiser to covet the crown. Some years ago, Steve used to dismissively refer to Mr Eubank's glorious title as the Wicked Body Odour title. Boxing is a funny old business, though. Next Saturday, they'll shed blood in pursuit of that Wicked Body Odour title.

Chris Eubank will prevail, he says, because Mr Collins has gotten under his skin with his 'rude, racial remarks'. Mr Collins has made Mr Eubank 'focused' and that, apparently, is a big mistake. Furthermore, Eubank will win because he is a good man.

Mr Collins will lose 'because he is a bad man with a bad message'. So there.

Why does the champion protest so much? Are the props and the poses not beneath the dignity of such a good man? Why does Steve Collins need to get right in under the champ's skin like that? Why do you folks hate him so?

Well, Eubank is not a chip off any block which the sporting world has previously known or loved. He's no pantomime plodder, like poor Frank Bruno. He's not loved for his simplicity, like 'Enry

Cooper. He's no sappy Barry McGuigan clone, thanking his manager breathlessly after every bout.

Nope. Eubank does what he does for the money. He's prickly and proud. He's haughty and baaaaaad. He's the super middleweight champ with the super heavyweight pretensions. He's the boxer who loathes his craft.

With his exotic vocabulary and his idiosyncratic fashion sense, Eubank is ridiculed easily and often, held up as the male hybrid of Eliza Doolittle and Mrs Malaprop. He struts and he poses. He proposes marriage to his girlfriend on live television: 'Marry me, Karron, marry me.' He is coolly disdainful of the grunting masses who populate the boxing world. He makes pompous pronouncements about the wretched state of this wee planet. He wears monocles and he wears jodhpurs. At the same time.

However, the package of spite delivered to him daily isn't filled with mere ridicule. Chris Eubank is unbeaten and unscarred and quite rich. Nothing draws barbed resentment quite like that combination. The good news? Well, he doesn't really care for your hang-ups. He knows you hate him and, frankly my dears, Chris Eubank doesn't give a damn.

He is a child of South London – Dalston, Stoke Newington and Hackney were his early stomping grounds – although part of his infancy was spent in Jamaica and much of his adolescence was passed in the mean streets of the South Bronx. His accent offers no hint of those tangled roots, though. When he returned to England, in 1989, he spoke mean and quick like a New Yorker. Since then, he has reconstructed himself entirely.

'I have learned to speak and behave in a manner which is easily understood by the people among whom I live. That is a matter of common courtesy.'

That common courtesy earns him little gratitude. A black man in jodhpurs and monocle, a black man with marbles in his mouth, a black man with a great shining hog of a Harley Davidson in his garage, such a black man is deemed to have overreached himself. Even today in 1995. People don't wish Chris Eubank well. They whinge that he has forgotten his roots; they wish somebody would just punch his lights out. They'll bay for his blood next Saturday night. They've bayed forty-two times before and scarcely a drop has been spilled. Hate is a cumulative, festering thing, you see.

Eubank internalises much of it and turns what hate he can't deal with into a marketing tool. The landmark disasters of Chris Eubank's life are well known. They don't help a good man with his marketing strategy.

Take the far from elementary case of Mr Watson. One night back in September 1991, Chris Eubank was taking the pounding which Britain's bitter little boxing community badly wanted to see him take. Indeed, Michael Watson was beating Chris Eubank to a pulp, whipping him in a devastating series of jabs and uppercuts and dancing away unmarked. Chris Eubank cheerily admits as much himself. He was out on his feet.

In the eleventh round, a punch, a right upper cut ('all I had'), sent Watson's brain swirling inside his head. Watson is in a wheelchair to this day, half paralysed and brain damaged. Not Chris Eubank's fault. No way. No how. He'd always said that boxing was a brutal and degrading game of Russian roulette.

Afterwards, Chris Eubank did his best by Michael Watson but...

'Now I have not spoken to him in a year and a half. I don't want to talk to him. Michael Watson is a nonentity for me. In that he is a cripple, I am sorry.

'I am sorry that this happens in this business. It did happen and I have come to terms with that. His behaviour, though, has not been gentlemanly. So I don't care for Michael Watson. I don't care to talk about him. I don't care for people to talk to me about him.'

It's a sorry tale from a squalid business. Eubank visited Watson eight times in hospital in the course of his slow recovery from a deep coma. 'Those times, we had good, good conversations.'

Then Eubank learned from the front of a daily tabloid that every moment he spent with Watson was a misery for Watson. 'He could,' says the champ, 'have told me that to my face. That wasn't being genuine. I have no time for people who are not genuine.'

There was ample salt for the wound as well. Watson sued Eubank for some comments made in the dizzy, chaotic aftermath of their fight. Eubank settled out of court. Then Watson tried to sue Eubank again. This time for assault in the boxing ring. No more, Mr Nice Guy.

Then, as if that one punch hadn't delivered enough food for sombre and melancholy thought, Eubank knocked down and killed a council workman, Kevin Lawlor, in February 1992, in a driving accident.

'That is my greatest regret,' he says, drumming his fingers on his immense dictionary. 'Killing a man in 1992. It was not my fault, but you can regret things which are not your fault. I regret that taking place. I so regret it. I wish it didn't happen. It will always haunt me. But it's done. I have to live with it. There is no turning the clock back. There is no way to bring that man back. Nothing is going to console his mother.'

He trails off and gazes out the window, where a small army of workmen is busy reconstructing his splendid garden. His eyes are a little watery and his great nostrils flare, just as they do when he is strutting around a roped ring. Then the moment is banished. He jumps up, seizes a video tape and rams it into the machine in the corner.

'What can this be then? Let's look.'

Seconds later the screen is filled with Versace man. He is talking to Pat Kenny. 'I haven't seen this interview, would you believe?' says the champ, standing back and admiring his televised image as if it were an oil painting. We watch for several minutes.

'Yes. Very good,' he says eventually, and flicks off the video.

Strange man. Convinced, because he has 'always been very male', that he could never father a daughter, Chris permitted himself to be persuaded by his good friend, Pepe, that a daughter would make a fine companion for his wife Karron.

'May I be struck blind,' he says, leaning forward conspiratorially, 'but on the first night that Karron removed her coil I made her pregnant. I knew it would be a girl. I knew, because a good man always gets what he hopes for.'

Hey presto! The champ is father to a nine-month-old beauty. But how, Chris?

'If you are a good person, you must hope, ponder and wish. Don't tell anyone your wish. Pray, but not in a selfish way, in a wishing way. If you are a good man, it will happen.'

Without warning, he jumps up and disappears into the kitchen. His head suddenly appears through a serving hatch.

'Tea?'

Before you can answer, a thought has struck him. A great thought. 'You know something? I am not that good.'

His face begs a response. Not self-deprecation from a man who has called himself a demigod? Say it ain't so, champ, say it ain't so.

'I am not a great fighter,' he says in all humility. 'But I am a paragon of what I do. Intellectually, I am above boxing, I can articulate that. When I fight, I am boxing. I become what I do. I become boxing. Boxing is not in my soul, yet in the ring I am an animal. In the ring I am pain, I am war, I am confrontation. I become those things. I am a warrior.'

He withdraws his head and makes the tea. Perhaps he even becomes the tea.

Chris Eubank must sometimes look at his beautiful house and his beautiful wife and his beautiful car and wonder what he, even a paragon such as he, is doing here. His life before boxing is one long picaresque tale. The youngest of four brothers, he speaks of a bleak and miserable childhood. His mother left the family home when Chris was just seven. His father worked long shifts in a motor factory in Dagenham.

'We were Victorian. We were a cold family. My brothers beat me, not all of them, but they beat me. There was no affection. Only once can I remember my father lifting me up. Never did anyone say "Well done, kid." Still, in my family, nobody can say those words. We were cold. We never hugged. We shook hands with each other.'

Young Eubank soon discovered the wild side of life. Expulsions and suspensions from school mounted up in sensational numbers. Eighteen suspensions in one year became a de facto expulsion.

He was sent into care in Crystal Palace, but escaped through a toilet window and lived on the streets for two years, becoming an accomplished thief and conman, removing expensive garments from sniffy upmarket stores and selling them at knockdown rates around south London.

'We were good,' he says, in a moment of rare nostalgia for the bad old days. 'You needed front to do what we did. You needed to be an actor.' As an unlikely corrective, he was banished to the streets of the South Bronx, re-joining his mother. He graduated from high school and discovered boxing at a little gym owned by Adonis Torres on the corner of 150th Street and 3rd Avenue.

He knew he had greatness in him and began preparing for the day when he would have great wealth thrust upon him. He trained six days a week and expelled all the badness from his good soul. He studied secretarial skills, so he might be trained to handle the huge amounts of money which would soon be coming his way.

He turned pro ('to earn money and be a proper man'), and fought six times in the seedy glitz of Atlantic City without drawing either a defeat or favourable press attention.

Then Torres died and Eubank went back to England. He was a limited boxer, but he had front. More front than the average seaside resort. Front sells tickets.

Today he remains unbeaten after forty-two fights and is nearing the end of a £10 million deal with Sky Television which will usher him into retirement and simultaneously stop the incessant calls from the taxman about the £2 million or so Chris has forgotten to render.

Two of Eubank's elder brothers, Peter and Simon, made a living from boxing. Their experiences at the sharp end of the sport, being used as fodder to fill promoters' cards, living their lives on the promise of one day being granted the chance to be a contender, have shaped him and his career. He is hated and abused because he is an autonomous being and boxers should be lovable Punch-and-Judy puppets.

He doesn't fight boxers who are clearly superior to him. 'Why should I?' he asks. If he is to fight a brilliant American like James Toney and risk his health and the earning power of his unbeaten record, well, then he had better be compensated hugely.

'Why should I fight him? Why should people want me to fight him? Pay me enough and I will do it. Pay me the sum I feel it is worth and I will fight anyone.'

Beyond the gnostic pronouncements, the rhetoric about his heroes (Bob Marley and Mike Tyson), beyond the peacock feathers, Chris Eubank is a hard-headed manipulator of boxing's grim odds. A man who takes his money and runs. There is something calculated about that, something romantic too. He likes the romance of it.

He views his exposure to crime (and drugs and theft and boxing's bad times) as a crucible from which he has emerged shining and new. He is 'a warrior', he says, and in his chest beats 'a proud warrior's heart'.

'Whatever, ultimately, I was going to be, I was going to be honourable and correct. I am on the side of morality. It is hard to do things correctly. It is hard to reach the pinnacle. Now I am there and people think me weird. Strange.

Eccentric. I am only trying to be correct. Is that strange? I am a man. A romantic man. If you are a real man, you will be romantic.'

Suddenly, we are rummaging through his gigantic *Webster's Dictionary,* the only book in the room. We are seeking to define romance. The champ has had several, extempore stabs at it.

'The difference between rape and seduction is salesmanship?'

Hmmm. No, Chris.

'Romance is sharing your strength equally with the woman.'

Hmmm. Maybe.

We arrive at the right spot in the dictionary. The champ reads the work of other eminent lexicographers. He is not impressed. 'Too frivolous,' he says.

'Not what I had in mind.' Thump! The great book is snapped shut.

So it goes. We visit the dictionary again not long after to find the true meaning of the word 'cynic'. Cynics make him laugh because there is a 'grain of truth in everything they say'. Cynics and Tom Waits.

Suddenly Eubank is on his feet, mincing across the room doing an impersonation of Tom Waits carrying a tray of slugs, snails and beetles to some house guests in Dracula's castle.

'Would you care for some hors d'oeuvres?' he hisses. 'Most nutritious. Have a slug.'

The successful execution of his party piece cheers him greatly. He is filled with bonhomie. He proposes a tour of his gleaming gym in the replica house which he owns just across the garden.

'You know,' he says, 'life is too short. When I beat Steve Collins, I will tell him that. Then I will turn away and I shall never think of him again.' And he smiles a huge big radiant smile.

Soon there will be no Chris Eubank to laugh at or laugh with. He plans retirement and a long twilight lecturing to 'infants, juniors and undergraduates'.

They say he'll blow all his money within five years. If he does, he says, he will have enjoyed the ride. He won't look back in anger.

He has been a household name for some six years. Some of his bouts have been truly heroic. Others have been truly tedious. Chris Eubank has placed a monetary value on his brain cells and has refused to stray beyond his limitations unless the money is truly staggering.

Good luck to him. If he can leave the stage with his faculties intact, with his money in the bank and his unbeaten record in his pocket, he will be one of very few to have beaten the cruel odds offered up by the sweet science. Deep down, Eubank has never taken himself as seriously as his detractors claim.

'You see the front, but you don't see the man,' he says, laughing still.

True warriors laugh last and last longest.

Reaffirming the faith and 101 reasons why

15 May 1995

This column loves soccer but fears its wildfire spread. Here to fend off Wimbledon and global homogenisation is a reaffirmation of faith. One hundred and one reasons why GAA is better than soccer:

1. Paul Gascoigne.
2. Fitzgerald Stadium Killarney on a sunny day is one of the loveliest sights in sport.
3. Bribery scandals.
4. Because the championship has always been the championship. The League of Ireland has had more new-improved formulas than most washing powders. Indeed, it's not even the LOI anymore.
5. Because by and large GAA heroes don't turn into villains overnight. One week this column would have happily borne Eric Cantona's children. The next week Eric was playing with Manchester United and this column wouldn't give him the time of day. Same old Eric both weeks though.
6. Most GAA players lead fuller lives than your average pro-

soccer player, thus they have more to talk about and fewer clichés to use.

7.   The PA announcer at Lansdowne Road soccer internationals needs to be shot. We hate the Mexican wave.

8.   Bohemians never win anything anymore.

9.   The offside rule can be really tedious.

10.   Andy Gray.

11.   Jimmy Hill.

12.   Mícheál Ó Muircheartaigh.

13.   No GAA team would ever wear a jersey as vile as Chelsea's away strip last season.

14.   Nobody sings 'You'll Never Beat the Irish' at GAA games.

15.   When Jurgen Klinsmann did his witty diving celebration at the start of the English season, every lame-brain striker in the game did the same thing for three months. Why?

16.   Since Dalymount decayed, professional Irish soccer has no place to call home, despite two World Cups and a Euro championship.

17.   RTÉ would never foist Brendan O'Carroll on the GAA viewership.

18.   There is no piece of sporting equipment available anywhere that is as lovely as a well-crafted hurley.

19.   Vinnie Jones would bawl like a baby if he ever came up against Brian Mullins, Brian McGilligan, Brian Corcoran. And that's just three Brians who sprang to mind.

20.   If something goes wrong, the GAA always comes up with some excuse. 'The crowd arrived too early.' 'The cat was sick.' In soccer nobody is ever to blame. Rioting in Lansdowne Road can be put down to what insurers call an act of God.

21.   The GAA may not appreciate its women as much as it should,

but at least we all know who Angela Downey is. The most famous woman in English soccer is Dani Behr.

22. It's hard to feel passionate about any sport that John Major feels passionate about. Plus David Mellor never made love to anyone while wearing a GAA jersey.

23. *Clash of the Ash* was a lovely film about hurling. *Escape to Victory* was a soccer film with Pelé and Sly Stallone in it.

24. Here we go. Here we go. Here we go. Here we go. Here we go.

25. Spivs who asked Wimbledon to move to Dublin anyway.

26. People working for Irish soccer clubs who double as scouts for English clubs. Some mistake surely.

27. No soccer manager was ever as warm and as entertaining as Eamon Coleman.

28. No segregation at GAA matches.

29. No naff furry hats on men who should know better at soccer matches.

30. No naff gold jewellery on men who should know better at GAA matches.

31. There were 15,154 fans at Ireland's last home World Cup match pre Jack Charlton. Now you couldn't squeeze all the 'real' fans into the Maracana with a shoehorn.

32. The GAA player who performs in front of 70,000 at the weekend will be teaching your kids on Monday, or he'll be selling you meat or fixing your drains or representing you in court. The soccer player who performs in front of 70,000 people at the weekend will be moaning about too many games and trying to sell you his personalised brand of leisure wear.

33. GAA players don't sell stories to *The Sun*.

34. GAA players don't have stories that *The Sun* would like to buy.

35. Bungs.

36. Backpasses.

37. Barry Venison's dress sense.

38. Jack Walker can buy a league title. You can't buy an All Ireland.

39. Penalty shoot-outs. What was wrong with the old interminable FA Cup replay sagas, e.g. Leeds vs Ipswich 1975? Heartbreaking but memorable.

40. Jack Boothman doesn't care if America doesn't like GAA. Joao Havelange loses sleep over it.

41. Nobody ever proposed making GAA goals bigger. Not even Charlie Redmond.

42. GAA nicknames are better: Sambo Hunter, Fat Larry, Babs, Bingo and so on. Soccer players just add a Y to each other's surnames.

43. The Munster hurling final.

44. The Munster football final.

45. Dublin vs Meath is a real local derby. What does Liverpool vs Everton mean to Jan Molby or Daniel Amokachi?

46. You always remember what county your Irish teacher came from.

47. We care so much about the weaker GAA counties that we sensitively refer to them as the 'so-called weaker counties'. English soccer just makes the Premier League smaller.

48. How many soccer players does it take to change a light bulb? Eleven. One to stick it in. Ten to hug and kiss him afterwards.

49. Why can nobody agree on the size of the crowd at domestic soccer games?

50. Under-age players get to be part of the biggest days in hurling and football. The Irish under-21 team is sadly neglected. The 'real' fans seldom turn up to see them.

51. Soccer players go to Rumours. GAA players go to the pub.

52. If a GAA player ever jumped at a spectator in the way that Eric

Cantona did, the rest of his team would jump in. So would the rest of the crowd.

53. You can't play a defensive game of football or hurling.

54. Razzmatazz. OK, the Artane Boys' Band may be boring, but why does it take Sky three hours to show a ninety-minute soccer game?

55. Soccer players always describe the game they have just played in the same guarded way. There is nothing like a GAA player cutting loose. 'He ate the shite out of us,' said an Offaly player of Eamon Cregan's half-time speech in last year's All Ireland.

56. The Championship means summer. The FA (or FAI) Cup means winter.

57. D.J. Carey in full flight.

58. Barry Fry, Ken Bates, Ron Noades, Robert Chase. Take your pick.

59. Television runs soccer. Schoolteachers run the GAA.

60. Vinnie Jones grabbed Gascoigne's testicles. Páidí Ó Sé decked Joe McNally during the national anthem. McNally learned his lesson. Gascoigne just got worse.

61. Joe Brolly in full flight, on the field or off it.

62. Jimmy Barry Murphy was the coolest skinhead ever to grace a playing field.

63. There's nothing like seeing the bonfires blazing when a winning team reaches its home borders.

64. The GAA season always leaves you wanting more. The soccer season leaves soccer people demanding less. Fewer games please.

65. Three points for a win is a distortion of the game's natural balance.

66. 'Soccer isn't a matter of life and death, it's much more important than that,' wasn't such a witty thing to have said.

67. The GAA is just a part of life and death.

68. Gaelic games are harder to play. Niall Quinn and Kevin Moran got out and went to soccer. You never see anyone coming the other direction.

69. GAA players run faster, hit harder and last longer. Nobody reacts like a grenade just went off if they get tripped.

70. Soccer is so subtle that Wimbledon can win the FA Cup.

71. There's no bigot quite as bitter as a soccer bigot.

72. They think Ryan Giggs is the new George Best. Sure sign of decline.

73. GAA teams are numbered one to fifteen. Soccer teams read like the National Lottery results.

74. All soccer players wear shinguards. Some hurling players wear helmets.

75. Every penny we put into soccer stays at the top. Most of what we spend on GAA trickles down.

76. The GAA is about where you are from. Soccer is largely about who you like.

77. A scoreless draw in GAA would be quite a novelty.

78. The GAA offers a journalist the chance to travel to Kerry regularly.

79. The GAA won't sell us all out by starting a European Superleague.

80. Under 13,000 fans attended the FAI cup final. 'Real fans' would rather watch Wimbledon vs AN Other at a new characterless stadium built by suits for suits.

81. Old soccer players get testimonials. Old GAA players just slip down to junior. Dog rough it is too.

82. Bubble perms never made it to Croke Park.

83. Throw-ins set the adrenalin pumping faster than tip-offs.

84. GAA fans never have time for Mexican waves.

85. Rupert Murdoch doesn't own the GAA.

86. Ghosted soccer biographies.

87. All of soccer works to filter the best players to the top teams. GAA sides always get to keep their heroes.

88. Dual players still carry a certain romantic cachet.

89. The Dergvale. Gay Prior's Pub. Tommy Tubridy's. The Bradog. The Drovers. MacGleogans. The Pound Bar. McSweeneys…

90. No soccer team has a name quite as lovely as that belonging to the Fighting Cocks of Carlow.

91. Danny Lynch. The thinking person's PR man.

92. The InterToto Cup. The ZDS Date Cup. The Simod Trophy.

93. GUINNESS isn't inscribed in large letters on the Liam McCarthy Cup. CARLING is inscribed in large letters on the Premier League Trophy.

94. Doubling on an overhead *sliotar* is a more beautiful thing to do than volleying a soccer ball.

95. Roy of the Rovers was a prat.

96. GAA goalposts cast nicer shadows on summer evenings.

97. There are always two men in white coats behind each goal at GAA games. Very wise.

98. The new Cusack Stand. We call it space age.

99. Sideline cuts, high catches, summer schools to define 'the tackle'.

100. The Dubs.

101. The Championship is here again.

Danger of golf to mature male

3 July 1995

I have a friend who detests golf. Fearing that the game might one day creep up on him, like grey hair, he has taken precautions. He has explicitly requested that, in the event of him exhibiting the faintest interest in acquiring a backswing or learning remedies for yips, one of his friends should fetch a gun and shoot him down. He will be many things, but he will not be a golf bore.

Nevah, he cries as he passes overhead on his hang-glider. Nevah!

What standing his request has in law is a moot point. Would, for instance, his wearing of plaid trousers and naff shoes make for a defence of justifiable homicide if one of us were to misread the signals. Would it be a mercy if a friend blew him away on the suspicion that he was becoming, let's say, a wine bore.

What if he is caught dissembling in order to impress a workplace superior over cocktails one evening? Hasta la vista, baby? C'mon, Bertie Wooster, make my day?

Golf is one of those issues which must be confronted by every male who grows in affluence to the point of having discretionary income and the luxury of being able to take the morning off without having to forge a sick note or pretend that yet another relative has passed away.

To golf or not to golf. To put away the consoling wee vanities of youth and stride the fairways in a yellow V-necked sweater, wearing shoes that a New Orleans pimp would find distasteful and sporting comfort-fit trousers as worn by nineteenth-century dandies. If women must face menopause, then men must face golf.

Increasingly as one pushes on towards middle age and the shiny little placebo inscribed with the words 'life begins at forty', one notices golf's insidious influence all around. One by one, friends out themselves as golfers. Others, those who have been out of the closet longer, gather around them supportively.

Watch your approach at the blind thirteenth and you'll be OK, sunshine.

Being made of the very cheapest moral fibre, this column likes to keep a foot in both camps. Some of my best friends are ardent golfers, etc., etc. I don't want to know what they get up to out there; our enduring friendships are sufficient testament to my own broadmindedness.

My own last game was fully a year ago, in the company of three Kerrymen, one of whom was a novice and had the advantage of a splendid hurling grip with which he whisked the ball away into eternity, embarrassing the rest of us mightily. It was at the height of the soccer World Cup and we were in south Boston on a public course near Dorchester. Occasionally, the crackle of gunfire and the squealing of sirens could be heard in the distance. Nobody broke ninety (for the nine). Everyone wore shorts and runners and assiduously avoided the use of golfing terminology.

'Six feet from the hole, boy, take out the putter there and bang it in.'

'What, into the hole with the flag there?'

'Yeah.'

'Why didn't you tell me that back there at the start, ya bollox, ya?'

And so we went, a living tableau of physical comedy and barely glimpsed potential, wanting to play golf without actually becoming golfers. Insecure in our own scepticism.

Playing on public courses allows a man to paddle without becoming completely wet. More. You don't have to slink home and tell your partner that you have been playing with the boys out at that place where she can't actually become a full member.

It is golf's emphasis on the economic disenfranchisement of women that makes the novice most queasy about what really goes down out on the private fairways.

It's a jungle out there when the big boys arrive at the weekend whipping out their graphite shafts and haggling over handicaps.

So that's a crass generalisation (this week's one), but out there on the golf course, under the surface, it gets a little bit macho sometimes. The boss peevishly accepts strokes donated by the specky guy with the big mouth from accounts. Two good holes and the boss's own braggadocio leads him towards a sucker bet.

Handing over the money on the eighteenth, the boss passes on some bogus portfolio advice. Uh oh. Man. He hunt. He gather. He golf.

Golf clubs are eerie places. Instead of being a haven, they are infested by beetle-browed chaps whose Bible is the rule book, whose oxygen is etiquette. The Club has become a substitute for real life. Women, immune from the golf bore bug, are a threat.

Male victims need their privacy.

It is intriguing to watch golfers in repose. They gather for scoops and crane their heads towards whatever golf tournament is on television today. Players are referred to on a first name basis. Seve.

Cory. Ben. Arnie, etc. All except the one who best embodies their own worst fears, that Australian, The Great White Chicken.

Yes. Golf, which is a marker of society's divisions and inequities, laughs loudest in the face of its own victims.

All those little humiliations and clumsy divots. They can't be all bad, those duffers who choke once a week out there. They must have absorbed some gentle philosophy amidst all that imperfection.

We seek mitigation on their behalf because truly there is something pathetic and poignantly desperate about the man standing on the first, assembling the moves he has learned at some expense. He's slogged all week. Now he has fled his family. For what? For this? The feeling of belonging in male society.

He's bent at the waist. Slightly. Legs apart so that the feet are spread slightly wider than the shoulders. His knees are flexed and he checks anxiously to see if he can roll his weight on the balls of his feet. He grips his club. It feels like a medicine ball on a piece of string. He checks once more that he is pointed in the right direction. Takes a practice swing and makes a delightful little whoosh through the air. Faces gather at the clubhouse window.

The flapping flares of his own plaid trousers tell him all he needs to know about the wind. Yikes! His bag of clubs lies behind him like a great mobile home. He cosies his feet in fractionally nearer the ball. Makes his address. A pregnant hush falls. He draws the club back. He gets to the top of his backswing, suddenly finds himself thinking of marshmallows. Begins his downward stroke towards perfect disaster.

His spirits sag but he is having fun. The male way. On the eleventh, he hits a shot that Seve would be proud of and he clings to its memory. Later, he'll moss the entire round over into a clubhouse anecdote. A very male practice. As gender roles become blurred, the golf bore shall become increasingly prevalent.

The course is the arena of male dreams. It's where these kids are turning for their kicks.

What can be done? My friend has the germ of an idea. Golf needs to be controlled, not eradicated. Give them their clubs and their sordid rituals but regulate it. So what if they have means but not taste. As the country slowly turns into one great golfing theme park, there is a case for the annual culling of golfers. I know just the people.

'Fore! Look out! Duck, sucker! BOOM! Hasta la vista, darling.'

Fighting for travellers

13 April 1996

Knacker. Some fool called Frank Barrett by that name once. Frank was eleven years old and walking down Castle Park feeling the sweet press of life's promise. The shock of that word stopped Frank dead in his tracks.

'Don't be calling me any names,' said Frank, 'it's not right.'

Then, that he might be better heeded, he blurted out his solemn warning.

'I'm in the boxing club now and I don't want to be sparring you or anything like that. Call me that name again and I'll spar you, though.'

Not needed. He has never lifted a bare knuckle in anger. That word still carries its bitter sting though.

'Travellers are just gone used to the way things are,' says Frank. 'Used to the bad looks. Somebody will bump shoulders with a traveller on the street, the traveller says "sorry" but the settled person just keeps walking. You just know.

'If I came home from Atlanta with a medal and I could get just one thing for travellers, it would be respect. Nothing else. Just respect.'

R.E.S.P.E.C.T. For some people you have to spell it out.

Knacker lover. People used to whisper that word about Chick Gillen when he first took the traveller boys in and taught them how to box.

Chick heard the hissing of forked tongues and slithering minds, but Chick never was a man to give half a damn about what people said.

The club was born in 1966. Chick had been reading up on the Olympics and had liked all that stuff about every race, every colour and every creed. So the little club in Bohermor East was christened the Olympic Club. Later, one Colonel Divine got in touch and told Chick that he couldn't use that name. Copyright conventions. Blah blah blah. So for divilment Chick added the five rings to the club's logo and coloured them in and that's the way it's been ever since.

Eight years ago, Father Ned Crosbie brought a busload of traveller children into Chick's gym and Chick set them to sparring. Chick and Father Ned stood back and watched the lads whaling away. Father Ned, knowing the map of Chick's mind, spoke first.

'Well, Chick, will any of this lot make the Olympics for you?'

'The little fat fella over there is the best of them, Father Ned. He'd be the one.'

'No.'

'You just watch him, Father Ned. What's his name?'

'Barrett. Francis Barrett.'

They had Bishop Casey for a patron for a while.

Father Ned spotted his picture in a skip outside the *The Sun*. The roseate bishop photographed with a clump of shamrock in his lapel. They stuck the photo up above the mirror in Chick's barbershop. The bishop would send Chick a box of fish every year. For a long time it looked as if the fallen cleric would be the most notable thing about the Olympic Boxing Club.

Then young Francis lost the weight, learned the science, won his first Irish title at fourteen. Francis called Chick another name. Chicken Gill. Hey, Chicken Gill.

Easy friendship. Good days.

Family. No more road. The Barretts have lived in their cluster of caravans on Hillside for the last sixteen years. Six boys. Six girls. Plus Mamma and Dadda. No electricity, save that which is granted by a cranky generator that the family coaxes into life each day.

The washing line always sags with the dripping handwashed clothes of a dozen sturdy offspring. The smell of smoke always lingers. The Barretts are always busy. The family makes and repairs trailers. Puts this together. Takes that apart.

Frank, the third eldest, loves the feel of the hard work. One night he came down to Chick's place for training having filled 200 bags of logs that day. Split and stored to warm the family for the winter. Frank trained fresh as a daisy that night.

Warm people. When Chick calls up there is tea on the table before he has the seat pulled out to sit himself down. Often there'd be the leg of a rabbit and some spuds. Chick will say that it's little wonder that the Barretts are all so robust.

'Everything we have goes on the table,' they say.

They love the life they live. Mamma and Dadda grew up in tents and caravans when times were harder. They tried a house once but couldn't live in that choking confinement.

'The only bad thing I can think of about a caravan,' says Frank, 'is that settled people look down on you for living in one.'

Dadda loved the boxing. Passed on the lore and the love. Eight years old and Frank was brought to Mervue to see his cousin Tom Mongan fight, saw Tom's arm raised in victory. Was addicted.

'Why Dadda? Why?' Frank said, tugging Dadda's sleeve. 'Why can't I box?'

Three years later he had his wish, matched up with another lad in a draughty hall in Ennis.

'I wasn't scared but I got hit. I'd never had gloves on. I was just throwing big swingers. I won, though. After that Chick taught me how to box properly.'

Frank did his time, saw the country through the window of a bus, fought in every ring, learned every time.

Goodfellas. Wednesday in Brent Park. London for three days. Resting up after four bouts in the Olympic qualifying tournament in Denmark. His Auntie Winnie collected him at Gatwick, gazed sadly at the black eye Frank got from the rocking-horse head of an Austrian pug and then kissed him.

When they got back to the caravan, every man, woman and child on the site stopped by to shake Frank's hand.

The gypsies, as the locals call them, are packed inconspicuously in here between Tesco's and a home improvement warehouse. A grey, steady drizzle insinuates dampness everywhere.

Portakabins. Oil drums. Tyres. Rotting boards. Pieces of mangled metal scattered like weeds across grey gravel. A black mongrel puppy scampers under a caravan as a gaggle of short-haired kids gather to catch another glimpse of their champion.

Their chatter is speculative.

'Are you boys from the radio?'

'No, the papers.'

'*The Sun*?'

'No. *The Irish Times*.'

'How come you don't see no travellers ever in the *The Sun*?'

'Couldn't tell you. Maybe it's best.'

'Frank is in the Olympics, mister.'

'Are you going to watch him?'

'Aw. Don't know. Maybe.'

'He'll be on the telly.'

'Frank will be on the television? Here? Frank? On the television?'

Frank appears suddenly slipping from behind a beige caravan door in a dazzling white O'Neill's T-shirt and blue jeans. He takes control.

He is going to borrow a car, bring us to a gym in Harlesden for photos. Do the interview there. Some of the boys will be coming down to get the photos too. Then he apologises.

'If it was home in Galway now, we'd be properly set up. I'd have everything organised.'

At home, boxing is the heartbeat. Frank and three brothers saved for half a year once and got Dadda to pay the balance for the body of an old trailer, which they have converted to a gym. £300 for a dream. Chick gave them a springball and a bag and they painted the wall. In the evenings they take it in turns to go inside and train.

Boxing marks the rhythm of their days. They leave the site at 7 am, scattering to do their running work. Frank goes to a field nearby, runs hills and runs sprints for half an hour. That always leaves him begging for breath.

In the afternoon the boys spar. They have an imaginary ring marked off on the grass of the site.

'My body has turned to stone,' says Jimmy Barrett ruefully. 'That's from the way Frank likes to spar.'

'You see,' says Frank, 'Jimmy comes at me with the jabs and the head shots. I always go to take a boxer down with body shots. I hit him in the body all the time.'

There are no ropes. No backing off. John Barrett spars differently. He dances around and Frank chases.

It's a job for Chick to get the lads on the pads and the bags. When Frank came to Chick first, he wouldn't skip, but now he dances like Sugar Ray Leonard.

'He'll always learn,' says Chick.

In Harlesden the boys slip confidently up the stairs of a gym which specialises in something called Aerobics. Frank likes London. Nobody cares what you are or where you live. He hits the heavy bag for the camera while the others dawdle. The boys rub shoulders and raise their fists for a group shot. They line up before a long dance mirror and make shapes, like a fighting cancan line. They have neat jabs and tidy uppercuts and driving overhanders and they look sublimely happy.

Local hero. Frank is a light welterweight in the ring but much more out of it. Nineteen years old and he has a lot to carry.

When he won the Irish senior championship last December, the local priest Father Brady made him stand up at mass the next Sunday. Everybody clapped. 'You'd feel embarrassed,' says Frank, 'but at sports awards you have to walk up through everyone else. That's worse.'

More to come, though. When he was in Denmark fighting for a place in the Olympics, the family followed the drama by watching the teletext pages. When Frank won through finally and the news came blinking onto the relevant page, he wasn't just their Frank anymore.

'Now there is much more for me to think about. Every time I talk I am talking for travellers. Even if I didn't want to be, I am. I like that. I suppose I'm going to be doing a lot of talking between now and the Olympics. For travellers. That's how people judge me.'

He talks about traveller life. Cold nights lying in bed in the dark with the heat of the stove for comfort. The name-calling. The business of being barred from pubs and being followed by security guards in shops.

There is a reception for him when he comes home to Galway next week in a big Galway hotel.

'I'm not sure if any traveller was ever in that hotel,' he says. 'Even if they'd be let in, I'm not sure they'd try. Travellers are gone used to that.'

He knows the edge of bigotry but he loves the life. Air. Freedom. An uncluttered head. The boundaries between small means and few wants. Can't imagine the drudgery of mortgages and offices.

Some days he just gets on a bike and heads away for a feckless day of fishing. The Huckleberry Finn of the Atlantic Coast. Chasing fish in Oughterard or Spiddle or Clarinbridge or Kilcolgan. Just Frank and his thoughts from dawn to dusk, with the sun beating off the trouty water.

No such days this summer. A pre-Olympic tournament in Atlanta looms later this month. Then nine weeks of training camps and trips and the briary tangle of media interest.

Afterwards he is going to take a few months off. Get a little caravan and travel all alone. A few months on the road. Some fishing. See his girlfriend.

Think it all through for himself. The recent past and the unfolding future.

Then he'll fight on, because that's his life. When he finishes fighting he'll train fighters, he says.

Boxing has made his life in Galway easier, he thinks. Two local gardaí and the local bank and the local radio station have started a fund for him to go the Olympics. A sponsor has a sweater ready for him. 'Francis Barrett, Olympic Hope', says the legend.

Caravan to bandwagon. He appreciates the affection but can't forget where he is coming from. When he qualified for the Olympics, the Mayor of Galway came to the site in Hillside to congratulate Mamma and Dadda. Frank was sorry he wasn't there to meet him. For sixteen years the site has been looking for electricity. For sixteen years that project has been on the long finger.

'Am I representing Ireland or am I representing travellers?' asks Frank. It is something he has thought about often. 'I am proud to represent Ireland, but I know that I represent people who'd discriminate against me too. I fight sometimes and I wonder what I am doing it for. I represent Ireland, but I represent travellers more.

'If I come back from the Olympics with a medal and the minister is at the airport, I'll do a good speech on behalf of travellers. I'm looking forward to that speech now if I win a medal, really looking forward to that. Maybe we'd get some electricity out on the site. We'd buy a machine and the mother wouldn't have to be breaking her back every day.'

Francis Barrett. Olympic hope. The Games have seldom entertained such a sweet dreamer. He says thanks very much. See you again. Turns and disappears into his caravan once more. Outside, the drizzle is still falling.

A match between past and present

6 July 1996

Your first Munster final. You've forgotten many things, but you remember your first Munster final. Your father brought you along, holding your four-year-old hand as your fair head bobbed low in the crowd, your saucered eyes gazed about at the shiny black pants, razor creases and best braces of the other men.

He'd put you on the crossbar of his stern black bike and carried you to early Mass while the dew was still on the grass. Home again and he inserted you into two pairs of socks lest it rain and entrusted you with the safe transport of tea and sandwiches. All set, he pointed you towards Thurles. Always Thurles.

The square in Thurles. You remember the good white shirts and the innocent detonations of colour on the crinkly rosettes. Great hamfisted men made light work of cool pints of porter. Your father there in the thick of it with the blinding sun lifting years off his face. You can see him now. Perfect as a photograph.

He pointed to the dowdy frontage of Hayes's Hotel and it stuck in your mind.

He walked you out of the town towards the ground, talking all the while to his cronies. The day seemed filled with talk. He stood at the town-end terrace and had you on his shoulders till the game began and somebody let out a roar at you.

The afternoon was unblemished. Ring or Mackey or Doyle played sublimely that day. Hurling fit for the gods. Sawdust in the square. Scarcely a hand put to the leather, so brisk was the striking. Through the thickets of legs and posts you saw what needed to be seen and tattooed it on your memory.

Afterwards, tired and hungry and braced for home, you walked up town and Ring himself caught your father by the sleeve and complimented him on a marking job well done in some minor game two decades earlier.

You shook the hand of the man from Cloyne. Your father, who voted Fianna Fáil all his life and who scarcely ever took a drink in the presence of your mother even at Christmas, had marked Ring out of it once. Not so predictable.

He seemed seven-foot tall that day, the father. On the train home you noticed that you were still clutching the tea and sandwiches. Surprise was never a more splendid companion. Later, when the train broke down, your father carried you on one shoulder all the way back to the village. He carried the train on the other shoulder.

After that you never missed a Munster hurling final until you were in your mid-twenties and working in England. You'd taken holidays for the sake of attending a couple of funerals earlier in the year and, come the summer, you couldn't get home. Between one thing and another, the spell was broken. Anyway, hurling is like soda bread, always better in the old days.

Look at you now. As old as your father was then, heading in pilgrimage to Limerick on a July weekend, one part of the greatest conglomeration of spoofers, sciolists, sentimentalists, snobs and soaks ever to descend on any Irish sporting event.

The Munster hurling final. The Munster bloody hurling final. Is any other game so celebrated, exaggerated, mythologised, eulogised, analysed and merchandised? Is anything else so neatly a part of what we think we are? Nothing comes near. This Munster hurling final business is the repository of all that is sacred and holy in our past lives, a vestige of ourselves which we might have discarded like pioneer pins and black berets and boys' sodalities, but instead we have turned into an arm-wrestling match between past and present.

If you attend just one hurling game all year, the chances are it will be the Munster final. You'll dig up the weather-worn cronies and make the pilgrimage to your past. Munster hurling finals appeal to the strangest constituencies. Once a year suffices for these gatherings.

You can forgive yourself your infidelity to the game. Winter hurling is an abomination which turns your stomach and in August you holiday in the Dordogne.

One game a year. So there. Absolution granted.

If the GAA is ever to introduce an open draw as a remedy for its structurally lopsided championships, you will fight it tooth and nail. What would happen to the world without the Munster hurling final?

There have, of course, been many bad Munster hurling finals, stodgy afternoons that couldn't be digested by the refined palates of the south. They are quickly forgotten, however.

There have been many fine Leinster hurling finals, too. Yet illusion wills away the facts when it comes to hurling. Leinster is second-rate stuff and the All-Ireland series is a mere postprandial brandy.

So you put on your grey suit and leave both cars in the driveway and by the time you hit the station the reminiscences are fizzing gently inside you. You have seen the past and it works. For spoofing and slurping on Munster final day, the train is your only man.

You know just how the day will open itself to you. Early on, you will open the bidding with a soft opinion. All Munster hurling finals should be played in Thurles, you'll say. Limerick ceased to be a shrine when they built the desecration that is the Mackey Stand, you'll say. Affirming nods all round.

By the time the locomotive hits Limerick, the Ireland you grew up in won't have differed in any significant way from a decade-long episode of *The Waltons*.

At some stage, beyond sobriety and hopefully beyond the sightlines and earshot of anyone in your employ, you will tilt your head back and belt out a verse or so of 'Slievenamon' and, before you're done, some hoor will start up with 'The Banks' and you'll subside into laughter. You'd great time for Clare and hats off to Limerick but for really great Munster finals, it's Cork and Tipp that you want.

You'll invoke the great names and the great dates, of course. Right back to Cuchulainn. Tread softly, for you tread on each other's spoofs. Ring didn't play that day actually. It wasn't in Thurles that year actually. No, sure, he was scoreless and they took him off with quarter of an hour left actually. Your man never spoke to your father after the game because he'd thirty-nine stitches in his tongue that day. Careful there.

The game will ambush you some time in the woozy middle part of the afternoon.

Seventy minutes of frantic heroics, during which you'll sit basking in the harmony of the spirits, hoping that Tipp will bring on Nicky English because you know the cut of his dash by sight.

You'll feel the sun on your pate and worry about burning. You'll let your heaviness settle into the grooves of the infernally tiny seat until you wonder with a start if the credit cards in your back pocket aren't being bent out of shape.

Your judgment afterwards will be damning. Hurling is in crisis.

The striking is no longer as crisp or as sweet as when first you came to Munster hurling. It may well have been a fine game, but you won't feel certain of that till next year.

For the moment it doesn't stand up to the glories of the past. No game ever did. Even in the long and glorious past of Munster hurling finals.

The power and the glory

27 July 1996

Pictures and sounds. Tricolours. Tears. *Cúpla focail ó Seán Bán*.
Cancan lines of cheering journalists. Michelle Smith's clenched fist
raised up out of the churning blue water, as if bestowing the sword of
Excalibur on Irish womanhood. The perfect sports story.

More. A none too subtle twist of partisan rivalry has been added
to the cocktail. Janet Evans has obligingly played the role of the ugly
American, allowing us to become red-faced and defensive about the
extraordinary events of the past week.

What has all the fuss been about? Has it been about ungracious
Americans who can't take their licking? Has it been about a big
country doing down a little country? Has it been about Irish
journalists lining up with pompoms and twirly sticks to do
cheerleading routines at press conferences.

No. This past week, beyond the glory and the images of glory,
beyond Bill Clinton and Mary Robinson, this past week in the pool
has been about an extraordinary improvement in one woman's
performances at a time of life when such quantum leaps seemed out
of the question. What Michelle Smith has done is to completely

mutate the body of physiological and biomechanical science surrounding women's swimming.

Picture this. If Michelle Smith trailed home all week beaten by a phenomenon as unique and surprising as herself, we would ask the questions coldly, stridently and curiously. Then we would decide whether or not to grant our trust.

If we are to be journalists and not cheerleaders with typewriters, we must pause to listen to the questions. If we are to be lovers of sport and not mere worshippers of success, we must ask for answers. If we are to cherish Michelle Smith as a true hero, we mustn't do her the injustice of demeaning her by means of whispered innuendo. Her achievements have been of such a magnitude these past seven days that they almost defy comprehension. The further you delve into the science of swimming, the more unusual all that gold seems. It was right that the questions should have been amplified and not whispered.

The questions have been asked, not just by Americans, but by all those interested in the sport. It wasn't an American who asked one week ago tonight if she could explain her sudden explosion at twenty-six. Nor was it just Americans from whom Erik de Bruin stormed away that same evening when asked about his own experience with illegal substances. Nor on Monday night, beneath the chorus of cheerleading, was it solely American voices that sought answers at a fraught press conference. Irish journalists were among those asking the hard questions. Furthermore, it is worth pointing out that the American media hasn't been nearly as ugly, racist or partisan this week as their Irish counterparts in the wake of Sonia O'Sullivan's troubles at the hands of the Chinese in Stuttgart three years ago. The US media asked questions of Chinese swimmers. They asked questions of Flo Jo. They asked questions of Frankie

Fredericks. Where there is an aberration in improvement curves, they ask questions. What's wrong with that?

That questions are asked is absolutely no proof of guilt. That they need to be asked at all reflects on the scale of achievement and the failings of sports administrators.

Let's not kid ourselves. The Americans have had a week of almost constant celebration in the pool. Irish success is good news here. The perfect sports stories always beg questions, though.

Michelle Smith's performances have been astonishing. She herself has recognised that the questions which have been asked have to be asked. That is the horrible cleft of modern sport.

There is no absolute proof of either innocence or guilt.

Pharmacology has galloped years ahead of testing procedures and even those quaint phials of urine being ferried around Atlanta this week will scarcely withstand a sustained legal challenge by an athlete at whom the finger is pointed.

Michelle Smith will point to the eleven drug tests performed on her in the past twelve months and those within sport will know that human growth hormones or erythropoietin can never show up in those tests, that the failings of sports authorities have left acres of room for innuendo and inference and rumour mongering.

We have to take athletes on trust. To defend Michelle Smith is a reflex.

She is one of our own. She only became a serious full-time athlete three years ago. She just lost weight and gained upper-body strength. She improved her technique. Bulked up on carbohydrates and protein. She went and trained in the flume, analysed her speeds and her strokes. By the next Olympics, perhaps, all female swimming medal winners will be her age.

Erik de Bruin's failed test and subsequent appeal can't be boiled down to the clumsy shorthand of innuendo and can't be permitted to taint someone he loves by mere association. Furthermore, just because Erik and Michelle were occasionally poor at handling the media prior to the Games doesn't mean that they don't deserve trust.

Yet, all the factors – the age profile, the mediocre career, the huge improvements, the coach who knew nothing about swimming, the faint taint of association – all those things make questions inevitable.

Michelle Smith's performance in knocking nineteen seconds off her own personal best time in the space of fifteen months in the 400-metres freestyle, for instance, is worth looking at in the context of the world record progression in that event.

In 1970, in Los Angeles, Debbie Meyer of the USA swam 4:24.3 for a new world record in the 400-metres freestyle. Six years later, Barbara Krause of East Germany took the time down to 4:11.69. In the same city, in 1978, Tracey Wickhan of Australia made another leap with a swim of 4:06.28. With the historic swim of a seventeen-year-old, Janet Evans, in Seoul, 1988, the time eventually fell to 4:03.85, the current outer limit of achievement in the event. It took twelve years for the best international swimmers in the world to pare eight seconds off the world record.

In twenty-six years, the greatest swimmers in the world have taken the mark down 20.45 seconds.

Michelle Smith lopped 18.93 seconds off her personal best in the space of fifteen months without even specialising in the event. She swam a national record of 4:26.18 on 1 April 1995, almost three years into her current training regimen. Then, this summer, in Fort Lauderdale, she astonished the world by turning in a 4:08 time out of the blue, having been encouraged to try the event by a good 200-metres freestyle swim in the Dutch national championships in June.

'Straight after the Dutch championships, Erik said to me that I was fit enough to try a 400-metres freestyle. We looked everywhere for one and found a race in Fort Lauderdale on July 7th.'

On Monday night, she equalled Mark Spitz's 1968 men's 400-metres freestyle record and swam fifty seconds better than Johnny Weismuller's 1923 record set in New Haven. Fifty seconds better than Tarzan. It's trivia perhaps, but jarring.

In the context also of a week of competition, the level of exertion and achievement has been a quantum leap on anything otherwise achieved.

In 1988, twenty-two-year-old, 6-ft, Kristin Otto won four individual swim gold medals, an achievement which was considered remarkable at the time. Her successes came in 100-metres and 50-metres sprint events. Cumulatively, she raced 700 metres in individual heats and finals, plus another 200 metres in relay events. Nine hundred metres of competitive swimming in all to become a legend of the pool.

In 1994, incidentally, after the fall of the eastern block, declassified documents revealed Otto to have been fed a lifetime diet of testosterone and other performance-enhancing drugs.

This week, Michelle Smith swam 2,400 metres' worth of top-class racing, breaking personal bests and leaving behind times which rank amongst the top ten in history in several events. Any wonder that the pool deck has been gape-mouthed.

It has been stated that her European championship performances last summer should have served as ample warning for competitors.

Yet Smith's times in Vienna last year, achieved in the absence of the great swimming powers of China, Australia and the US, would have placed her among the also-swams in Atlanta. The surprise this week has been the sight of a twenty-six-year-old breaking personal best times by more than a second (more than three seconds in the 400-metres individual medley) in a succession of events.

Make no mistake, twenty-six is old for a champion female swimmer, an extraordinary mutation in the historical pattern. The last ten Olympic 400-metres freestyle champions, for instance, have ranged in age from fifteen (Shane Gould and Petra Thurner) to twenty-two (Dagmar Hase) and have had an average age of 16.9 years. Michelle Smith will be twenty-seven this winter.

The physiological argument runs that the gains which can be made in a change of training styles and body shape should be offset at such a time in life by the increased water resistance of the mature female body and the leveling out of potential.

In a sport where times and improvements are measured in such fractions that the removal of body hair is considered a routine essential, the question of physiology is a moot one. Besides, being older than almost all her rivals, Michelle Smith is also smaller and in many cases heavier. She doesn't enjoy the advantages of reach bestowed for instance on the 5'10" world champion, Yan Chen.

When you look for a nickname for her, 'The Albatross' doesn't come to mind.

Instead, Michelle Smith has packed astonishing power into her upper body.

The power and sheer aerobic physiological fitness can't but impress the onlooker. In a week of stress and hard, competitive swimming her body has recovered faster than anyone else's, suggesting extraordinary levels of cardio-respiratory fitness and a remarkable durability in the musculo-skeletal tissues.

Again, this has been acquired late in her career.

The aggressive approach to racing has been a factor, too. The confidently aggressive approach, fostered by the 'us against the world' mentality of herself and Erik de Bruin, has given a certain mental edge.

It is the physiologists and not the sports psychologists who remain most fascinated, however.

Jay T Kearney, head sports physiologist at the US Olympic centre in Colorado, has no axe to grind concerning Michelle Smith's achievements, yet confesses that they run against the grain of what he has come to expect.

'If you examine the rate of development of records across age groups, especially in females, they are very, very flat after the age of about fifteen or seventeen.

'Physiologically, with Michelle Smith, I don't know precisely where she was three or four years ago, or when she should have been peaking, but to make the physiological adaptation necessary to improve that much competitively, well, just like everyone else, I would have to say that it would be unusual to accomplish that much in that length of time.

'If having already competed in two Games she has radically changed her training programme and diets and factors like that, even then these would be truly exceptional gains.

'For instance, our oldest-ever female gold-medal winner in swimming is twenty-nine years old. She would have a completely different career profile, however.'

Indeed Angel Martino was winning gold in the Goodwill Games some ten years ago. Interestingly, also in terms of the way the American media has been portrayed this week, she is seldom allowed to forget a positive drugs test in 1988 which kept her off the US Olympic team. In terms of associative guilt, it is often dropped into profiles of her that her husband, Mike, is a biochemist.

Angel was getting on with it this week, winning golds and being charming. Like several other Americans, she went out of her way to praise Michelle Smith's achievements and express some solidarity as Smith faced down the innuendo.

Michelle Smith has turned a sport on its head in the space of seven days. She has turned a modest career into something glittering and golden, altered a nation's mood and perhaps pushed back the barriers of female physiology. A lifetime at the nation's bosom lies ahead. The choice of commercial endorsements are spread at her feet like rose petals. This weekend, the Sunday papers are rumoured to be offering £20,000 minimum for the rights to her story.

Her achievements have been remarkable. The rewards, both material and spiritual, will be immense. Answering a few questions as to how it all came to be was a small toll to pay. Some would say it brought out the best in her and the worst in the rest of us.

Sonia O'Sullivan's failure to finish race shocks fans

29 July 1996

John O'Sullivan, from whose gentle stoic face his daughter draws her features, stood in the thick of the storm. Cameras. Recorders. Officials. Questions. Questions. Questions.

'Lads,' said John quietly, 'nobody died tonight.'

Nobody died. Yet there were the tears and the keenly felt grief of a wake as Sonia O'Sullivan's career came apart at the seams on the night that was supposed to mark her coronation as the world's greatest middle-distance runner.

In one of the most astonishing and poignant twists of these Olympic Games, she failed to finish her 5,000-metres final, vanishing quickly and in tears into the Georgia night.

'She'll be back,' said John O'Sullivan. 'We'll all talk tomorrow.'

The shock has scarcely registered. Sonia O'Sullivan, the indomitable force in her field for three years, had just left the track with two laps of the 5,000-metres Olympic final left.

The principal drama of the night had been robbed of its most scintillating character. The world looked for answers rather than track times or winners' quotes.

Shock and disbelief. Tears streaming down her face, she packed her gear into a small black rucksack, slipped into a white T-shirt and black leggings and fell into the embraces of her loved ones.

Quick whispered words with her physio, Ger Hartman, and then she just vanished beyond the eyes of the press. These wounds will take some healing.

The nature of those wounds remains a mystery. No explanation was left behind.

The forensic examination of the race revealed little, either. There had appeared to be bumping in the field on the fourth or fifth lap, but no incident more robust than the sort that O'Sullivan usually takes in her stride. Nothing else.

Following the pattern of the heats, the early running last night had been made by Sara Wedlund, the mono-paced Swedish runner.

Olympic finals aren't occasions for frail hearts, however. By the 1,000-metre mark, O'Sullivan's friend and sometime training partner, Pauline Konga, was taking the field through in 3:06.15 and O'Sullivan was looking safe and comfortable.

With six laps to go after much shuffling, Konga still led as the field suddenly strung out. Alarmingly, O'Sullivan, looking heavy limbed and sluggish, found herself trailing the field badly. The deficit opened up further and further over the following 400 metres and, when Sonia O'Sullivan's face shot up on the huge videotrons in the Olympic stadium, there was no doubt that she was struggling.

With four laps to go, running as if on a floor of glue, pale and wreathed in sweat, she was some 100 metres off the pace being set by Pauline Konga and the Chinese runner, Wang Junxia.

The cluster of Irish flags which brightened the elegant stadium hung limp and redundant.

With two laps remaining, O'Sullivan came around the bend and slipped straight out of the stadium down the exit tunnel, leaving

83,000 spectators and a worldwide television audience baffled and mystified. Her departure left Wang Junxia of China and Pauline Konga of Kenya to take the gold and silver medals respectively.

It was a night when the fates had appeared to be conspiring approvingly with the Cobh woman's ambition. The much-feared Atlanta humidity never materialised, a balmy Georgia evening freshened by a light breeze providing the backdrop for one of the Games' set pieces. Regardless of the pace, it was whispered, O'Sullivan was never going to want for kick in the closing stages.

We never got to see the closing stages.

'I don't know what's wrong,' said John O'Sullivan, forced in a time of pain to answer a million hasty questions. 'We spoke today and she was in top form. She went driving around at about 4 o'clock and she was feeling great. I just don't know. It must have been bad to make her quit a race.'

It was at a children's party in John O'Sullivan's Cobh workplace when she was five years old that Sonia O'Sullivan's running life began, a life which brought her numerous national school championships, a Villanova university scholarship and a fourth place in the 3,000-metres event in the Barcelona Olympics four years ago.

Sonia O'Sullivan has hit setbacks before, but none as shocking or as debilitating as this. The possibility of recovery and rehabilitation in time for the 1,500-metres race later this week will depend on the precise nature of whatever affliction befell her last night.

If her record of fighting against the odds is anything to go by, we will see her running again this week. Encouragingly, as she left the Olympic stadium, the signs of distress were emotional rather than physical.

Nobody died. The sun will rise this morning. So will Sonia O'Sullivan.

Say it ain't so, Tony, say it ain't so

3 November 1997

Tony the barman slams the shot glass down on that particular piece of mahogany most adjacent to my left ear. My left ear, which is at that moment cushioning my head in a pool of stale liquor. The familiar percussion of glass on bartop rouses me.

'Whadd's the story, Tony?' I say. 'Whadd's the story?'

Tony carries a switchblade behind the bar in case I cut up rough and start pumping him full of it with facts about dope in sport. Got me barred from most of the dumps along this stretch. No intention of messing with Tony.

'Whadd's the story yourself, you got no work to be doing?' he says.

I've been running from this, but Tony, he's got family and all that baggage and wants to get away. Workaday sap, I think bitterly, but I don't say nothing out loud.

'Yeah, sure I got work to do. Sure I have. I gotta column to write. I'm still somebody.'

I wipe the dribble from my chin. Tony blinks, turns and adjusts the rusty horseshoe hanging above the mirror behind the bar. Keeps tipping over upside down and spilling all the luck out.

'Go do your work,' says Tony, 'get outta here and do work. It's getting bright outside.'

'Give me something to wash this down with, will ya.' I knock back the glass of Four Roses. Feel a column coming on. Anything to take the edge off the morning.

Hotshot bastard editors will be on the case soon. Last chance saloon and all that heavy stuff.

'Ya even know what you're goin' to write about?' Tony mutters, shaking his head.

He steals a look at his wristwatch as he tips the tequila into the glass.

Thinks I don't notice him looking at his wristwatch. Sneaky homebird.

'Ya even know what your doin'?' he says. Louder this time.

'Yeah, sure I know,' I tell him. And I'm lifting my head out of the wet, wiping my ear with my sleeve. 'Sure I know. I'm gonna tell it like it is, Tone. Sport is shagged. Sport is dead. Sport, my little measure-cheating friend, is a goner.'

'That's what you write every week,' he says. 'People get sick of it.'

'Yeah. Like you'd know,' I say. 'What makes you such a hotshot expert media consultant goddamn Marshal MacLuhan know-all type? Who died and made you Fintan O'Toole for the day? Huh?'

'I'm just saying,' says Tony, not backing off, 'that people need something to believe in. Ya could write something positive once in a while. Must be something good.'

'Tell me about it,' I say. 'Nothing good under heaven and earth. No heroes left, Tony. Sport is a jungle with little moral pygmies running around in it, Tone. It's a dirty job, but somebody has to do it. What's your story?'

He hits me with it then. Paid £200 for a pair of hurling final tickets. The Credit Union still has him in a headlock since the last World Cup.

He's doing extra shifts to go to Brussels. Dreamy saps like Tony can't be saved.

'Tell ya what I want,' says Tony. 'I want to not know how much Phil Babb gets paid and what will happen when his contract finishes. I don't want to worry about where swimmers get their muscles. I get a temperature when I read about the business of sport. I want to believe.'

'Yeah, Tony. And I wanted Adi Roche for president. Dream on, flower child.'

'Shut up a minute now, dogbreath. I don't want to be forced to do the Mexican wave in Lansdowne and I don't want to believe in the Clare Shout. I'm not a halfwit. I don't want to buy Nike runners off Michael Jordan or Oki printers off Mick McCarthy. I just would like to be able to be allowed buy tickets to see them at work.'

'I don't see your point, Tony.'

'Shut it, wiseass. Listen and learn. I don't want to be held to ransom by Sky Sports. I don't want to listen to the Celtic Warrior boasting. I don't want to be bitter about executive boxes. I don't need to know about Roy Keane and his next-door neighbour.'

'But Tony, I've been saying all that…'

'I don't want stupid dances and celebrations after footballers score. I don't want athletics to be dirty. I don't want Don King anywhere on the premises. I don't want rugby to die. I hate agents and I hate public-relations types and I hate sponsors' advertising on jerseys.'

'Just let me interrupt here, Tony. Newsflash, Tony.'

'No. I hate hype and groundless transfer speculation. I hate contrived sports events. I hate GAA players fighting. I hate awards ceremonies and I hate that nearly all sport is for somebody else. If you're just an ordinary Joe, who will sell you a ticket? They'll sell you everything except a ticket to be there. The jersey, the computer game, the bumper sticker, the dedicated credit card. I'm a fan, not a customer.'

'I hate those things too, Tony. I could cry, Tony. I hate all those things too. Welcome to my world. Don't bother wiping your feet.'

He lifts his finger to his lips. Sssshhh.

'But most of all I hate having it all rammed down my throat by you every Monday morning, ya big fat self-righteous high-horse-on-the-moral-high-ground loser ya. I hate having it all picked apart by some hypocritical, expense-account lump who hasn't paid into a game in a decade.'

'Oh.'

'Give me a hero. Give us the romance. Give us one hero, that's all. Something to believe in. One hero, one thing to hold up to my kids. Something about joy and sweat and pride. Just about the game. Leave us something to believe in. You don't have to pull the stitching out of everything, do ya?'

'Hurling,' I say to him. 'Believe in that. There's lots of it about, lots of good sport. But you know something, Tony? You are my hero. You're the last real hero left. The last to believe in the good things.'

'Go home,' he says. 'That phoney won't run. I'm starting to feel sick.'

'Just goin',' I say.

Religious support of bigotry of ugly sisters

27 April 1998

From Central Station, up Argyle Street and out Gallowgate towards Celtic Park, you could have been in Ireland, so familiar were the accents around Glasgow on Saturday afternoon. Tricolours trailed from bulging waists and men wore T-shirts which said 'Celtic, Pride of Ireland'.

In the battered little public houses that line the grimy main drag towards the ground, men held dark, cream-headed pints in their hammy hands and committed atrocities against 'The Fields of Athenry'.

As a race we are smitten with Celtic in a way which precludes the possibility of rational thinking. You can be a Manchester United mind-slave or a freethinking renegade; you can be an anti-GAA bigot or an anti-soccer dinosaur; but, by reflex, you will have reserved part of your brain for the goodwill you feel towards Celtic.

Next New Year, try going into your local saloon bar and roaring for Rangers in the New Year derby. Your first exposure to parity of esteem will be when you receive the same treatment as the other patients in casualty.

Soccer isn't central to our lives, in that no city in Ireland can claim to be a soccer city and we dole out the love for our national team in proportions directly linked to the size of the stage they occupy. We have no immense floodlit cathedrals of the game; indeed the GAA possesses at least two dozen grounds more impressive than the best-appointed League of Ireland precinct. So Celtic are a symbol of the footballing attainment of the race.

They are like the football wing of the Kennedy clan, proof positive to us that those Irish who suffered economic expulsion are doing well. An indication that there must be a crumb of genius in the national gene. We expect so much of them that they, like the Kennedys, are exempt from the clear-eyed scrutiny that distance should allow.

On Saturday, Celtic were awful. A middling team topping a substandard league and pretty damn fretful about it too. If they win two more games, they will win the Scottish league for the first time since 1988. It will be the least stylish of triumphs, but we will celebrate in a tight-lipped spiteful way. Given the choice, we would swap three unbeaten years and a European Cup for the chance to deprive Rangers of their tenth title in the jammiest fashion imaginable.

Celtic and Rangers are the ugly sisters of sport. The pokey way in which one's poverty is the other's riches is the best argument yet for a European superleague which might broaden their vision. And ours.

Rangers, as a literal matter of faith, are masonic nuns. Celtic, of course, lovable rogues, still serve as a vent for the dopiest kind of kneejerk republicanism, the beery waving of tricolours and raucous chanting of songs by those at the safe end of the Northern conflict. The Saturday afternoon patriots are still with us.

It's easy to sing 'Up the RA' and imagine that you would happily die for Ireland when you are in the midst of 50,000 Celtic supporters at a football match.

Outside Celtic Park many of the scarves and flags still suggest in three words of Irish that our day will come.

You meet plenty of decent football-loving men and women on an afternoon in Glasgow who will lament the excesses which have distinguished the rivalry, yet that middle ground hasn't grown big enough just yet. This column asked about twenty people in the course of the day if things had got better or worse between Celtic and Rangers. Still the same, said most of them. Worse, said the balance.

Glasgow is an interesting goldfish-bowl study of muddied perceptions.

Underpinning all Celtic theology is the cast-iron belief that the club and its disciples are morally superior to those who play and worship at Ibrox. Strangely this isn't recognised as a self-evident truth by Rangers fans.

Certainly no fuss is made about the religion of any player who wears the green and white hoops, whereas Rangers clung for the longest time to a more institutionalised form of bigotry.

Rangers were founded by a Presbyterian boys' club and have never got over it. Celtic were the recreation ground of Irish emigrants. They, too, are mired in the past. No matter how much money comes into the game in Scotland, no matter how many sponsors try desperately to paper over the cracks, no matter how sumptuous the spreads in the executive lounges, the ugliness at the centre still remains. Rangers are orange bigots. Celtic, of course, just burn the Union Jacks, sing the songs, beat Mo Johnson's father up in a pub, firebomb his house and expect us to see the funny side.

On Saturday, I met three sets of Celtic supporters who told me in exasperated tones of the havoc which is wrought on the visitors' end at Celtic Park every time Rangers visit. The seats are ripped out and the toilets are broken and, all in all, those bluenose Rangers fans are unreconstructed savages.

The taxi back to the airport was driven by one such season-ticket holding unreconstructed savage with a bluenose who explained to me in tones delicately designed to convey understanding, but not offence, that he has always been afraid to take his son to see Old Firm games at his beloved Ibrox because of the sheer savagery of Celtic supporters. You should see them.

He went on to muse about how the homes of the two teams illustrated the essential difference between the two tribes.

He goes into Ibrox and there is a central corridor beneath each stand which is thirty yards wide at least and dotted with TV monitors playing highlights and player interviews. There are soothing lights and well-painted walls and food concession stands as far as the eye can see. And Parkhead?

'No offence, pal, but Parkhid is a shit-hole, but that's them for ye.'

It is a depressing place to be. Liverpool and Everton have got over their religiously divided pasts and been united by the fetid poverty of their city and the common passion for football. Glasgow is a comparable city in many ways, but progress is impossible.

You find that, by reflex and by breeding, you are a Celtic fan and your sympathies are distressingly rigid. You look for signs to reinforce your prejudice, hoping the cab driver will slip the words 'fenian bastards' out between his lips and give you an excuse.

Sometimes sport is smaller than the world around it. Celtic and Rangers, in their eternal bitterness, are a museum piece dedicated to our own past.

The relationship between ourselves and our club in Scotland is warm and unique and worth preserving. Some of the trappings, though, need ditching before the rest of the world begins a new century.

It is an embarrassment that so many of our own mindlessly play their part in preserving the sporting wing of a sectarian conflict which moves gradually towards hard compromise while Celtic and Rangers never change.

Running up that hill

The sun was splitting the rocks on Carrauntoohil a fortnight ago when John Lenihan brought a group of friends scrambling up the mountain. One of them got as far as Hag's Glen and felt his brain telling him that he was a man, not a goat. He turned back.

Lenihan called him later.

'Thought you were gone back to get the suncream, boy?' said Lenihan.

'It's not suncream you want, Lenihan,' said his friend, 'it's a brain transplant.'

He's right. John Lenihan and his ilk need help. You have to be cross-eyed crazy to do the things John Lenihan does. There is only one thing stranger than people who run up mountains. People who run down them. Lenihan does both. Nobody has beaten him on Carrauntoohil for a decade.

In Zermatt, Switzerland, back in 1991, he was twenty seconds behind the front pair at the top of the mountain. He was thirty seconds ahead by the time he reached the bottom and heard the voices in the crowd telling him there was nobody else in sight and he was about to become World Mountain Running Champion.

To get to the place where John Lenihan lives and was reared, you have to tackle a few ascents yourself. If there is an off, off Broadway, then Glounageenty represents the outreaches of off, off the beaten track. Ask Denis Mannix in the post office, go past the church, the graveyard, the school and left where the Earl of Desmond met his end. On then up a boreen which climbs with a shocking gradient and offers views which you would enjoy if you weren't afraid they'd be your last sight on this earth. Finally, into a yard where four wag-tailed dogs greet you before Lenihan emerges, long haired and baseball capped.

He has 160 acres of land here. Soil which he is master of and slave to. A couple of years ago, he milked his cows in the morning, drove up country to Croagh Patrick, won the race up the mountain and drove back home again to milk the cows that night. 'The cows would tell you I was a bit cranky that night maybe,' he says smiling.

One hundred acres of mountain and none of it fit for anything but taking up his own turf and his time. He took the farm over from his father four years ago and, in the first year, he nearly went under.

'Working with him all those years, I was used to doing the things as he laid them out every day. On my own, having to plan it myself, well I nearly went under.'

In a way, running saved him. He had a career-long habit of taking notes and records of his training and he did the same with the farm and compared the results every night with leaflets and pamphlets he got from Teagasc. He got through it.

He loves the land and the animals and the belts of fresh air and his easy-going metabolism is tuned to the rhythms of this extraordinarily lonely place. There are regrets, though. When he was younger he got the chance to go to America on a three-year contract with Team Adidas to run the roads. The family and the farm kept him at home, though, and he speaks about that junction in his life with wistful regret.

'I went out afterwards for three months on my own steam.' In San Diego he got a reputation for ferocious road racing, which got him invitations up and down the west coast. He did odd jobs to keep himself going and the southern California sun kissed his head from morning to dusk every day.

He brought some American friends over to his lonely eyrie when he came back and, the first day the skies spilled, he couldn't keep them in, they were so desperate for the novelty of running in the soft Kerry rain.

He wasn't so enamoured with the familiar clouds and found it hard to settle on the mountain again after the three months in America. Guilt at having left the farm for such a period drew him back, but America and the sunshine of San Diego washed around his brain.

'I've never been on drugs, but it's what I imagine coming off them is like. It was hard. If I had gone for three years, I don't know if I would have come back at all. I regret not having been a full-time athlete, but I wonder when I look back if I could have enjoyed it all any more.'

He'll never know. He came home and he farmed and worked in the factory for four years, toiling over braking systems and dreading the effects of the dust which thickened the air. You could put on a white shirt going out at night and, within an hour, no matter how much washing you had done, a million little specks of red dust fresh from your pores would be performing a polka on the white cotton. So, he settled on the farm and the 5.30 am starts and reconciled himself to being a farmer first and a runner second.

It might have been different. He came to running by accident but loved it from the first footfall. He went in for football as a kid, but his family creased themselves with worry about him, the only boy and the extra hands on the farm out risking broken limbs chasing leather. He persevered. He got called in for some trials for a Kerry vocational school team at fourteen, but the family didn't want him to go.

Touching seventeen, he felt the need for some sort of outlet away from the mountain and joined Ballymacelligot GAA club for the company and fitness. The Sunday papers were serialising *Be Active Be Alive*, a series of leaflets produced by the Department of Health. They became his Bible. He used the information for getting fit for football and halfway there he saw a race advertised for Castleisland the following Sunday. He put his name down, for the *craic*, came seventh and was a member of an athletics club by the time he got home that evening.

Ballymacelligot GAA club had lost him forever.

The running has been his valve, his daydream and his escape. He never wrung an Olympics out of it, but he got some good travel and met some heroes. Willie Counihan, a local runner, who first caught his eye, met him, raced him, befriended him. John Treacy and Gerry Deegan were good to him, he says, and, once in Czechoslovakia, he met Lasse Viren, the king of kings.

Towards the end, the discipline of hill running and the lure of Carrauntoohil drew him in. The rush of the mountains and the fellowship of the field kept him there.

He has been up Snowdon and down, out ahead of the posse. Up Croagh Patrick for the last three years, winning each time and breaking his own record last year, getting up and down the mountain in forty-three minutes, twenty-three seconds.

'I like Croagh Patrick. It means something to people who know it from walking up it, it means something when they think of you running up it and down it.'

But Carrauntoohil is the mother lode, the magic mountain. He missed the first running of the race but entered the second time. That was ten years ago and he hasn't been beaten since. Tomorrow he is looking for eleven titles in a row.

'Carrauntoohill,' he says, rolling the word around on his Kerry tongue. 'How do I explain it? Close on 3,700 feet of climb on the 8.5-mile course. If it's a bad day, you wonder what the hell you are doing up there. If it's a good day, you are close to heaven.'

Close to heaven. Or very dizzy and close to fainting. John Lenihan describes the course like a gourmand reading aloud from a menu.

'We go up an unsurfaced road for a mile or so, then onto the shoulder of Caher mountain, there's a fair sting in the tail getting up that, then a series of descents and ascents to get around the ridge up Carrauntoohill, then back down. Mentally, I look at Caher as the finish, if I make it there, going downhill. That's the race, but I suppose there is more to it. Carrauntoohil is special.'

You look out John Lenihan's kitchen window at the trees and cow parlours huddled on the side of the mountain and there is a connectedness with land and rock which life in a suburban rabbit hutch doesn't provide. Lenihan is in thrall to those rugged contours of the landscape.

'I love mountains. I wouldn't be in the running game now, only for the mountains. The beauty of them and I suppose the fact that I can compete on that terrain. There's the attraction for me. There is something special, maybe a bit spiritual. Nobody says I'd really love to run the road between Tralee and Castleisland, but running up Carrantouhil has something special about it. People come from all over to it.

'I just get a rush of adrenalin from being on the mountain. I can't think of any other experience like that. The mountain gives you a strength you don't get anywhere else.'

The injury risk is there, but it's overstated, he says. Going up, the gradients are so steep that you barely go fast enough to do damage. Some people walk up the steeper bits, but Lenihan keeps jogging, just for the momentum.

Sometimes, he looks and sees walkers gaining on him as he jogs.

He is a ferocious climber, leaning into the hill and moving all the time. He has a trackman's awareness of the tactics of racing as well, keeping one eye on the good climbers, measuring out what sort of lead he can afford to grant them if he is to pull them in when his moment comes, that thrilling second when, having conquered gravity, he turns around and embraces it.

'I love coming down,' he says, with a smile looping from ear to ear. 'I love descending. That's the thrill. A lot of people find it unnerving. Bouncing through heather… You'd be destroyed coming down on rocks. That can be a bit embarrassing, because people have this idea built up that I'm a ferocious descender. I am, but on my own terms and my own sort of terrain.' There is friendship everywhere you look in hill running and mutual respect, too, but the kudos and the genuflections go to those brave souls who come down quickest.

Lenihan knows his rivals and he feels the breath of the best descender on his neck.

'Francis Cosgrove has been closing in on me every year. He caught me on the way down on the rocky terrain last year. God, he was flying. I got onto the heather and we were back on my terms. On the heather, you can just blast it. Francis is coming down this year. He rang me the other night. I'll have to be ready.'

This week he has been laid low by the flu, but a friend in Castleisland gave him a restorative which he is trying. Some *poitín* boiled up with water, lemon and honey. It'll kill him or cure him, but either way he'll be on a mountain tomorrow, preferably one step ahead of Francis Cosgrove, with heather under him and Caher in sight.

'I suppose if the run ended, if I stopped winning Carrauntoohil, I might ease off, step back a bit. I'd still go out and run, I'll do that as long as I'm able, but the competitive thing might be gone a bit. I'll never stop running, though.'

The cows need emptying and the land needs attention and the dogs are barking.

Farmer first, runner second these days, but no final summit in sight for the man who runs headlong down the mountains.

Black spots and dull pains – Scenes from a World Cup

11 June 1998

Scene One:

Charles de Gaulle Airport. A journalist approaches a flight desk. Unlike his esteemed colleagues, Mr Byrne, Mr Malone and Mr Lawrenson, the journalist is not a polyglot. Mr Byrne, indeed, contributes soccer snippets to the *Esperanto Telegraph*. That's another story. The journalist knows nothing of languages, merely that Polish is the loving tongue and Irish apparently killed the ancient Romans.

The journalist is carrying a small phrase book and a blue tote bag which takes so much stuff that the journalist can hardly lift it.

Journalist: '*Bonjour, Madame.*' (Hello.)

Woman at internal flight desk: '*Bonjour, Monsieur.*' (Hello, Sir.) '*Comment allez-vous?*' (How are you?)

Journalist (fumbling with phrasebook): 'Uhm. *Je suis...*' (shrugs shoulders expressively, rolls eyes, shakes head, conveys notion of hernia incurred from lifting big blue bag) '... uhm, *mais c'est la vie.*' (Uhm. I am a singer in a popular girl band.)

Woman at flight desk: *'Je suis desolée, Monsieur.'* (Sorry for your troubles, Mister.)

Journalist (confidently): *'Pardon?'*

Woman at flight desk: *'Je suis vraiment desolée.'* (My heart bleeds for you, fatso.)

Journalist (locating correct page in phrase book, smiling broadly): *'Je voudrais acheter un billet.'* (I want to buy a ticket. Your job is safe.)

Woman at desk: *'Ou êtes-vous allant et puis-je voir votre passeport?'* (Where are you going and can I see your passport?)

Journalist (looking through phrasebook in panicky manner): *'Ah. J'aimerais faire nettoyer à sec cette jupe.'* (I would like to have this skirt dry-cleaned.)

Woman at desk: *'Il y a une grève, Monsieur.'* (Have you been living up a tree pal? There's a strike on.)

Journalist: *'Ah! Très bien! Est-ce bien le vol pour Montpellier?'* (Ah, OK! Will the next flight to Monpellier…?)

Woman at desk: *'Le prochain vol part a…'*

Journalist: *'Aha. Prochain. Oui. Oui???'* (No. No. I'm well out of my depth.)

Woman at desk: *'Noël. Peut-être.'* (Christmas. Perhaps.)

Journalist (spotting phrase with jocular potential): *'Je voudrais essayer le ski de fond.'* (I'd like to try cross-country skiing.)

Woman at desk: *'Pardon, Monsieur?'*

Journalist: *'C'est une plaisanterie? Une ho ho ho?'* (Jaysus, it's only a joke.)

Scene Two:

Eighteen hours later. An airport arrivals terminal in southern France.

Journalist realises he has no work done yet. Reaches for media guide and phrasebook. Heads for payphone.

Journalist: *"Allo. 'Allo. 'Allo. J'aimerais parler à Ronaldo.'* (I want to speak to Ronaldo.)

Receptionist: *'Il dort.'* (He's asleep.) *'C'est de la part de qui?'* (Who are you anyway, pal?)

Journalist: *'C'est Nike. C'est cas urgent.'* (I am Nike. It's an emergency.)

Receptionist: *'Pourquoi, Monsieur?'* (This should be good.)

Journalist: *'Er. Ma machine chauffe.'* (My engine is overheated.)

Receptionist: *'Au revoir, Monsieur.'* (Drop dead, Mister.)

Journalist: *'Mais j'ai rendez-vous avec mon cher ami Ronaldo.'* (But I have an appointment with my dear friend Ronaldo.)

Receptionist: *'Non. Tu as un rendez-vous avec chômage.'* (No. You have an appointment with unemployment.)

Journalist: 'Kimmage. Paul Kimmage. *Ah oui, oui. Desolé.'* (He's with Kimmage. Buck-toothed Brazilian bastard.)

Journalist: *'C'est vraiment cas urgent. Je suis un point noir.'* (It's really an emergency. I am an accident blackspot.)

Scene Three:

At the hotel. The journalist surveys his lodgings. Fumbles for the phone.

Journalist: *'Hallo, reception? J'ai réservé une chambre avec une ampoule.'* (I asked for a room with a light bulb.)

Scene Four:

End of day two. The journalist has yet to file. Fumbles for phone.

Journalist: *'Bonjour, le service en chambre? Je voudrais trente-cinq litres de bière.'* (Hallo, room service? I'd like to order something to help me forget.) *'Je suis une douleur sourde.'* (I am a dull pain.)

Room service: *'Une douleur sourde? Parlez anglais, Monsieur.'* (Speak Eengleesh, Sir. I speeek eet.)

Journalist (in Maurice Chevalier accent, speaking slowly and very loudly per modern linguistic technique): 'I – need – zumtheeng – to – 'elp – me – furget.'

Room service: *'Vous devez payer un supplement.'* (You have to pay extra.)

Journalist: *'Envoyez votre facture à* Dr A.J.F. O'Reilly.' (Send the bill to the *Indo*. They'll bankroll this.)

Room service: *'Vous appelez-vous Monsieur...?'* (Name?)

Journalist: 'Burke. Raphael.'

Scene Five:
Journalist, lonely and desperate, dials number at random.

Voice: 'Bonjour.'

Journalist: *'Nicole?'*

Voice: *'Papa?'*

Journalist: *'Non. C'est Bob.'*

Exit lines the same in familiar tale

2 July 1998

In a funny sort of way, we are going to miss England. They are the lousy, noisy neighbours who have suddenly upped and left the area which they have inadvertently defined. We have depended on them for the friction, the saltiness, the fly-in-the-ointment awkwardness.

Without the English, we journalists, we professional pedlars of sports clichés, have no texture to our lives. We are just fat geezers off at the World Cup in sunny France. Without the English, we have no chance to call up our offices on the mobiles and announce, à la Kate Adie, that it's 'going off' outside.

'Can your hear me, hello, can you hear me? Oh God. Hello? Hello? Is there anyone there?'

'Eh, yes, sports desk here. Hearing you fine. Is that you? How are ya? What's the weather like?'

'Listen. This could be my last call. My last call. If I get cut off, Jesus, tell the sports editor that I love him, will you. It's gone off outside. Do you hear? It's gone off. It's too dangerous to walk to the media shuttle, four of us are going to try to call a taxi. It's our only hope of getting to the hotel bar before it closes. Pray for us.'

'Any chance you could do 500 words on the scenes you have witnessed? Eyewitness account. "My terror" sort of thing.'

'Well, it's just too confused. There was some pushing I think. I got the suede bit on my runners scuffed coming down the stairs to the press restaurant. You can't repair that. I'll never get that back, that brushed look. That's gone forever. I'm not going to let myself cry.'

'Eh listen, I'm going for me bus now. Speak to you in the morning.'

'Well don't call too early and, erm, if anything happens, put it in the paper that I was working on a novel and "ironically, this might have been his last assignment". You might say "he had seen too much, begun taking too many risks". Should I send you over some obit stuff? Tragically, I'm younger than I look. I think the paper had yet to see the best of me.'

'We were wondering about that alright.'

So there's that. No more adrenalin rush for those of us hooked on danger.

From now on it's just sappy crowds singing together and hugging and swapping jerseys. That and the Germans.

We'll miss our colleagues, too, not the solid English chaps we are friendly with from the trips with the Irish team, but the big league full-colour tabloid guys. They are the best thing to watch at the World Cup. We Irish sit around and discuss them in press-centre restaurants, like old Cubans spitting tobacco juice and lamenting the state of baseball pitching in the major leagues in the US. We have only a sketchy grasp of what we are lamenting, but even from our little island home we can see that it's worth lamenting.

You haven't begun to understand the sociology of the English hooligan until you've seen an English tabloid big hitter slightly inconvenienced.

'Taxi driver. I-WANT-TO-GO-TO-THE-STADIUM. GOTTIT? DO-I-HAVE-TO-SPELL-IT-OUT-TO-YOU?   STAD-EE-OENTE PLEASE.'

'Can't you see I have customers in the back, sir? I am stopped at the traffic lights.'

Witnesses to the tabloid warriors' last foray into the post-match mixed zone on Tuesday night came back blanched with fear, or convulsed with laughter. As happens most evenings, the winning manager and players arrived in first to provide the media with their thoughts. Argie thoughts were of absolutely no value to the boys. After two minutes of Daniel Passarella and his team, you could hear the French press liaison guy over the TV monitors pleading with the gentlemen to please calm down. What we couldn't hear was the journalistic side of the debate. Inside the mixed zone, the air was blue. The tabloid boys were shouting at the victorious Argentinians.

'Now f**k off. We've got deadlines. Go and f**k off.'

Argentinian journalists and neutrals were trying to do their jobs and gather the thoughts of the winning team. The tabloids turned on them.

'You've got six f**king hours to do your work. Six f**ing hours. We've got deadlines now. F**k off out of here. Go orn, f**k off.'

Beautiful.

We'll miss Glenn Hoddle, too. Like Richard Nixon, we won't have Glenn to kick around anymore. Glenn is a little luckier than Tricky Dickie, though. He didn't get found out.

It was all shaping up for an ugly finale, with the tabloid boys keen to gut and fillet the chap for the enjoyment of their readers. Hoddle's post hoc rationalisations of decisions, which suggested that he was making the World Cup up as he went along, could only work so long as England still had a chance of winning. Nobody thought that he could still manage to look like a winner if England went out in the second round. The laughter was barely suppressed among the ranks of the fourth estate when Hoddle announced, without irony, that it had always been his plan to have Beckham in the centre of midfield by the time England played Colombia, that he was always going to introduce Michael Owen little by little and so on.

All along, Hoddle seemed to be fondly watching himself spooling these yarns out, smiling approvingly at his own cleverness. The old quote about Graeme Souness was much used in the past week. If Hoddle was made of chocolate, he'd eat himself.

The focus has shifted a little now. The mass market papers generally follow the national mood and, in England, this week's defeat has played out as a heroic failure. Nothing wrong with that, but four weeks ago losing to Romania, failing to top the group and then going out to Argentina in the second would have been classified as a calamity by the English football public.

Hoddle reacted to his team's departure from the competition by stating that they had no luck, that destiny had it in for them, that Beckham's departure cost England dearly. In the short-term past, he could get away with those claims. The truth is a little more prosaic, a little more damning than that, though.

Beckham, for instance, was on the field for the last fifteen minutes of the first half on Wednesday night when the Argentinians played their most irresistible football. Under the sort of pressure England experienced for that period, the lightweight, non-tackling feel of England's midfield looked as if it would be the factor which cost England the game.

With Beckham's departure, the English had to reorganise themselves along emergency lines. At this point, Sol Campbell, Tony Adams and Alan Shearer intervened to save Hoddle's bacon. In a state of blissful paralysis on the sideline, Hoddle took forty-six minutes to introduce David Batty, leaving poor gangly Darren

Anderton to experience a crash course in tackling in the centre of midfield as the Argentinians swept through again and again.

Three things kept England alive. Some extraordinary tackling by their defence, heroic work by Alan Shearer, who bailed water all night, and a disconcerting bluntness to the Argentinian attack. Ortega apart, they never looked like scoring.

So Hoddle goes home having slipped the hangman's noose. The drama of a third English exit from a major competition by way of penalty shoot-out gives a flavour of heroic martyrdom to the exercise. It will take a while before the damning context of dry history shows Hoddle up in a more stark light.

We'll miss them, with their carping, their arrogance and their spirit. One moment from Tuesday's match of the tournament summed up the best of them.

Shearer had just taken his second penalty of the night, England's first of the shoot-out. England looked somehow doomed, what with three of their designated five penalty takers (Anderton, Scholes, Beckham) being unavailable for one reason or another, but Shearer scored with aplomb and shook his fists to the heavens.

And the cameras picked up the look on his face.

Up against it, but exulting in that fact. They were like that all the way through. They left at the end of the best match of the tournament, one of the best of any World Cup.

If you are leaving the party early, you might as well make your exit memorable. They got that right at least.

France stage *coup de monde*

13 July 1998

La Metamorphose! One glance at St Denis tells you how hard pressed it is. Grey boxes strewn on a concrete wilderness as the train shuttles by from wonderful Paris to the cool halls of the airport. Last night it was the centre of the world. The surreal, beautiful stadium which has been set down here shook, quaked and rocked.

Tricolours rippled the sky. Songs rattled the roof. Men cried. Women danced.

Fireworks crackled. People got kissed who've never been kissed before. France became Champions of the World.

'This group of players was born for the World Cup,' said Youri Djorkaeff, the French midfielder of Armenian stock. That was just the point, though. They weren't born for it. They grafted. Brazilians are born for it.

It must have been like this when the men in the Bible stepped from the boat on to the surface of the water, when the first plane stayed up in the air for breathless seconds, when Armstrong got moondust on his earthly feet. Achievement which defied comprehension.

In St Denis they danced on air, walked on water, went over the moon. France won the World Cup and men in blue shirts mounted the steps and lifted the gold.

What a sensational night. The outsiders with nothing to offer except their nation's hospitality and their extraordinary defence beat the Brazilians, brand leaders in the romance business. Beat them well, with three goals, two of them functionally crafted, one of them the crowning moment, a thing of beauty.

And they didn't even have a striker. They didn't have Laurent Blanc. And in the end they didn't have Marcel Desailly; but they had the World Cup trophy hoisted into the Parisian sky.

Seldom has sport presented such a dramatic consummation of hope and achievement. This was an evening when France was subconsciously prepared to celebrate gallant defeat, to wonder at the journey their largely workaday team had taken. Instead, men grew into giants before their eyes. Their goals came from midfielders. Two from Zidane and the final one deep in injury time from the superlative Petit.

It was an extraordinary night.

Zinedine Zidane, a child of hard streets in Marseille, knew the feeling of having his name chanted in every corner of the republic. 'Zizou! Zizou! Zizou!'

The little man with the bald patch and the snake's smile was everywhere. Every blade, every screen, every mouth, every keyboard. 'Zizou! Zizou! Zizou!'

Two matching goals, both from near post headers in the first half, elevated Zidane to the pantheon. The son of a poverty-strained family of Algerian immigrants, Zizou was the story of the evening, the story of the World Cup, the story of France. Work, integration, achievement. Zidane missed two games earlier in this World Cup, having copped a suspension for a silly foul. Last night he added atonement to the list of his credits.

He was overshadowed in midfield, perhaps, by Emmanuel Petit, the pony-tailed Arsenal midfielder who filled in at centre half when Desailly was sent off and still found time to charge up field and score the goal which finished the tournament and lay the Brazilians in the ground.

Brazil were never what we had expected them to be. For a few mad minutes before the kickoff, indeed, they were something else entirely, sending out a team sheet without the name of Ronaldo on it. Another appeared minutes later and Edmundo's name had been erased and Ronaldo's name included.

Stories ran like bushfire around the stands of the Brazilians having taken Ronaldo to hospital within an hour of the start of the game, of dissent and turmoil beyond the dressing room door. On the pitch, the reality looked depressingly prosaic. Ronaldo unfit. Dunga tired. Bebeto uninspired.

'Everybody was very upset and very down about Ronaldo,' said Brazil's coach, Mario Zagallo, afterwards at a bad-tempered press conference which left more questions unanswered, 'and the team played to less than their full potential. It was indicative of the major problem with Ronaldo. We were very inhibited.'

What happened to Ronaldo is a little yarn for today or tomorrow. Last night the Brazilian defence was the tale. More anaemic than their history entitled them to be, they seemed shaken by the vigour of the French support and the ambition of the French attacks and the defiant panache of the French defending.

Brazil's defence had been rickety throughout this tournament and last night it fell to dust. Junior Baiano was awful. Aldair slightly less awful. The French knew they were on to something early on when they drummed out three scoring chances in the first ten minutes.

They pushed and pushed and felt the door scraping open. Djorkaeff missed two.

Guivarc'h began a chain of misses which, on less charitable occasions, would have had him guillotined. Instead he's moving to Newcastle.

A couple of goals up at half-time, with a million tricolours fluttering in front of their eyes and the words 'Allez, Allez, Allez' buzzing in their ears. They hadn't dared to have dreams of this.

The second half was a metaphor for the tournament France have had. Defiance and defence. Resistance!

The Brazilians, treated to an interval with the smelling salts, had come to.

The French defended with passion. Adversity mounted before them. Brazilian near misses drew the breath from French lungs. For the second successive game, France had a centre half dismissed. The perfection of Marcel Desailly's tournament performances was marred by a slightly harsh sending off for a second bookable defence.

It was the sort of setback the French have learned to deal with, though.

Petit dropped back. His clubmate Viera arrived in with regal coolness. The ship steadied.

There will be those curmudgeons who will say that the best team in the tournament didn't win. Perhaps, but it was splendid none the less.

France defended with such passion and cunning, went forward with such naive enthusiasm, and sung the song of football like it is meant to be sung. Last night the French won the best World Cup final in years.

Great occasions can do nothing for the terminally mean spirited and this was a great occasion, a great story, beautifully climaxed.

The inside story of what happened when the dope testers called to Michelle de Bruin's house in Kilkenny

7 August 1998

It was still dark when the Guys pulled up outside Kellsgrange House, Co. Kilkenny, on January 10th last. The trip was a familiar but scarcely enjoyable part of their strange job.

The couple who had previously been responsible for randomly testing Ireland's most famous athlete had quit the task because they felt uncomfortable with their role, deciding that, at fifty dollars a test plus mileage, it was more trouble than it was worth.

So it had fallen to the Guys to present themselves periodically at the home of Michelle and Erik de Bruin and demand 70 mls of urine from the triple Olympic champion. They were recruited by the English drug test expert John Whetton, and had undergone the training which the job required. If the road to Kilkenny was well worn, the results were often frustrating.

Typically, the Guys and other testers from the world's leading testing agency – the Swedish company, International Doping Tests and Management (IDTM) – followed the details supplied by the swimmer, which informed FINA she would be training at the local

St Paul's pool at a given time. But in over a year of testing, Michelle Smith had never been located at the pool.

The Guys had made the journey just two days previously, registering a 'no show' as they failed to locate the swimmer at either the pool or her home.

Michelle de Bruin's record of no shows for random tests was public knowledge and she had received a warning from FINA the previous year.

Her reluctance to deal with the officials charged with doping-control duties was well known within the sport. In July 1995, her own federation, the Irish Amateur Swimming Association (IASA), had written to her in stern terms threatening that if the 'doping control consent form for the National Swimming Championships… is not received in this office by return duly completed and signed by you, your entries will be withdrawn from the National Championships'.

The text of the letter was surprising, the fact that it had to be sent to her parents' address in Rathcoole and faxed to a mysterious number in Holland more so. Despite the fact that it was well over a year since Michelle Smith had emigrated, she had still failed to provide IASA with an address.

This chill Saturday morning was different, however. As the cold insinuated itself into their car, Al and Kay Guy drove towards the de Bruin residence, Kellsgrange House; a large and picturesque house, structurally three buildings knocked into one and protected by a chest-high wall.

The de Bruins had purchased it just before house prices in Ireland went through the roof. With twenty metres of driveway between the gates and the front door, it made for an impressive sight in summer with the sunlight pouring through the trees and playing on the whitewashed house walls.

Early on January 10th, however, the sky was still charcoal, no lights were on at home and the front gates were heavily padlocked. The Guys sat in their car, waiting for a sign of life.

Early morning is a good time for random testing.

In cases where the athlete has proved difficult to locate, or has given unreliable information regarding training schedules, the start of the day is the perfect moment for testers to arrive. Combined with the element of surprise is the fact that the quality of the urine to be had from the athlete after a night's sleep, when the metabolites have settled, makes for rich pickings in the laboratory.

The occupants of Kellsgrange House had reason to be cheerful on 10 January, 1998. A minor road accident at a T-junction in Co. Carlow late the previous autumn had resulted in a neck injury that kept Michelle de Bruin away from the World Swimming Championships in Perth.

Not being in Perth was a blessing of sorts. That morning, the papers were full of the new buzz phrase of swimming. Human growth hormone was one of a number of new designer drugs which were undetectable through urine tests. In Perth, the swimming world was speaking of little else: one of the Chinese swimming delegation had been caught passing through customs in Melbourne with a hip flask full of HGH.

The principal plank of Michelle de Bruin's defence since the controversy of the Atlanta Games had been her claim that she was the most tested athlete in the world. So her presence in Perth, while the swimming media frothed about a substance entirely undetectable in urine samples, would have been irresistible. Tucked up in bed in Kilkenny, she was better off being far away from the World Championships and the microphones.

Things were looking good in other respects also. The three gold medals she had brought home from Atlanta had proved to have no alchemic powers for altering the couple's financial situation. Expecting a major windfall, the de Bruins had been disappointed to lose the backing of their major pre-Olympic sponsor, the courier firm TNT, just after the Games.

New endorsement opportunities had been scant. Michelle had appeared on TV advertisements for shampoo and for the promotion of the Irish language, and had featured in a poster campaign for a dairy company. But Speedo, whose Aquablade suit she had worn with such prominence in Atlanta, had steadfastly ignored her.

So had the rest of the commercial world.

The poor financial yield and the drugs question had hurt de Bruin, but there were other factors. She was an Irish phenomenon and Ireland is a very small market. Furthermore, as with many other sports, the Irish only show an interest in swimming once every four years, when an Olympic celebration invades their living rooms.

Michelle de Bruin had thus been unable to cash in on her Olympic glory. Her attrition rate with agents didn't help either. She had hired and fired two since her rise to prominence and was on the third.

Yet this January morning the couple were getting over their financial disappointment. Michelle, ironically perhaps, had expressed an interest in working in the media after her swimming career wound down.

The previous summer she had co-presented an Irish television programme, *The Sporting Press Gang*. The pay was poor but Erik had also been paid (as a consultant) and the reaction to Michelle's cool broadcasting style had been positive. A long-term career within the ranks of the despised media was a distinct possibility.

In the short term, meanwhile, swimming was beginning to yield a moderate wage also. De Bruin had generally eschewed the attractions of the world swimming circuit, missing grands prix and high-profile events in favour of smaller competitions which generally didn't include drug testing unless records were broken. All her pre-Olympic swims in 1996 were in small events with no drug testing.

This tactic was beginning to pay off financially in 1998. Small events, whose cachet would be considerably enhanced by the presence of a triple Olympic champion, were prepared to pay up to £5,000 a time for her presence in the pool.

Michelle was also cashing in on the growing trend for skins, or winner-takes-all events, and was exploring the possibilities of making guest appearances for clubs in exchange for cash. She had swum a skins event in Australia earlier in the winter, taking a disappointing A$4,000 (£1,762) out of an all-expenses-paid trip. Later she flew to Brazil and guested for a local team in the national championships.

Cash was also flowing in from other sources. The Leinster branch of IASA had paid Erik and her a couple of times to get into the pool with youngsters on coaching courses and the previous summer she had attempted a number of Irish and European short course records for cash rewards put up by Irish sponsors.

The IASA had also contributed £4,000 to her training fund for the Perth World Championships, but her road accident neck injury forced her to pull out not long after the payment was received.

At around the same time, the de Bruins returned the Opel car which they had been lent by General Motors when a prominent businessman presented them with a Lexus and made Michelle an honorary member of the prestigious Mount Juliet golf club.

So life was good, getting better, when Michelle de Bruin opened the front door to Kellsgrange House twenty-five minutes after the Guys' car pulled up at the gate.

The details of precisely what happened next have been slow to emerge. The Guys have drawn a discreet veil of professional silence over the whole affair, refusing to elaborate in even the most general terms about what transpired.

However, FINA officials close to the case have become aware of what allegedly went on through their familiarity with the report sent by the testers to the Swedish testing agency, IDTM. The Guys supplied their employers with a detailed timetable of all the events of the morning. Some details conflict with statements made by Michelle de Bruin after the story broke in late April, but, by then, IDTM had checked and rechecked the facts as reported to them.

Michelle de Bruin took one look at the Guys' car at the gate and went back inside the house. The Guys waited. Not long afterwards she appeared again, this time walking slowly down the driveway. A brief conversation took place through the locked gate. The swimmer turned to walk back up the driveway but then apparently remembered the gate.

She came back, turned the key in the padlock and walked quickly back up the driveway to her house. Al Guy got out of his car, removed the padlock and chain, opened the gate, drove through and left the car in order to close the gate again.

The Guys had been in the kitchen of Kellsgrange House with Michelle de Bruin for perhaps ten minutes when Erik de Bruin joined them. He appeared to have just woken and was surprised to see the testers waiting downstairs. A conversation in Dutch ensued between the de Bruins.

After some minutes, Erik addressed the testers in English. He was sorry but a test would be impossible that morning because his wife was due at Dublin airport at 10 am to meet an incoming flight. It was now about 8.20 am and Kellsgrange house is eighty miles from Dublin.

It was suggested by the testers that the rules made provision in these cases. If a trip to Dublin was unavoidable, the testers could travel with the swimmer, one accompanying her in her car, the other following behind. Whenever she felt capable of supplying 70 mls of urine, the cars could pull in somewhere; the women could visit the toilet and the sample could be taken and sealed.

Finally, the de Bruins announced that Michelle would stay.

According to her own testimony, Michelle de Bruin had just urinated when the Guys called that morning. Empty bladders are a common problem for testers, who bring sealed beverages with them to help the athlete aid and abet nature.

Michelle de Bruin chose a sealed bottle of Aqua Libra. They all waited.

Drug testing is the ugly side of sport, the dirty police work which sponsors and television companies would rather not know about. Every time we watch an Olympic gold medal being hung on an athlete's neck, we must assume that not long afterwards the victorious medal winner finds himself or herself in a cubicle in the company of a person paid to watch them urinate.

They will choose a small plastic beaker and, using mid-stream urine, endeavour to fill it to at least the 70-ml mark. It is an unseemly business and the price that must be paid for the joy of sport.

The flying squads of doping control officers whose job it is to collect the urine samples of the world's elite athletes are familiar with the techniques of deception. Athletes are often difficult to locate, despite the requirement that they fill out forms on a quarterly basis detailing their training schedules and availabilities.

Michelle de Bruin had some form in this regard. In February 1997, *The Irish Times* published documented evidence of a series of problems which FINA had encountered in attempting to keep track of the swimmer. Her own federation had complained that no address had been supplied for her after her move to Holland in 1994. Less than three months before the 1996 Olympic Games, de Bruin had informed FINA that she didn't know where she would be training for the Games. By February 1997 de Bruin had received an official warning on the subject of missed drug tests.

If she was often hard to find, the samples she had submitted over the years since her first random test in 1994 revealed nothing more unusual than a fluctuating testosterone level. Regardless of the levels of discomfort sampling officers may have experienced when calling to the de Bruin residence, the tests had always been carried out without breach of procedure.

Again the case history file in this regard was thick. Cases have been recorded of athletes submitting clean urine which transpired to have come from the bladder of a different person entirely. Contamination of samples is a rare but not entirely uncommon problem. The addition of a tiny amount of a foreign substance like vinegar will cast sufficient doubt on the process to ensure that the case won't withstand a legal challenge.

The Dubin inquiry into the case of Ben Johnson, the Canadian runner who tested positive after taking gold in an Olympic 100-metre sprint, learned he had consumed a mixture of honey and vinegar before testing in a futile attempt to confuse the testers.

Occasionally a female athlete wishing to contaminate a sample will run a finger quickly down across the anus and let the accumu-lated bacteria on her fingertip wash into the plastic container in the flow of urine.

It was not known until quite recently that Michelle de Bruin needed two attempts to supply the necessary amount of urine on the morning of 10 January, 1998. Having supplied about 40 mls on her first visit to the lavatory in the company of Kay Guy, she came back into the kitchen area and sat for another twenty-five to thirty minutes before departing to the lavatory a second time.

On this occasion when the athlete and tester returned to the kitchen, the small container of urine had a noticeable whiskey smell coming from it. Al Guy's past life as a customs officer had included a spell as a distillery inspector and the distinct odour would immediately have struck him. Testers are not encouraged in these circumstances to challenge athletes. In a circumstance with sufficient underlying tensions already at play, the suggestion by a tester that something has occurred which may potentially damage the athlete's career is not a good idea.

Both parties observed the sealing of the sampling vessels. Michelle was asked to inspect the code numbers and to fill out the standard form confirming the matching of the code numbers, and her satisfaction with the proceedings as they had taken place.

On the form, there is a comment area where the athlete may bring to the attention of the testing agency any irregularities they feel may have occurred.

Both Michelle and Erik de Bruin were familiar with this facility. Erik had availed of it extensively on his infamous trespass into the doping control area at the 1995 European Swimming Championships in Vienna when he acquired the accreditation badge of a Belgian official, gained access and began listing objections to the procedure in Dutch on behalf of the Irish swimmer. The incident came close to getting Michelle de Bruin expelled from the championships.

With all vessels sealed and packed away, the Guys took their leave of the de Bruins. Their subsequent report to the testing agency IDTM suggested that both had noticed the whiskey odour emanating from the second sample, and that there may have been slightly unusual sounds while the liquid was being passed.

Rather than the expected hiss sound of water being passed, there was a 'plonk, plonk' sound as though something was dropped into the liquid.

There the involvement of Al and Kay Guy all but ended. The

samples travelled by special courier to a lab in Barcelona, where science confirmed what the sense of smell had first suggested.

IDTM, which has never lost one of its own doping cases, checked and rechecked the chain of events that morning. Any failure by the testers could lead to costly legal proceedings and a severe loss of reputation.

In Barcelona, the samples were checked and rechecked, and FINA's office in Lausanne was informed of the findings. More checking and more consultation and the passage of events brought Michelle de Bruin to Lausanne to face the music on a Friday two years to the day after she had listened to her national anthem being played after she won her last gold medal at the Atlanta Olympics.

Johnny we hardly know ye

April 1998, Guinness Press Release for Psyche-Up Ad Campaign:
The hurling hero is psyching himself up... camera moves back to
reveal another figure... new character brings with him a sense of
foreboding, of dark forces... back to the hero, who takes a step
further, swings his hurley across his torso and gazes down the
corridor unflinching... the other figure mirrors these actions...
close-up reveals he is the same person... the first hurler's alter ego...
the demon within... the demon cracks the base of his hurley off the
floor... a fracture appears and travels down the length the tunnel... it
is white hot and molten, spitting and bubbling... with a fluid
movement the demon takes up a scorching ball of molten material –
a *sliotar* from hell!... with a sudden tremendous burst of speed the
demon hurler knocks up the ball and fires it down with awesome
power and pace to the hero facing him... our hero holds his
ground... he tenses himself in anticipation and...

Johnny Pilkington leans back in his seat and runs his hand
through his hair. Looks at the ceiling. Yawns. All the good things and
all the bad things in Johnny's life are stored up in his brown eyes. He
is considering hurling just now. Good and bad.

'The whole idea of it actually is ridiculous,' he says. Johnny never saw a bush he wanted to beat around. 'Training in muck and dirt. A big chunk of life gone for a little chunk of metal while an organisation is making millions. It's a so-called amateur game with a professional way of preparing and nothing but a clap on the back or a knife in the back at the end. "Why bother," I'd think to myself sometimes.'

And he grins, showing a wrecking yard of imperfect teeth. On the table is the round plastic ashtray, a mass grave for the cigarettes Johnny has sucked the life out of this morning. Johnny drums his fingers. No fags left. Forgot to buy a pack at lunchtime. The tension of a looming All-Ireland final can't be found anywhere on his face. The fiancée says he gets a little snappy in the week before a big game, but he hasn't noticed it himself. The way he's been for the last year or so, well, it's not molten lava or *sliotars* from hell stuff. Forgot the fags. Tut.

Take this summer and the game with Meath. A done deal after ten minutes. Game over. Johnny found himself just standing in Croke Park in the middle of the field. Wondering and wandering. What's the point in beating these by twenty-five points? Could have done with a fag.

Even when he has been with the programme, it's not been his best season. His detachment from the game and its molten passions has become more distinct.

Sometimes he listens to the table-banging speeches and the boys who are going to do or die and his ironic mind is leading him away from it.

'In the dressing room every game is the important game, you know. Win this one and ye'll be alright lads. The All Ireland, we'll go out and play that and it's the biggest thing ever. Two weeks later it's the club championship. We have to win that to get into the semi.

Then we have to win that to get into the county final. We've never put one back-to-back or something, so that's the most important thing and so on.

'Sometimes in the dressing room, I think, "Wouldn't it be more important if one of us lost his job. Then we'd be in trouble."'

He bodyswerves. 'Then again, though, you wouldn't be without the hurling.' He wouldn't be without it, but there are times when just being a hurling man in a hurling town closes in on him, days when the world seems a small place. If he didn't have hurling, what would he be?

He works for Minch Norton, the agricultural supply people. Apart from farming, every customer has one thing to talk about. Hurling. All hurling. All the time. Goodfellas and blowhards and bad debtors. Hurling.

Listen, Johnny might say, you owe us money, you've owed it this long time. Johnny, there'll be some hurling done to beat Kilkenny a Sunday, some hurling done.

Once, not long liberated from the ag. block in UCD, Johnny and another ag. graduate went out on a professional mission to see a farmer, a former Tipperary hurler actually. For half an hour, Tipp asked Johnny's colleague about farming. Then, business done, he turned to Johnny for the hurling chat at the end of it, as if Johnny was some sort of hurling bimbo included as part of a special offer.

'You have to get away,' he says. 'You need to escape it sometimes. There's not much point in stopping hurling and staying around in Birr. You'd have to go away altogether. Go somewhere where nobody knows you and nobody knows hurling... Kildare maybe.'

He got away for a bit last winter and fled to the sanctuary of the local rugby club, where he hid out for the duration of the Towns Cup campaign. The town buzzed with rumours that the rugby was eating

Johnny Pilkington away like the ebola virus. Little to be talking about.

'My rugby career wasn't exactly what it was made up to be,' he grins. 'I was playing in the worst division in the worst league in the worst rugby country in Europe. Didn't exactly have my head turned.'

Yet he appreciated it greatly. The lads on the rugby field with him two nights a week and on Saturday afternoons put the work in and pulled out less reward than hurlers are accustomed to. The GAA is the hub of life in Birr. The rugby boys go about their toil facing every problem except acclaim.

Babs gave him the call, of course, summoning him back to the fold. Johnny told him he'd a couple of weeks left with the rugby lads and, if Babs didn't mind, he'd like to see it out. Glad he did it. No idea what was down the line with Babs.

That's life, though. He shrugs in a way that's part of him.

It's twenty minutes after the All-Ireland semifinal in Thurles has finally finished up. Offaly aren't yet done with their whooping and hollering. The dressing-room door opens. He stands in the dustmoted light, drained, drawn and a cigarette in his mouth. Lets his mouth crinkle into a smile. He-eeeere's Johnny!

People sit Johnny Pilkington down for these sketches every year or so. They fiddle away while he sits there. Shade here, light there. And when they hand him back the portrait, he's king pogue, the Shane McGowan of his game, burping his way through the seasons, indifferent to hurling and stone mad for the drink.

He doesn't recognise himself.

It started maybe in 1994, before the All Ireland. Ger Canning asked him what an All Ireland would mean to Offaly. Johnny said it would mean a lot of drink. Looking back now, it was a stupid thing to say…

'But I was twenty-four and young and fresh out of college, no clue about tax or PRSI or those things. My reputation would be very exaggerated from then on.'

If there are ten rumours out there, he reckons six of them are wrong and he hasn't heard the other four yet. His fiancée's family own a pub. Brian Whelahan owns a pub. His car is parked outside one or the other most nights. Quick tongues do their work about the place. Johnny Pilkington had six gallons of porter and went home in the batmobile.

Johnny? He's not a soak. He's not telling you he's at home listening to his Jane Fonda workout tapes either, but he's not a soak. He has a life is all, and, if he sits drinking minerals till his woman finishes work at two in the morning, he's no need to reckon it with you in the morning.

'Look. Probably I drink a little bit more than I should, too much for inter-county hurling maybe. Maybe sixteen, seventeen pints a week, but there is a limit. I know the rumours, but where I'd be the people who'd talk about me don't be.'

He has the face and the character for it, the mixture of humour and sadness, the attitude and the walk. It all provokes gossip. In a town consumed by hurling, he cradles his genius for the game with such nonchalance that he must infuriate the right-thinking fundamentalists.

'What damages me is being the lad with the one-liner, the smart answer. I'm the messer. And sometimes I feel that, because of that, people don't take me seriously. The people that matter know me.'

Some guy bellied up to him the night before a wedding once. Johnny's fiancée's sister was getting hitched and the do was held the Friday before an All Ireland. The wedding was at two o'clock in the afternoon, and back in the hotel Johnny set into drinking minerals, tipping along nicely, enjoying himself despite the parade of people coming up to him all night with wagging fingers and soppy stern faces and drink taken.

'You're not to be drinking too much tonight.' So this guy bellies up once and says his piece. Fine. Then up the second time. Bit more strident this time. Not long later, he's along for the third speech from the pulpit. 'I can look after myself,' said Johnny. 'Look, I'm standing here drinking minerals.'

But this guy is in Johnny Pilkington's face, all froth and fervour, pushing him around like he is a piece of public property. So what happened?

'I says, well fuck you anyway, I'm tired of you coming up telling me what to do. I went off and had a few quiet pints. Came back and had two more. I drank five or six pints at the wedding from two o'clock in the day.'

And every one of them counted threefold by the time they got spilled into the rumour machine the next day. He knows how the machine works, multiplying his consumption exponentially.

Take the year they won the Fitzgibbon in UCD. As it happened, the semifinal was on the same Saturday as another wedding, which he had promised the fiancée he would attend. No matter what. Hell or high water.

Then a month later he realised it was Fitzgibbon weekend in Waterford. So he went and played the semifinal, hopped back into the car, drove home to Birr and was at the wedding before anyone was any the wiser. He had three pints, went to bed and drove to Waterford the next day. He played out of his skin and UCD won the Fitzgibbon.

Fast forward to a couple of months ago. Johnny meets a young fella still yomping through the groves of academe in Belfield. Said scholar pipes up to Johnny that in Belfield his legend still lives, preserved in alcohol as it were.

'How do you mean?'

'The Fitzgibbon,' says he and nods and winks.

'Eh?'

'The Fitzgibbon. The lads were saying when you turned up for the final they had to pump coffee into you and put you under a cold shower, just to get you on to the pitch.'

'Never happened.'

That's life when you have a big name in a small world. Part of you is hurling property. The bits of your life you might call your own are sequestered. 'I know what I'm doing,' says Johnny. 'I'll always go where I normally go. I'll do the same thing and, if somebody wants to say that Johnny was in the pub and he had ten pints and he fell out the door and next day he raised the hurl, well it doesn't bother me at all.'

Press him on the subject though and, rightly, he gets irritated. The business of players and their own lives blurs the borders in this amateur game. 'It's made out to be the wrong thing,' he says. 'I enjoy a pint. I'll have a couple the night before the All Ireland. That's me. I'm easy-going, relaxed. Other fellas will miss a night's sleep with the tension. No big deal.'

He's baffled by the curiosity, but it's been a baffling year. Why hasn't he been dropped, for instance? 'Seven games,' he laughs. 'About seven different partners in midfield. It's some kind of punishment. I can't work out if it's me or them that's being punished.' Strange times. Not too long ago he came into training and there was a new fella sitting in the corner. Shiny top, red face, nothing to say. Johnny whispered an inquiry. 'He's the new physical trainer.'

'Hmmm.'

Next thing, the imposter was on his feet.

'I'm Michael Bond. I'm from Loughrea. I trained the 1983

Galway under-21 team. I love Offaly hurling. I don't want to change Offaly hurling. I expect respect and I respect commitment. I give respect and I give commitment. Let's go train.'

Johnny was loping out the door thinking to himself that the lack of bullshit was a commendable change when he heard the order, 'BROSTAÍGÍ!' Jesus, what was that?

Another turn in a convoluted season, that's what. He's hogged headlines without hurling well at all. 'Did the Leinster championship exist at all?' he asks. 'Must have been the dullest ever.'

It would have been, if he and Babs hadn't added the strange coda to it after the Leinster final. There were a few words said in the dressing room that day they lost the Leinster final. Babs Keating said something or other. One of the players stood up and said there were too many lads acting the mick on the team.

Nobody in Offaly was playing well and Johnny felt that they were hinting at me and a couple of others. That stuck in his head.

He can't really remember what Babs said. He'd tuned out, but in the car later he heard the sports news coming on, heard this business with Babs, washing his hands, telling the world that Offaly just weren't listening to him. It got in under his skin, and the next morning the phone rang. Liam Horan from the *Irish Independent*. Johnny cut loose.

'I thought afterwards that maybe there'd probably be holy war at training. We'd either knuckle down or, if he wasn't happy, well me or him might have to go. Then, just before it came on the news, I heard he had resigned.'

Sorry it happened?

'Well, he was wrong to say what he did say. I was wrong to have a go back in the media. He was wrong in a lot of things he wrote about me after that too. I don't know him as a man, but he doesn't know me as a person.'

Seen Babs since?

'Babs isn't from Birr. He doesn't be where I be.'

Glad he's gone?

'Am I glad he's gone?' Pause.

'Well, to be honest, I don't miss him.'

Johnny Pilkington grins again. Easy come, easy go. The words sound harder than he is. He's not a fella for confrontation. Not a fella to hide from it either. Just not driven.

You pick away at him, talking about D.J. Carey and Brian Lohan and those sessions they talk about, alone in handball alleys battering a *sliotar* against the wall. Ever do that, Johnny? He smiles at the mischief of it.

'Hmm. Did it once or twice maybe. When we were kids, we'd be at home batting a ball off a wall all right. I'd never go off on my own though. Horses for courses really. D.J. Carey and Brian Lohan, they're the top hurlers in the country. I'm in the top fifty on a good day.'

When he's warmed up and talking hurling, his erudition on the topic is clear.

This is his life, after all, even if he tires of every dog and divil looking for a word.

'Sure I like to hang around. When I was working in Kilkenny, I knew a fella in Piltown, and, if he went into a pub and he couldn't see anyone there to talk to about farming or hurling, he'd just leave. I could talk farming and GAA and sport and beyond that, well, what is beyond that? I don't know. The salt of the earth, the hairy bacon and bit of cabbage kind of thing. That's what I grew up with.'

He grew up with perhaps the most gifted bunch of hurlers playing the game today. Grew up with them and learned to take them for granted. 'We're just a group of friends. Nothing special. We play hurling. We train. I remember in national school, I was eleven and

Brian was ten. I got a phone call to come out and play an under-
fourteen match in Banagher. I'm not too big now, but I was very
small then and Brian was worse. The two of us got sent in as corner
forwards. He's been there on teams with me ever since.'

Joe Errity was in his class. Always exceptional, and Johnny
reckons that, bar serious knee injuries, Joe might have become the
best hurler in the country, or one of them.

'We grew up together. We went to places. Féile. The community
games in Mosney. The *craic* in the chalet. All that.

'Daithí Regan was around, he was a year or two older, but we'd
be on the same teams. Daithí would have been a mad hoor, but he's
settled down now. I remember he was so big he'd solo up to me in
training and handpass the ball over me and solo around the other
side. Thanks Daithí, making me look good here.' They never fell out.
Johnny can't remember ever having a bad word. They'd have their
arguments when they were out having a few pints, but nobody ever
got wound up and walked out. There was always a third lad as
referee. Anyway, it was more of a jeering thing. If you made an eejit
of yourself at some stage, it would be coming up forever. 'If you
couldn't take it, you wouldn't really be in the group.'

That's what keeps him ticking over really. No lava or flaming
sliotars or burning passions. Just that feeling in the dressing room.
The comfort of friends. 'It's 3.15 on Sunday and everything else is
forgotten about. I like that. All that matters is the twenty lads togging
out, plus the management. The lads who have put in the effort. You
don't want to let them down. Everything is forgotten about, all the
troubles, all the worry. You have a job to do. It starts then and you
tune off the other things. You'd be worried about missing the first
ball, what you'll do if you win it.

'Everybody is focused in on the one thing. Some of the lads
would go through a steel door. I'd be more inclined to open it first,

but we're all going the one way. You know the sounds, fellas chatting, balls banging, lads getting rubs, all the talk, fellas a bit nervous.

'It's a nice place to be actually. Gets you away from everywhere, no trouble, no bitterness, no anything else. Just some lads out to do a job.'

Three-fifteen on a Sunday with the lads. That's it, the heart of it, the Johnny Pilkington psyche-up.

Sucking up to the Sports Editor

14 September 1998

I never expected to fall in love with the Sports Editor. I was surprised that I did. It started one day when he called me into the hallowed sanctum, what IT insiders call the Rugby Ball-Shaped Office. He was puffing a cigar and I felt a tightening in my gut. I could feel him undressing me with his eyes. But I get that a lot around the office, especially when I wear polyester.

He felt that day that we should be more controversial. He told me he was throwing his weight behind Proposition 123, which demanded that all columns be very controversial. This measure would put an end to whimsy, reminiscence and what the Sports Editor aptly termed 'that old shitetalk you go on with'.

I thought it was the most sophisticated thing I had ever heard.

There would be no more sentimental *Cider with Rosie* columns, no more painful stabs at humour, no more pieces dedicated to the purpose of conveying that Johnny or Mick or VHF (no derogation for rugby, even) were great fellas altogether.

He rolled his piquer smoothly on his lip as he expanded upon this new policy.

I could feel the static rise on my shirt. Sport had been taking the controversy war to the newspapers. Especially hurling. Beating us over the heads with controversy. The Sports Editor was getting tough. The light shone in on his face. He looked tough.

I suggested an idea I had borrowed from one of the really big hitters on the New York newspaper scene.

'What about a hero and idiot of the week?'

'With your picture at the top of the column, it kind of takes half the guesswork away,' he drawled. We laughed together, and I realised then that something was happening.

The Sports Editor would encourage me to do things which I didn't feel comfortable with. Work. Making phone calls. Checking facts. Attending to personal hygiene. He asked me to stop having tequila slammers in the morning.

For a while I lost my confidence. I felt isolated from my colleagues. We took risks. Once he was taking an important call on the phone when I did it to him. I got down on my knees and begged him to sign my expenses' slips. He did. I later learned he had been speaking to somebody about golf at the time. I felt soiled and dirty.

This stuff is extremely tough for me to talk about. Once, in August, I went all the way with him. It just happened. You might as well know, you'll find out anyway. With two other men present, I played golf with him.

He urged me to do it. He assured me that this was a kindness disguised as cruelty. He gave the impression, without stating it explicitly, that it would help me to get a job later. I said, 'What do you mean, 'later'?'

It turned out to be cruelty disguised as a charity outing. He forced me into an expedient alliance with one of the other men. I felt insignificant. I asked him not to do this with me. He said, well, you're both crap and you won't score too many points. So we played off the ladies' tees and they didn't write down any scores in the high two-figures range.

The Sports Editor performed wonderfully, and when he made mistakes he covered them up with persuasive argument. We did the whole lot that day. Eighteen holes in every position. I was tired, but I tried not to laugh in the wrong places. We shared a cigarette afterwards. The worst thing was I had to give him £25.

There was an understanding between us that, if we were ever asked if there was golf between us, we would both deny it. The Sports Editor said that, if people play golf and never hand in their card and then deny that they ever played golf, well, even if their shoes have spikes and tassles and their trousers are naff, the golf just never happened.

Despite the Sports Editor's warnings about secrecy, I told the GAA Correspondent (in confidence) that there had been golf between us. The GAA Correspondent asked me to tell him every detail of what had happened. What had the Sports Editor worn? What had his demeanour been? Where had the golf occurred? Had I worn anything special? I told him that the Pringle sweater I had worn for the occasion was destroyed, what with the Sports Editor spitting tobacco juice at me.

The GAA Correspondent told me not to get it cleaned, just to keep it. He asked if I had worn anything else that day. I told him no. He just nodded and said, 'Nothing else at all?'

He asked if the Sports Editor had put this idea in my head. I said not exactly. But maybe. Everyone else did it. Everyone knew he had a huge appetite for golf.

We never played full golf again, but at times the Sports Editor would allude to it in company. I would see him with the other two men from that day and feel uncomfortable. I felt they were laughing at me.

Not much else happened between us. Once, coming back from the shops, he made me carry his orange. He ate it and said, 'Tastes good.' I thought that a little strange.

Not long afterwards, he broke off all contact with me, but I continued to pay money into his account just to get my columns into the sports' section.

Proposition 123 has forced me to reconsider.

This has been very difficult for me to talk about and I have done so only in the hope that it will fill a column and I can go off to lunch. I am sorry if I have brought shame on the man I once loved.

There's no way my family can find out about this, is there?

Bad guys make the ring go round

9 November 1998

Isn't it strange when people go to the pantomime and confuse the dancing cows and the rosy-cheeked dames with real life?

Every time Naseem Hamed fights a fight, the aftermath is clamorous with solemn bells ringing their grave consternation. Naseem Hamed is a pup who, for disfiguring boxing in a manner unprecedented in memory, deserves the ultimate sanction of being planted on the seat of his leopardskin pants.

Sure. And Daisy the cow is an insult to bovine history and boxing needs to attract more humanities graduates.

The point about Naseem and the strutting, the posturing and the bragging is that there is nothing new under the sun and those journalists who throw up their hands in horror should know better than to become part of the PR machine. Is anyone in Sky Sports telling Naseem that he needs to come across as a bit more of the boy next door?

Naz is a mouth and the only point worth making about him is that, in the long lineage of gabby braggart boxers, he can hold his place with the best. He pours on the spiel without bothering to tip us the wink, he gets innocent folk genuinely wound up and, for all the talk about how his grinding win over Wayne McCullough would hinder his American push, he enjoyed the highest ratings HBO have had all year. Better than Oscar De La Hoya, in whose saintly mouth butter wouldn't melt.

When it comes to panto, Hamed knows his lines and he knows his boxing history. He knows that, from Jack Johnson to Sonny Liston, from early Ali to middle and late Tyson, the box office has hummed and sung when the bad guys have been in the ring. Boxing's bad guys come and they go and most of the time they are just spinning us a line, conforming to their profession's need to present itself as a morality play.

Sonny Liston was a genuine bad guy, a thoroughly troubled soul, but his drift across the dark sky of the heavyweight boxing scene was no less filled with pathos for that. He was a bad man, forlornly trapped in the world's view of himself, and his story puts Hamed's in its lighthearted context.

'There's got to be good guys and there's got to be bad guys,' Sonny Liston said ruefully. 'That's what people pay for – to see the bad guys get beat. So I'm the bad guy. But I change things. I don't get beat.'

Is there a sadder story in boxing than that related by David Remnick in his wonderful new book, *King of the World*. Liston, having beaten Floyd Patterson in just over two minutes, was on a plane back to Philadelphia talking earnestly with one of the few journalists he could trust. He had just beaten Patterson in Chicago to become world heavyweight champion, a title which had some genuine social resonance back then.

And on the plane Sonny spoke. Sonny was going to make himself a black champion that black people could be proud of. He was going to reach his people and tell them that they didn't have to worry about Sonny Liston disgracing them, that he wouldn't be stopping their progress. He spoke of his own heartbreakingly tough and lonely life and how he was going to reach out to kids and tell them that, if he could make it, anybody could. His experience would be the currency of change.

And they got to Philadelphia and there wasn't a soul at the airport to greet the new champion. Liston gave a shudder, 'adjusted his tie and put on his hat, a trilby with a little red feather in the band'. And he got on with his lonely life.

'I didn't expect the president to invite me into the White House and let me sit next to Jackie and wrestle with those nice Kennedy kids,' he said later, 'but I sure didn't expect to be treated like no sewer rat.'

Redemption came for Sonny Liston right at the end, when the boxing public found somebody to hate more. If white America feared a big dark brooding former thug, it found it feared a confident beat poet like Ali all the more. The late Murray Kempton captured the transition beautifully in *The Champ and the Chump*, his report on the changing of the guard.

'"I am a great performer. I am a great performer,' said Clay...

'Suddenly everyone in the room hated Cassius Clay. Sonny Liston just looked at him. Liston used to be a hoodlum. Now he was our cop. He was the big negro we pay to keep sassy negroes in line and he was just waiting until his boss told him it was time to throw this kid out."'

The morality play with sassy lippy negroes stretched back beyond that. Jack Johnson was the great black devil come to pillage white America. Joe Louis was reviled. Generation after generation turned harmless pug after harmless pug into that lucrative form of loser – the great white hope.

And then came Ali. This column wouldn't be alone in hoisting him high as the greatest sportsperson this century has known, somebody who changed the face of sport, changed the way we think of black people, retired with an enduring heroism which has made him the most-loved sports figure of our time. They should have stopped boxing when Ali finished. Just before then, in fact.

And yet, seldom has a boxer taunted and humiliated with such devastating combinations of lip and glove. Pummeling Ernie Terrell, who refused to recognise his new Muslim name, around the ring. Bam. What's my name, Ernie? Bumph. What's my name? Jab, jab. What's my name?

It was Ali who dropped into Floyd Patterson's training camp with arms full of lettuce and carrots to drive the scaredy rabbit back into his hole.

And subsequently Patterson was humiliated like few fighters before or since, beaten so badly by Ali that he later admitted that he hoped to be knocked out, freed from the humiliation. Ali carried him for twelve rounds, taunting him. White American. Uncle Tom. White man's nigger.

Seeing Naseem, a Muslim kid from the east end of Sheffield, coming over all mouthy uneases some people. Ten generations of deferential black boxers wouldn't have made the impact for their race that Ali made. One visible and mouthy Muslim is such a jarring change from the cultural stoicism that informs the Asian experience in Britain that some people can't stand it.

It was Naz who said no to having the names of his beaten opponents painted onto polystyrene tombstones. It was Steve Collins who went to Millstreet in the wake of Michael Watson and Gerald McClellan and fooled an opponent into believing that he had been hypnotised into feeling no pain. One is pure brown panto. One is pure white cynical.

Maybe Naseem Hamed isn't a nice guy, but since when did men who are paid to beat each other up have to be nice guys?

A nation turned its lonely eyes

9 March 1999

Joe DiMaggio represented the last curling wisp of blue smoke, the last fading big-band note of a more elegant era. His celebrity was enduring enough to have survived into the buffeting, chaotic time of the paparazzi and the tabloids, but mostly he will be remembered and revered as the last of the matinée idols to have graced the sporting imagination.

From Hemingway to Paul Simon, he was duly name-checked as an American cultural icon. The son of Italian immigrants, he and his brothers, Dom and Vince, made it in the Klondyke of major-league baseball, and Joe married a goddess of the silver screen to underline the great American dreaminess of his life. He has been part of the American consciousness since before World War II. His bumpy hitch to Marilyn Monroe in 1954 bought him another spin on the merry-go-round after baseball had stopped for him, but it was the sport he graced and its place in America's vision of itself which made DiMaggio such an enigmatic and enduring cultural phenomenon. The tickertape of statistics gives some measure of his sporting stature but little idea of his sociological importance. He replaced Babe Ruth for the New York Yankees and also stepped fully into his shoes in terms of mythmaking. He was on nine World Series winning teams, but his fame and significance outlasted them all.

'I would like to take the great DiMaggio fishing,' said Hemingway's old man.

'They say his father was a fisherman. Maybe he was as poor as we are and would understand.'

Born in 1914, in Martinez, California, DiMaggio might indeed have understood something about poverty. He left high school after just one year to work in a local fish cannery, and not long afterwards began playing baseball with the San Francisco Seals of the Pacific Coast League, despite the objections of his father, who thought he was becoming 'a bum'.

He joined major league baseball and the New York Yankees in 1936 and his first game in Yankees stadium attracted 25,000 Italian-American New Yorkers waving DiMaggio flags. He would go on to play 1,736 games for the Yankees.

He was an instant sensation, but his greatest year came in 1941, when he created a record which still stands. With Americans just forgetting the Depression and beginning to fret earnestly about the war, DiMaggio hit safely in fifty-six consecutive major league games. From May 15th through to July 16th, he hit in every game. Picture Robbie Keane scoring every day for a season and you have some grasp of it. His record should survive for many more years, but it was the sociological impact of the feat which was so interesting.

Rival ballclubs began advertising his pending appearance in newspaper advertisements. Bandleader Les Brown caught the circus atmosphere of it all with his summer hit, 'Who started baseball's famous streak/That's got us all a glow/He's just a man and not a freak/Jolting Joe DiMaggio'.

The streak ended in Cleveland when third baseman Ken Keltner threw DiMaggio out as he headed for first base. DiMaggio's friend,

Lefty Gomez, blamed the death of the streak on a taxi driver who had jinxed DiMaggio on the way to the stadium.

For DiMaggio, shy and weary, the end of the run brought nothing but relief.

After 1941 the real world intruded and DiMaggio was drafted at the end of the following season. He returned to the Yankees in 1946 and retired in 1951. For the final three years of his career, though, he earned $100,000 a season, a statistic which grabbed the popular imagination even more firmly than his 1941 record. As fame overtook him and his celebrity became an uncontrollable monster, DiMaggio became increasingly withdrawn. He was remote even from team-mates, who used to refer to his hangers-on as boboes, a slang word for caddies. They fetched errands for DiMaggio but were never close to him.

Famously, in his prime, he once drove with two team-mates in a car from California to Florida, a journey of three days. He didn't speak for the first two, until one of his companions asked him if he would like to drive.

'Can't drive,' he said, and continued looking out the window.

In *The Summer of 1949*, David Halberstam's elegy to that great post-war baseball season when the simple pastoral rhythms of the great game were finally fully restored to American life, the author captures some of the splintery awkwardness of DiMaggio's celebrity: 'There was a contradiction to DiMaggio's shyness. He wanted to touch the bright lights of the city but not be burned by them.'

Undoubtedly he got burned by Marilyn Monroe. The waning of his prime and the dizziness of hers made them beautiful but doomed. Their honeymoon in Tokyo was an augury, with Monroe interrupting their bliss to go to play for US troops stationed in Korea. She returned to Tokyo. 'Oh Joe,' she said. 'It was so wonderful. You never heard such cheering.' 'Yes I have,' the old athlete said wistfully.

Still, after their marriage ended, the sincere broken-heartedness which DiMaggio quietly exuded was markedly different from today's quote-friendly jilts. He never spoke of her, but he sent fresh roses to her grave weekly and kept friends and acquaintances of whom he disapproved, most notably the Kennedy brothers, away from her funeral. Red Smith, the great American sportswriter, told a story of DiMaggio which shed light on his loneliness. DiMaggio loved to frequent Toots Shoor's bar in New York City. When there, friends and fans would gather around him respectfully and his privacy would be breached in only the gentlest ways. One evening, in the company of some sportswriters, his friend and team-mate Lefty Gomez passed the table on his way to the front door. Gomez paused, then launched into a machine gun burst of anecdote and ribaldry which left the company giddy with laughter. As Gomez passed out the door, DiMaggio said quietly to Smith: 'I'd give anything to be like that.'

Through late middle age and into his drawn-out old age, he inhabited an intensely private world. He moved back to San Francisco and immersed himself in his two great loves, family and fishing. Even his death was a drawn-out drama of defiance. For months the reports seeped out about his last stand, braced against the inevitable with one foot in the grave and one foot in this life, dodging in and out of coma, on and off a life-support machine, playing hide and seek with the obit writers. His streak ended yesterday. The last line of the last column written by Red Smith, who was to sportswriting what DiMaggio was to baseball, read:

'I told myself not to worry, there would be another DiMaggio.'

Wrong for once, Red.

The fine art of training champions

13 March 1999

Racing is another country. They do things differently there. Earlier anyway.

The electronic gates open. The black jacket security man materialises against the early morning charcoal.

'Straight on up, Benny,' crackles Aidan O'Brien's voice over the walkie-talkie.

'Straight on up,' instructs Benny, 'and if you see a horse anywhere, stop and kill your engine.'

And away into the heart of Ballydoyle. Past the looming statue of Nijinsky, up the long road to the cluster of stables and barns that are the hub of life here. The flat horses are circling on the loam in a lofty barn. An endless almost unbroken circle of them, they issue great cloudy snorts of warm breath into the cool morning air and, for a minute, to see them is to be Jeff Goldblum getting the first sighting of dinosaurs in Jurassic Park.

The stable staff sit atop them, stiff-backed and slow-eyed in the early light. They look as if they could do this slow walk forever.

The jumpers, just a half-dozen of them these days, are off some place else just now. They live apart from the flat racers down amidst the jolly blue painted halfdoors of Margot's Yard in one corner of this lovely fold of Tipp countryside.

'Jumpers have different schedules and different temperaments,' it is explained. Perhaps they smoke and drink.

The flat horses circle in their steady hypnotic rhythm. In the middle of the barn's early morning gloaming, the red tail-lights of a jeep can be picked out.

The Boss. Aidan O'Brien spots the newcomers, waits for a gap in the procession and beckons us inwards.

He is a small man, jockey's build if not a hand or two higher, and he exudes an authority and bearing that is almost military in its clipped style.

Throughout the morning he will talk about the teamwork at Ballydoyle, the sense of interdependence that all the inhabitants have on each other, but there is only one Master, one terminus where the buck always stops.

He is just twenty-nine, which is startling enough given the huge legends which have barnacled themselves to his name, yet he looks younger. Unblinking, intense yet controlled.

'It's a fresh one, isn't it?' he says and we nod, not knowing if they are all fresh or not.

Each horse looks identical in the dust-moted light. For warmth each is wearing their striped blanket with the AP O'B logo stitched into the corner.

Some have a distinctive blaze, but they all have the cut, almost sculptured look of athletes or ballet dancers.

Aidan O'Brien stands and quietly names each horse as it passes, giving a concise biography of each animal. This is as chatty as O'Brien gets. He studiously avoids anything resembling hubris and questions about his training techniques usually draw short oblique answers and the little kicker 'just makes sense, doesn't it?' or 'do you understand what I'm saying?'

The tape recorder won't be spilling over with anecdotes on the journey home, but the trip is about understanding, getting the feel of this world. O'Brien, understated and quiet in a very Wexford way, wasn't born to this world of high rolling and grandstanding.

They used to say that nothing brings out the boor in a man quicker than his first good horse. O'Brien's quiet nature has inoculated him against that.

He has been up and out since 6.15 am, an announcement which diminishes the sense of martyrdom among the visitors. His face is fresh and content beneath a navy baseball cap. He smells pleasantly of aftershave. He separates the group according to task. A photographer is dispatched to a watching post where he might get a good shot of the star of the day, Istabraq. The flat horses begin filing out. The rest of us await our instructions.

We are encouraged into the jeep along with Tommy Murphy, assistant trainer, and Joseph O'Brien, five-year-old son of Aidan, who has been muffled and wrapped well for the morning portion of this idyllic life of his growing up amidst the horses.

O'Brien drives us out of the barn and on to one of the little roads which run like veins around the acreage. He stops there awhile, seemingly unaccountably. Before he pulls away, you notice he has been getting his jeep filled with fuel from his own petrol pump. Before you came here, they told you about the airstrip and the horseflesh and the sublime facilities, but a petrol pump. Nice touch.

Ballydoyle reveals itself like an equine theme park. O'Brien trucking around in the jeep, apparently aimlessly, pokes out and parks in a succession of spots just in time to see his line of horses go past. The realisation dawns quickly that precious few minutes in Aidan O'Brien's days are wasted.

He took over Ballydoyle in 1995, transferring the bulk of his operation from Piltown to this mecca of Irish horse training when John Magnier invited him down to make use of the facilities.

Today the string comprises about one hundred flat horses, all of impeccable pedigree. O'Brien has a love of Ballydoyle and its dependable rhythms and rare beauty which suggest that this is a spiritual as well as physical home.

'There is something about Ballydoyle. It keeps the horses focused and alert. It challenges them every day and you just see them getting fitter. It's the perfect place for them.'

And for him. He seldom travels to races any more.

'My work is here. If I do it properly, I don't have to be at the races. I don't enjoy travel too much anyway.'

Vincent O'Brien (with whom he doesn't share a bloodline) bought these acres under the crook of Slievenamon back in 1951 and it has been horse country ever since. It is a place which thieves the breath. Gallops and tracks rolling off across the gentle hills, queues of horses about their daily business, a quiet industry which keeps itself close to nature.

The flat racers are in a long, long line now, walking the roadway towards their undulating gallop. O'Brien nips ahead of them every now and then.

'Okay, Pat? Okay, Nadine? Okay, John? Okay, Michael? Nice and easy…'

And inside every greeting is wrapped a hint of inquiry. The words allow him a quick flashing inspection of horse and rider.

It takes maybe two or three seconds for a horse to amble past. O'Brien processes everything he sees like a whirring computer. He processes it instead of a computer, in fact.

'We wouldn't keep it all on database or whatever,' he says. 'This is our day-to-day business. I know in my head how they are going and what they are aiming for. Day in and day out till it becomes second nature. You see if the horse is happy, if it's stiff, uneasy. You know what to look for.'

The talk on the drive bounces between Tommy and Aidan mainly, with young Joseph making occasional polite corrections on the biographical details of each horse. Three generations of horsemen. There is an easy friendship there and O'Brien constantly defers to the older man's knowledge.

'Those Sadler's Wells horses, they keep getting stronger for longer, don't they Tommy?'

'They do, they get bigger and stronger every year.'

'Istabraq's ahead of where he was last year, I'd say, Tommy.'

'I'd say that all right, Aidan. Bigger, too.'

Then an astonishing thing happens. We are talking about Istabraq, the wonderhorse, and, without saying anything, O'Brien turns the jeep, points it to head down the gallop. You are looking straight ahead, but to the right is the percussion of pounding hooves. Istabraq and Theatreworld lead the jumpers off down their mile-and-a-furlong morning gallop.

Startlingly, the horses are just the other side of the white rail, inches away. Touchable, if that wasn't such a trespass.

Big brown eyes alive with excitement. Necks strained forward. Pat Lillis up on Istabraq. Hoof music. Thumpety, thumpety, thump.

They are building towards full tilt. Theatreworld, wide-eyed and snorting as he stretches his limbs full and furious. Istabraq, self-contained and peaceful, just eating the slipstream. The two stable lads like little commas on top of the flying animals. The clock on Aidan O'Brien's jeep tips forty miles per hour.

Theatreworld is flat out like an Olympic sprinter, but even to this untutored eye Istabraq is taking it in his stride, still within his gears.

These elemental moments, as the sun struggles for purchase and the horses pound the earth, are hypnotic. O'Brien manages the remarkable feat of being absorbed totally in the mechanics of the racers while steering the jeep effortlessly down the track. This is what this life is all about, the heart of it.

'Looks good, Pat,' O'Brien calls up to the rider when they walk out, finding regular breath again.

'Keen for it this morning, Aidan.'

Istabraq is a creature of mood and habit. Pat Lillis is the only rider the horse knows apart from Charlie Swan, who is in the saddle on race days. O'Brien chose Lillis for his intuitive knowledge of horses and for his own temperament.

'Pat would know horses and he would be good at reading their moods, how they are feeling, if there is something bothering them. 'He is good at getting that and communicating it. He suits Istabraq's personality, too. There is no point in teaming an aggressive horse with an aggressive rider, they'll annoy each other. The pair of them complement each other. Pat is quiet and takes it in his stride.'

Istabraq is weighing in at 510 kg, heavier than he has been on previous journeys to Cheltenham. The weight expresses itself as pure strength. Most days he spends in the company of Theatreworld. He will be transported the day before to facilitate his progress through Cheltenham traffic on race day.

'The sort of horse he is, he gets moody and highly strung. You'd prefer to move him on the day of the race, but with Cheltenham you'd never get into the place. Istabraq just likes to be left alone. He has his habits. He knows Theatreworld and he'd be kept together with him and with people he knows. No surprises. Being highly strung, he'd leave form behind him very quick.'

Istabraq is unusual in that he keeps improving, long past the point where he should plateau. O'Brien is constantly amazed by him. Cheltenham is still twelve or so days away this morning as we talk.

Istabraq is already unbackable, but: 'Lot of work to be done between now and then,' says O'Brien. 'Whole lot of work.'

This morning's work, though, is reaching a hiatus now, with the horses heading back to the yards. We are rejoined by the photographer, somewhat envious at having missed the chance at shooting from the jeep. 'Well,' says O'Brien matter-of-factly, 'sometimes a lens would give a glare which would startle a horse. We had one strained a leg here a few years ago and I'd be a bit of a coward now about ringing J.P. McManus with that sort of news.'

No news is very good news for McManus in the run-up to Cheltenham. O'Brien doesn't wear a face which betrays signs of pressure, but piloting the form of so many rich men's playthings must take its toll. 'Pressure?' he says, playing with the word as if it were an old toy. 'Well, the easy month is December. From January on it's work and races all the way through. You wouldn't be putting too much weight on anyway. It's a lot of pressure, yeah.'

Ballydoyle has about eighty staff who live in, enjoying facilities which include tennis and squash courts. O'Brien and his family live in a lovely low-slung house in one corner of the place. With half a day's work done, he walks in among the morning fuss of getting kids breakfasted and to school or nursery. The breakfast room is sunlit and inviting. Horse books line the wall, from *The Turf Guide* to *The Horse Whisperer*. Joseph is away to school, and before his father has lifted his first slice of toast he is deep into the racing paper, absorbing more of this world which will eventually revolve around him.

Method man in a swingin' groove

3 April 1999

A Day In The Life (Beatles 1967, by the way).

Belfast, and the morning has broken misty and moist. Brian Kerr shapes out of the Forte Crest Hotel, all woolly hat and anorak. Drinks in the scene. 'Yis all in fighting order?'

His players are loitering on the brink of the bus. The backroom boys are loading up the boot like it was an aircraft carrier. The driver is getting his instructions for later in the evening when Kerr's boys play Northern Ireland in the first leg of a qualification play-off for the European finals.

'Listen,' says Brian, 'we're supposed to be there an hour and a half beforehand, but that's time enough to be leaving. Where's the official observer from?' Pause. 'The Faroe Islands? He's not going to be making a song and dance.'

And that's decided. The bus duly pulls away out of Dunmurray towards the Malone Road and training. Kerr and his confederate, Noel O'Reilly, sit up front. 'I used to know this city,' says Brian. 'Ma and Da came from here and every summer we'd come up. I know the little houses, but with the motorways now I don't know how to get around it any more.

Frank and Margaret Kerr came down from Belfast and settled around Drimnagh way. Frank tailored for a living and coached boxing for pleasure. He passed on a sense of the dapper and a genius for teaching to his son.

Outside, it's Belfast. O'Reilly and Kerr have an appreciation of travel and its opportunities, which is rare in the football world. One sight sparks remembrance of another. The Malone Road triggers talk of big houses in Cape Town, the training ground sparks a conversation about Jerusalem and so on.

The roadway to the Queen's University training ground is called Dub Lane.

'Ah, home,' says Brian quietly to himself as the nose of the bus passes the corner. A minute later, the body of the bus is manoeuvred around the corner.

People are shouting the name out. Jaysus, Dub Lane. Dub Lane. Very nice. The bus draws in above the pitches and the hydraulic door hisses open just as the last line of the tape spools off in the cassette machine. 'Oh my name it is Sam Hall, chimney sweep, chimney sweep,' rasps Ronnie Drew.

On the pitch, sixty seconds later, Kerr is pacing, head down, determination pasted on his face. The training ground is about three feet narrower than the pitch which tonight's game will be played on. He gets some cones and redraws the border.

Then he gathers his boys together. He has decided to tell them the team now.

Only fair; he told them what Northern Ireland's team would be last night. Now fresh faces blink at him hopefully. Does any manager like this bit?

'This wasn't a handy one to pick, lads,' he says from beneath his green woolly cap, his eyes dancing around catching theirs, 'and even if you're not picked I want you to be in the spirit of the thing. We all need each other tonight, lads.'

And quietly he goes through the team. 'Dean in goals, Colin right back, Kevin and Jason, centre backs, alright – which of you likes playing on the right, by the way…?'

This is the last training session before the game. Time for tinkering, time for varnishing the setpieces. He spends an hour or so in tutorials. Richie Baker of Shelbourne makes the little decoy runs. Shaun Byrne thumps the frees. He lines up the stringy centre halves and the big strikers to meet the corners from headers. Different choreography for every situation. You could say anything to Brian Kerr; he doesn't make people fear him or shrink from him. His trick is that people like to listen to him. You can never guess the next tangent. Bobby Charlton couldn't coach footballers. Brian Kerr has been doing it since he was fourteen. He can link any vision with the words and make it interesting.

'Do you hit it with your left as well, Trevor?' he asks Trevor Fitzpatrick. He absorbs the assent, computes it into all the situations he has already devised.

Trevor is new; a big posse from Dun Laoghaire are coming to see him play tonight. Kerr has been breaking him in carefully, rooming him first with Shaun Byrne, whom he knew at West Ham, then putting him in with Gary Doherty, who he will be playing up front with tonight.

Then there was the quiz. Nothing loosens them up like the quiz. Noel O'Reilly devises the questions, keeps their heads busy.

Kerr sorts out the teams in a certain way. 'There might be one culchie with a Leaving Cert and one Dub who never sat an exam in his life and one in between fella with an English accent. We give them different questions, some of them set up so fellas have to know the answers. Gets them talking and arguing.

'Who is bottom of the Scottish first division? The fellas playing in

Scotland have to know that. That brings them in. Or the one last night: Name the United States manager in the World Cup; the clue is it has biblical collections.'

He thought everyone would get Steve Sampson, but half of them come back with Moses or Ed Moses. Still. It's not University Challenge.

BBC's Jackie Fullerton is pacing up and down the far touchline. The players watch him twitchily, like fretting wildebeest eyeing a hungry lion. They aren't confident enough yet to make their own decisions when it comes to speaking to cameras. Ger Crossley is an obvious angle for the media pack. The Celtic player comes from Belfast and might be wearing a different jersey tonight if things had been different. The northern media have been stirring up some controversy on the issue already. Kerr is keen to defuse the situation, steering Crossley away from the wolfish Fullerton and doling out his own time and bonhomie freely.

'Wasn't me who first picked Gerry Crossley anyway,' he says with a chuckle when the bus door is closed and Crossley is tucked away down the back. 'They'd only be gettin' it up for us anyway.'

Back in the Forte Crest, the background music which wafts through the lobby might have been picked for Kerr. An eternity of '80s hits thread their way through his conversation. A discussion of 'GhostTown' by The Specials leads to a debate over the merits of The Blades' first album which leads to a soliloquy on the death of the old TV Club in Harcourt Street and so on.

Music trivia is a speciality. Ian Dury and the Blockheads' first hit?

He orders tea and sits back to talk, about old times with the boys. Paul Weller's first band? He pours, handing the plate of biscuits around, too. The bass player with Graham Parker and the Rumour?

Music and football.

'Moxy,' he says, describing an ancient performance which he rated somewhere between manky and poxy.

'Yeah, moxy.'

'Remember stabbers,' he says to John Fallon, the kitman. 'Little butt of the cigarette that you could only hold between your thumb and your forefinger. "Those medals they used to give us were like stabbers." Nobody says that any more.'

'He could put a cross in, a real put-that-on-your-miraculous-medal cross...'

It could be corny, all this remembrance of times past, but Kerr has a wryness and a sense of irony which keeps it spinning and fresh. This is the time of his life. No need to dress up the past.

The talk turns to England, of course. Who's making it over there. Who's coming back soon. Who's never going to make it. One of the under-sixteen kids at Nottingham Forest has been on tenterhooks. One of the under-eighteens has been filling Noel O'Reilly in.

'He says to me that the young fella is "getting tellt" today. That's what he says. "He's getting tellt today, Noel." I'll give him a call later, maybe. See how he's going on.'

The endless queue of young fellas willing to take the tightrope walk that is English football is a matter of mixed feelings for Kerr. The kids are going earlier, which he doesn't like, and they are getting used up quicker and more ruthlessly, which he doesn't like either. He tells people to keep their kids at home until as late as possible, but for many of these kids football is their shot...

One young buck is back from England with his tail between his legs after what papers would term an incident in a nightclub. The spark quickly goes out of young fellas like that. Six weeks ago this kid was breaking into first-team football, pranking the manager by laying out wet kit for him, and now he is at home and maybe untouchable.

Brian Kerr remembers Derek O'Connor from the last Youth World Cup. Oco they called him. Oco took sick during the last Youth World Cup, before the US game.

They visited him in hospital in Malaysia, the infirmary cooled by oar-blade fans whirring quietly and Oco sitting up in crisp linen, half-zonked. 'I want to play.'

'Can you play?'

'Sure.'

So they got him to the game in Alor Setar and Oco was white as a sheet. Sure you're okay, Oco? Ah yeah. And they're warming him up tossing footballs at him and Oco is moving to the left, moving to the right with the stiff alacrity of Frankenstein with rheumatism. 'I says, "Oco, you might be alright in the slow motion replay, but let's hope they're not coming at you at normal speed."'

But he goes out and plays the game and saves the day. The punchline is that he gets booked for wasting time in the first few minutes, because he has a little shuffle in his run-up to the kickout. Sixteen minutes from time he's sent off for the same kink and misses the next round anyway. Oco was with Huddersfield then. Star of the show. Now he's with the amateurs at Bradford Park Avenue.

'Goes to show you never can tell,' says Brian.

'Chuck Berry,' says Noel quietly.

You never can tell. For Nigeria he has a better, more experienced team than he has brought anywhere. He also has a better draw. On this morning in March he is confident of winning the tug-of-war with English clubs to get his players, too. He should be whistling. 'You don't know how it will break. You get the best fellas and the thing doesn't take off as a group and you're thinking I'd sooner have ordinary fellas who'd die for each other. That's half the secret, getting them to work for each other. You'd look at who we had in

Malaysia and say we should go further next time. You can't say, 'til they've played a match or two. That's the beauty of it.'

At lunch, Noel and Brian and Declan the physio get a table in the corner.

'Has to be the same table we sat at last time we were here,' says Noel. 'We won from that table.'

They've won from a lot of tables. Indeed, they lost only twice last year in the space of thirty-two matches.

'What's the grub like?' says Brian.

'Chicken or pork or something,' says Declan the physio.

'Buffet?' asks Brian.

'Yeah,' says Noel, 'what was her big hit?'

'Who?'

'Buffy Saint-Marie.'

'Aw, give us a minute and I'll think of it.'

'I saw you having a word there with Podge?' says O'Reilly to Kerr during dinner.

'Yeah. I just told him he was brilliant.'

'He is brilliant. And you're right. Kid needs to be told.' Podge is Padraig Drew, a lank-haired winger who enjoyed his fifteen minutes of fame when Everton told him he could be the next big thing. His year at Goodison went badly, though. The English club squeezed the dove too hard instead of letting it spread its wings.

He's back at Home Farm looking for a transfusion of confidence. 'That's all he needs,' says Kerr. 'He was a year over in Everton and never got anything but this in his ear.' His line of fingers jaw up and down on his thumb.

'Same in his school,' says Noel. 'They said to me, "Look at him, he's useless," and I said, "No, he's better than the rest of what you have put together." They didn't even understand that.'

Players are what keeps Brian Kerr going. He's fascinated by them and their possibilities. He knows the shape he likes players in each position to be, knows the colours they need to have on their palette. A guy can look like a centre half or he can look like a playmaker. Kerr will seldom guess wrong once he has seen the physical appearance. Players keep coming to him. He's had an e-mail telling him about a player in Dortmund with Irish parents. There's a big bruiser of a centre forward at Blackburn he has his eye on. His father is a Dub. Come at it the right way and well… 'the young fella can score goals'. He has just missed out on a kid whose mother was from Sligo. He had a hunch and didn't go quickly enough on it. The boy's father was a Kiwi who played for Sligo Rovers in the '60s. Kerr saw the name in the South-East Counties' league and vaguely remembered the Kiwi marrying a Dublin woman. Stored it in his head. Next thing the kid was picked for the English under-16s and scores twice on his debut. Now he'll never know.

It is not long after 4.30 in the afternoon in a little room upstairs in the hotel. The team are shoehorned inside to talk about tactics. While the boys have been napping, Noel O'Reilly has been drawing the battle plans.

Shaun Byrne is dispatched for the second time to get Michael Reddy of Kilkenny and Conor O'Grady of Sligo Rovers, who haven't shown up just yet.

'I told them already,' says Byrne. 'They didn't believe it was time to come down.'

'Jaysus,' says a streetwise Dublin voice, 'D'Unbelievables play for Ireland.'

O'Reilly and Kerr play the next hour like a double act. Xs and Os on white paper is a little abstract for football tastes. They have to keep the banter coming. Kerr accuses O'Reilly of filching the blue and red markers. O'Reilly counters that Kerr is a chancer. The kids forget to be nervous as O'Reilly flicks over the sheets. Here's how we defend when they have the ball and Richie Baker is working the right wing, here's how we drop back for a free kick to the left of our area, here's how we line up for a corner when they leave the two centre halves inside…

Kerr runs down through the Northern Irish team. He knows as much about them as he does about his own players. Show him the outside and he won't beat you.

Let him know you're there and he doesn't like it. Run at him, he's clumsy going backwards. Play the diagonal ball out to Richie, it'll baffle them…

'Any questions, lads?'

Silence.

'Right, lads. It'll be a short journey home tonight.'

The Oval is half an hour away and it is soaked in Belfast gloom. In one corner of the ground is a huge sign with the word JESUS on it. It's about the only thing that isn't dowdy or crumbling. Brian gets the team bus to pull up near the dressing-room door and ushers them off the bus under the sixty-watt bulb at the doorway and down into the dressing room.

'Settle down, boys, it'll be a long night,' is the last thing you hear him say before the door rattles to a close and another rip-roaring chapter begins.

Stories for Boys (Uhm, U2 1980??)

Golf – a poorer friend than drink

5 April 1999

The late Jim Murray of the *Los Angeles Times*, whose canvas was frequently the US Masters, once noted that golf is not all Ben Hogan, Sam Snead, Arnold Palmer, Jack Nicklaus and Tiger Woods.

He was right. More right than he knew. Golf is nothing to do with those things. I know this because I have golfed. Twice in twelve months. Forgive me, father. I know not what I do.

Golf is not all Millionaires' Row, it is losing good cash on the front nine, a double or quits on the back nine and your dignity over the whole eighteen. Golf is not about birdie-birdie-eagle, birdie-par. These are just words, just rumours.

Like foreplay, the free lunch, and job satisfaction, golf is keeping the per hole score in single figures and cheating as much as possible to make up for the lack of physical contact.

Golf is not about making the cut. Golf is about making it out onto the course in a pair of jeans and T-shirt. You will not master it, but neither will you be its slave.

Golf is not about sponsors pleading with you to enter and your locker being lined with appearance cash. Golf is about journalist societies putting the arm on posh courses to get a free game. Yes, golf is ethics.

Golf is not about the hushed gallery in the cathedral of pines and the air-cutting swoosh of your first drive. That's just done with animation and special effects. Golf is about the divot going further than the ball. Golf is about the greenkeeper in his tractor keeping the engine idling just beside you as you take your shot. Golf is about hearing his snort above the engine noise when you whiffle it. Golf is about burying his body.

Golf is not about an orthodox grip, a sweet arc trajectory and follow-through smoother than a Cary Grant line. Golf is about hurley grips and hoping to keep one foot on the ground and being allowed to tee off without loss of a shot.

Golf is not about the tyranny of purity. Golf is about finding your own way to the ball. There is no such thing as a lovely swing. You hit it like an axe murderer? Fair play. You hit it.

Golf is not putts that slide home on greens as smooth as plate glass. Golf is deciding to putt from five yards off the green because the blade of your wedge is in the greenkeeper's skull.

Golf is seeing the putt from five yards off the green skip off a tuft of grass and across the green and into the far bunker. Golf is bad language. Lots of it.

Golf is not elegant. Golf is trickier than catching a greased pig on ice. Less fun, too.

Golf is not all scratch players and Pringles. Golf is fundamentally unfair.

Golf is an unfair handicap system. Why not arrive at handicaps by dividing the age you started playing at by your annual income.

Golf is not about the two good shots per round which allegedly keep you coming back. The law of averages is about that.

Golf is about fear of snakes and using a compass to get back to the short grass and overcoming the fear of drowning when you go looking for your last decent ball.

Golf is not about being in the zone. Golf is about being in the plus fours.

Golf is about being in a quandary. Golf is about seeing your playing partners as dots on the horizon. Where is the zone?

Golf is not a game where you get money only for what you accomplish. That's TV golf. Real golf is where the breadth and ambition of your approach to the dog-leg left is rewarded with laughter and scorn.

Golf is undemocratic. Forget about women being locked outside the gates. They should have more sense than to be rattling them.

Golf is about growing up taking hand-eye co-ordination for granted and then being humiliated by a four-eyed computer nerd in a sweater who never got fresh air before he was thirty.

Golf is not relaxing. Golf is the short cut to inadequacy. Golf is lonely.

Golf is socially unacceptable. Golf is destabilising.

Golf is not about Big Bertha. Not unless Big Bertha is the woman whose head I hit in the Superquinn carpark. Golf is about big hernia. Big score. Big Hook.

Big Divot. Big Mistake.

Golf is not David Leadbetter. Golf is the guy behind you shouting helpfully just as you are about to scud-bomb the local peat bog: 'Clench your buttocks and keep the head down.' Who does he think he is? The president?

Golf is not just about lifestyles of the rich and famous, but being one or other helps.

Golf is not always staying at the home of a rich friend at a tournament, golf is a Motel 6. A Marriott. Golf has been known to be sleeping in your car.

Golf is not about companionship, comradeship or good buddies.

Golf is a poorer friend than drink is. Golf friends are no friends at all. No game should force you to cheat on your friends. Golf does.

Golf is not about fairway-splitting drives. Golf is not about fairways as such. Fairways are usually narrower than a Portadown resident's mind-set. Greens are about the size of your friend's bald spot. Golf is not a game.

Golf is not shirts with alligators on them. Golf is water hazards with alligators in them.

Golf is not broomhandle putters. Golf is debris. Golf is looking stupid without the broomhandle putter. Golf is what other people do on weekends and you do early in the morning for privacy's sake.

Golf is not The Masters. The Masters is better than golf. The Masters is just a TV programme.

Twisted life of the artful begrudger

26 April 1999

What's with you people? Slack-brained, impressionable, band-wagon-hopping bunch of no-marks that you all are. Be warned, I'm curmudgeonly and I'm dangerous.

If I am approached by one more person shaking his or her head and smiling beatifically as if they had just been faxed the third secret of Fatima, cornered by one more fat Cheshire cat who purrs and says 'United, you couldn't begrudge it to them all the same', just one more of these shuffling zombies intruding in my no-fly zone and I shall come over all Bob de Niro in *Taxi Driver*.

For crying out loud, I thought there was an immutable principle here. I thought all things were begrudgable. I have been brought up to believe that, as a race, begrudgery is what we do best, begrudgery is the Riverdance of Irish conversation, the bitter thread running through our history. *Táin Bó Cuailgne* to Peig Sayers, to, well, to me it seems. Here in Ireland begrudgery is not strained. It droppeth as the gentle rain from heaven. At least, it used to.

The good grace lobby will have to prise begrudgery from my cold, dead fingers, I'm afraid, because begrudgery is an inalienable right and I begrudge Manchester United. I begrudge them the notion that they are Britain's team and I begrudge them the right to be Ireland's team, too. I begrudge them the current bias against begrudgery. If that is the price of freedom, it is a price I am not willing to pay.

I begrudge Manchester United their success, but I am not inconsistent here. I am no mindless, begrudging gobshite. I begrudged them in their mediocrity and failure, too, begrudged them not having enough of either, begrudged them that time didn't stop when they were in the second division.

Of course I did. I begrudged them their last success with that talking plank Bobby Charlton and gummy old Nobby Styles and the bleedin' Busby Babes. Even when they were second division failure fodder, I begrudged them not being in the third division. I begrudged them when they were improving and now I am begrudging in Europe.

I am not a mindless begrudger. I begrudge them everything except maybe Roy Keane, who I consider to be a victim of English begrudgery in that they fail to recognise him as the best player in the Premiership. My begrudgery is not a crude thing, see. It is nuanced and calibrated and layered. I can begrudge a team, but not their leading light. If Keane played for Leeds, I would feel very passionate about the manner in which he is usually overlooked by people who are fawningly grateful to that breed of player who appears on TV advising one not to bring two bottles into the shower. To be intellectually consistent, I must bear the same begrudgery on his behalf, even though he has made the wrong choices in life.

I begrudge them everything else, though. I begrudge them Cantona, who they got for a song as part of some conspiracy, and I begrudge them bloody Denis Irwin, who, when he was at Leeds, might have tipped somebody the wink that he was going to be a top-class defender.

I most solemnly begrudge them the Manchester United Superstore which they are opening fifty yards from the desk at which I sit. If I'd known when I moved back from England at the end of the 1980s that England was just going to follow me around, I might have stayed put.

I passionately begrudge the damage that they are doing to my two daughters, poor mites, who, although they play camogie week-in, week-out, have never seen the game on television. 'Why is Manchester United always on telly, Daddy?' asks my five-year-old curiously. 'Are they like Coronation Street?'

Yes, they are, but I am forced to sit her down and speak softly to her about what begrudgery means in our family, in our nation.

I sincerely begrudge them their ability to make converts out of the feeble-brained. All those people you knew in school who were in that glamourless limbo whereby they were neither academically gifted nor sportingly inclined, they're the ones hollering the loudest, giving RTÉ the impression that they are some sort of national movement. I fiscally begrudge them the power to buy Stam, Yorke and Blomqvist with their loose change and still masquerade as a home-grown side.

I enthusiastically begrudge them all the TV coverage, too. I am always curious as to how our national broadcaster can afford the European Cup and the Formula One season (two events which I associate with a particular type of middle-aged, middle-class, fair-weather sports person) and seemingly can afford quality coverage of little else.

I begrudge them their Sky coverage also, because the loot they get from it merely perpetuates their advantages over other clubs.

I begrudge them the manner in which they are annexing imaginations quicker than the worst dictators in history annexed neighbouring states. Sports hacks get it bad, you know.

Questions come in ominous pairs.

'What do you do?' Here goes. 'I'm a sports reporter.' 'Oh.' Pause. 'So, what do you think of United then?' And then it's all a blur, your honour.

I respectfully begrudge them every penny they got for Lee Sharpe and, historically, I begrudge them their *X Files* seduction of Kevin Moran in 1978.

They turned him into a Stepford wife.

I spitefully begrudge them the bleached blonde bimbo Beckham, who has insinuated himself into the vacated slingbacks of Princess Di as Britain's most poignant victim. He'll never have her elegance.

I humbly begrudge them their good fortune in letting Blackburn discover that Brian Kidd has the brains of a rocking horse rather than finding it out themselves when Fergie goes. I inevitably begrudge them Fergie as well.

I reflexively begrudged them the Murdoch takeover when it was a runner and, inventively, I now begrudge them their failure to be taken over by Murdoch. I have lost five, maybe six, easy columns a year as a result.

I begrudge them everything. Never having been implicated in the Kennedy assassination, their role in the death of punk, their links to the mafia, appeasing Hitler in the 1930s, their promotion of decadent western lifestyles and the support of all those goddamn celebrities. I begrudge them my time in having to write all this down.

I begrudge them all those things, but I would like to finish on a more gracious and constructive note. I don't begrudge them the long odds – 7 to 4 – their foolish supporters are creating on Bayern Munich to win the European Cup.

The drinks are on me when the glorious Krauts win the penalty shoot-out.

Sport and politics – a lethal mixture

17 May 1999

I had just finished telling my shocked partner the details of my twenty-seven-year love affair with sweeties when *Liveline* came on. Joe was struggling.

Nothing identifies the character of the lesser-brained sports fan than the shrill call, usually heard in the long grass of radio phone-in programmes, to the effect that sport and politics don't mix. Every time we hear the light refrain, the thought occurs that naivety and stupidity have at last been mated successfully.

If you went to the game in Dalymount in 1955 between Yugoslavia and Ireland, you engaged in a political act. And well done. If you feel, however, that permitting Yugoslavia to play football here next month is no different or that waving a white hankerchief during the playing of the Yugoslav national anthem will somehow make things alright, you are sadly deluded.

By playing against Yugoslavia, by attending the game and treating it like any other match, we will be engaging in a political act even more shameful than that which we engaged in in May 1974 when the national team went to Santiago, Chile, and played in the national stadium before the blood had dried on the slaughter which occurred there.

We became the first country to visit there in the space of a year. We went for a friendly. There was a lesson there already.

The Soviet Union were supposed to visit for a World Cup game the previous November but conceded the points instead. Chile duly kicked off and scored into the empty Soviet goal, but it was the Russians who emerged with all the honour.

It doesn't really matter in the current instance whether or not you approve of NATO's hawkish, morally imperfect behaviour around the Balkans or if you are disturbed by the inconsistency with which the policemen of the world wave their truncheon, the fact is that we are being asked to partake in the frivolity of international football at a time when the state of the rival team is on the one hand being bombed and on the other is engaged in unspeakable acts of ethnic cleansing.

Let's not pretend that right now sport and politics don't mix. Yugoslav players all over Europe have made it patently clear that they do mix, by striking, by displaying banners, by urging each other to fight for the homeland.

Let's not flatter ourselves by thinking that the waving of white handkerchiefs in Lansdowne Road will be a topic of alarmed conversation in the bunkers of Belgrade or that Yugoslav television will linger wondrously on our peevish little faces as we make our facile little gesture. Let us not effect to imagine that the game won't be exhibited as an example of the Milosevic regime's happy relationship with another small and oft-beleaguered country.

Sport and politics has always mixed in Yugoslavia. Soccer and politics have been Siamese twins since the foundation of the state. The first club to be founded in Yugoslavia back in 1911 was Hadjuk

Split, named after local fighters who had railed bloodily against the Ottoman empire.

This is a country where teams play for the Marshall Tito cup, where they abandoned half-completed games in 1980 when Tito died, where Partizan are still the army team and where Milosevic stopped his comrade and rival Arkan (Zeljko Raznatovic) from buying Red Star Belgrade because ownership of the club would give Arkan too great a power base in the capital.

Instead, Arkan (whose Serbian Volunteer Guard or Tigers, formed from the dregs of Red Star supporters clubs, were to the fore in the slaughter of Muslims throughout Bosnia and have been reported to be in action in Kosovo) bought an apartment which overlooks the Red Star ground and a team which now rivals Red Star.

He took over Obilic two years ago, pumping in sufficient cash to get them to the head of the Yugoslav first division.

(The club, by the way, is named for a Serb hero who stabbed a Turkish commander to death before the battle of Kosovo Polje in 1389.)

It's not just cash which has buoyed what was once a humble division-two team.

There has been a good mix of bribery and corruption as well. The man they call Commandant has been seen grinning with amusement as the thugs who patrol his terraces chant 'score and we'll kill you' at rival forwards.

Two of the panel selected to play Croatia last month were from Obilic. No doubt the chattels of Arkan will be selected for Dublin too.

'Sport and politics don't mix,' bleat the woolly heads on the airwaves. 'We have no quarrel with the ordinary people of Serbia,' they say grandly. Well, perhaps the worst of them are only obeying orders and swallowing propaganda, but we have an obligation to ourselves not to allow soccer and our team to be fed into the grinder.

We owe sport a duty of decency.

Ask the dead of Vukovar and Bjeljina, where Muslim civilians were slaughtered by Arkan, if they might make a murmur about this game proceeding as mass graves are being filled elsewhere. It was in Bjeljina that Serb TV filmed Arkan leaning across the body of a dead Muslim to embrace Biljana Plavsic, soon to become Serb president of Bosnia.

Before we wave our hankies and do the Mexican wave, why not ask the players of FC Pristina if they are currently over the moon?

Or what about the trembling refugees whom we grudgingly allow to seep into our bloated little country? What do they think of us playing footie with the boys from Belgrade? Do they fret that the linen in the corporate tents will be crisp enough for us to dine on?

No doubt the FAI have moral concerns here, but the issues of fat money and three points appears to have paralysed them. The team just plays football, see.

Yet when the socialite Diana of Wales died in a car crash a couple of years ago, the team weren't beyond expressing their profound grief by wearing black armbands during a game in Iceland. And Mick McCarthy seems, regrettably, to have no difficulty misplacing his innate decency to appear grinning in newspaper shots taken outside a courtroom in which a journalist who once urged a Lansdowne Road crowd to boo Roy Keane had just been suing another journalist.

Synthetic grief, issues of journalistic pique and the assisted sale of Opel motor cars are matters in which the team or management are permitted to take sides. About ethnic cleansing they are perforce silent. If that is the case, let the government put an end to it now.

Politics and sport always mix. In grants, in swimming inquiries, in civic receptions, in anthems, on days of sheer flagwaving nationalism. They mix.

Always. It is time for politics to intervene on our behalf. After all, the Irish team do not belong to the FAI, they represent all of us and take our name with them on to the field.

You too could be a county manager!

5 July 1999

From the Files of the 'Locker Room' I Can't Believe It's A GAA Inter-County Management Correspondence Course! Read the testimony of our successful pupils and graduates! Some names and addresses have been withheld, but all are one hundred per cent genuine:

A Chara,

Many thanks for your recent dispatch of instructions and tutorials. I see now the point of Paranoia 101, and, even though it is too late for its implementation this year, my team will certainly be operating in an atmosphere of healthy and acute paranoia next summer.

I read and reread the work study exercise involving the former manager 'from the north' and his Technique in Random Atrocities Against the Media. And yes, as advertised, its bitter tones paved the way to my own Damascus. The avant-garde use of such delicate phrases as 'yiz all writ us off, ye b***ards (and then we lost)' was a revelation. Is there a corresponding course for teams which have been maliciously tipped as favourites?

I also found Ger Loughnane's essay on the history of human rights abuses within the GAA to be a most moving testimony.

My decision this summer to emphasise the positive character-building aspects of Gaelic games was ill-informed and naive. I shudder when I think of telling my players 'we may not win any medals but we might end up better people!' Thanks for taking the scales from my eyes.

Mise le meas (name and address withheld)

A Chairde,

I am a 1996 graduate of your course (you may remember the small controversy when my 'highly commended' final year thesis, 'Wearing Shorts on the Sideline in the Post-Impressionist Era', was submitted again in 1997 by a candidate from Derry under the title 'Wearing Shorts and Funny Hats on the Sideline in the Post-All-Ireland Era') and, while I have derived many benefits from completion of the course, there are areas where I feel extra tuition would be beneficial.

I am interested in post-graduate study opportunities which might deal with the following areas: the Philosophical Basis and Justification of Football Without Forwards, which seems to offer a palliative which would be applicable here; and What is the Basis for Local Authority Legislation on Sealing County Borders to Prevent Forwards from Migrating? Can they be extradited back to the county?

I received a flyer from your school some weeks ago advertising opportunities for further study (the one with the stark picture of Páidí Ó Sé and the Kerry team all gagging themselves), but I left it in my tailor's when he was taking my shorts up for the championship.

Please remit again.

Yours etc., 'Westerner'

Dear L.I.C.B.I.A.GAA.MCC!

How are you doing? I am willing to pay through the nose for

some unusual advice. I am a very successful former manager of my county team and have, as per the advice given in Colm O'Rourke's six-week course on the True Meaning of Success, parlayed my own achievements into a fine lifestyle. I have also improvised a role for myself in quasi-management based on the Mick O'Dwyer Kerry Principles; that is, the subtle art of giving the impression that Everything Would Be All Right if Only I was in Charge Again.

Things have taken a turn for the worse, however. Since being beaten out the gate in the championship, the county management team has resigned en masse and have been quietly conducting a campaign to 'bring back big mouth, he seems to know it all'. The team is full of fat, crumbling, prima donnas. No way will lightning strike twice. How do I do nothing while retaining credibility? There is a delegation of players coming on Tuesday and I need help quick.

Yours sincerely,

'Confused'

Sirs, I have followed your instructions through the winter and during the championship, right to the Objection to Provincial Council After First Round Exit Stage. I seem to be missing subsequent modules of the course. People are asking the dreaded What Now Smartypants? question. I am interested in details on two courses beginning next semester. Firstly, Talking Up The League (I'm assuming this covers all aspects, from championship failure to indignation at All-Star selections, and will, as usual, involve field trips with the Offaly footballers and Dublin hurlers).

I am also interested in Waiting for Round Robin... Waiting for Round Robin: Conceptual Approaches to Why the World is Wrong and Not Your Team. I have done some extra-curricular work already in the Waiting for the Round Robin area but am getting out of my depth. Is it a migratory bird?

Yours etc.

Sirs,

Help! Howler Alert! I accidentally gave out a team to the media on Tuesday last week and played the same line-up on Sunday. How do I get back my credibility?

Yours Red-faced

Dear Sir,

I greatly enjoyed the modules I took last winter. Prof Pete McGrath's ideas on a Montessori Approach to Difficult Teams were invigorating. I also gained academic credits in Eamon Coleman's Long-Term Strategies for Getting Satisfactory Expenses from the County Board (Exile and Beyond), and enjoyed Danny Ball's contribution to the Peter Canavan Broken Jaw Memorial Lecture on Media-Created Divisions Within Hypothetical Northern Counties.

I am now manager of Cavan and have some time on my hands before the league starts. What should I study next? I feel Mattie Murphy's media relations course (I'm OK, You're All Mouldy Hoors) would be interesting.

Yours etc., Val

Hello,

I am enclosing $25. Expect to get the advanced section of 99 Ways Not to See Incidents at Club Games by return. Yours etc., 'Big Success'

Sirs,

Took bad advice in my first years in charge and am now seeking to undo damage done through promiscuous dealings with media. Have seen your course Media in the Age of Sponsorship: Marketing Allies or Same Old Spawn of Beelzebub advertised.

Very interested.

'You Know Me'

You too could be a top inter-county manager! All Cheques and Postal Orders to 'Locker Room'.

Fear and nachos in Las Vegas

15 November 1999

Fight-day. Hours to kill. Sweet to be savvy. Take $40. Unwanted money. Leave room. Walk to slot machine. Pull lever 160 times. Lose 25 cents each time.

Sense that big win is due.

Return to room. Take $60. Run back to machine. Pull lever 100 times. Notice that woman beside me is talking to her machine. Pat my machine furtively. Pull lever 140 more times. Lose 240 straight times. Leave for fight. Pulling Vegas by the tail. Oh yeah.

Arrive at Thomas and Mack Arena. Sweating. Bump into Steve Collins. More sweat. Have written so many mean things about Collins' hypnosis caper versus Eubank. Mean columns about Collins flood into brain. Oh Lordee. Expect punch on nose. Eyes water preemptively. Plan to faint if he moves a muscle.

Celtic Warrior very forgiving. No. Celtic Warrior thinks I am just another Paddy in the sun. Self plays role of another Paddy in the sun with admirable verve. Friendly chat ensues. Nose unpunched. Good. Better than winning money on slots.

The Thomas and Mack Arena. Everybody has a credential. If you go to a fight in Vegas without dangling a credential, you can't look yourself in the mirror for the shame of it. Press credentials. Hotel credentials. Shuttle bus credentials.

International House of Pancakes credentials. People walk around ogling each other's chests. Insight: this is what it feels like to be a woman of notable bosom.

Seat is not good. Sweat and blood from fighters will not reach notebook. Too near fight fans for journalistic self-esteem. Grumble with other hacks. Discuss precise meaning of the word ringside. Bloody Don King. Too much to bear. Wander back to press room to eat Bloody Don King's Bloody Complimentary Nachos. Stick credential inside shirt in case of second Celtic Warrior sighting.

Nacho overdose. Take walk. Concourse is unpleasant. Lots of Brits. Long day for them. Three thousand of same were in the Tropicana at 6.00 am to watch the soccer at $30 a throw. Easy to see how they spent the rest of the day. Lots of middle-aged fat guys, too. No necks, chunky jewellery and blonde girlfriends. It's true. Women don't go just for good looks.

Outside, the limo drivers are hanging around in huge, gossipy herds. The stretch limos from the New York New York Hotel are the vivid yellow of New York taxis. They look like the long dribble of nacho cheese on my T-shirt.

The limos are the only cool thing in town. Even the drivers lounging on their hoods look cooler than their colleagues. Take credential out to hide nacho cheese stain. Turn credential backwards. Just in case.

From steps of Thomas and Mack Centre the world is visible. The Eiffel Tower. The Chrysler Building. A Pyramid. Imperial Rome. Venice. Monte Carlo. A Volcano. A Treasure Island. Any wonder this is the home of boxing? The planning regulations were drafted by the same guy who did the boxing regulations.

The under-card. Why do they have under-cards? Nobody cares.

It's like presenting some folk dances before the main event in a strip club. The under-card evaporates too quickly. People tumbling every time you look. This could create a vacuum in the schedule. Don King abhors a vacuum. Somebody thinks quickly. Ricky Martin is played very loud.

The ring announcer isn't the Le-hets Get Ready to RUHUUUUMMMMMMMM-BELLLL guy.

Politics or a sore throat. The new guy is understated. Maybe the Let's Get Ready guy scares Lennox Lewis. Anyway, the new guy announces the night's attending celebrities. Starts with the day-time soap stars and works up to Michael Douglas. Catherine Zeta Jones gets the biggest cheer. If it all goes pear-shaped for C.Z.J., she'll always have work as a round card girl.

Round card girls are the new rock and roll. How artfully they display their vital information. How admirable that they have held out against being replaced by computers. When the round card girls need to get into the ring, a guy with a tux helps them up. With his foot he presses the second lowest ring rope. Suave.

The girl stoops in. The guy winks to the guys below. They can see her knickers. Smiles all round.

Lennox Lewis arrives stripped for work. A firework goes off. Holyfield arrives in bishop's purple. Another firework. We wait for the God Is My Pal act from Holyfield. Am sick to death of sporting Christians. Plan to yell to Evander: There Is No Bloody God, Evander.

Remember lucky escape with Celtic Warrior. Opt not to push luck by shouting.

Reflect that, if there is a God, he probably doesn't handle sports matters personally. As in a newspaper, God would farm that business out to a wholly owned subsidiary. Staffed by culchies, if the Dubs' luck is anything to go by.

Memo: ask Evander for number of God's Sports Subsidiary. Send number to Mick McCarthy.

Ring is filled with more people than is legally permissible. This is the top tier of credentialed society. The Brahmins. The Cayman Island Account Club. The Into the Ring Before the Fight Credential Elite. They all stand squashed together in the ring looking out at us. The Brits chant 'You Fat Bastard, You Fat Bastard' at Don King. If a bomb went off in the ring right now, the rest of us would all be killed by jewellery shrapnel. Somebody whispers: 'Cops! Run!' Ring clears in an instant.

Bell rings. Fight starts. Lewis uses tried and trusted tactic. Stands there looking like a cow in a field. Holyfield plays the role of an irate goat. Butts Lewis. Runs at Lewis. Scampers back again. In seventh round, Lewis and Holyfield stand toe to toe and slug each other. Reminds one of boxing.

The fight finishes. Everyone says Holyfield has done enough. Judges give it big time to Lewis. Everyone shrugs. Holyfield just not Y2K compatible. Everyone heads for press conference in case Holyfield retires.

Taxi to hotel. Drive along Strip. Engage driver in banter about fight. 'What fight?' says driver. Vegas is filled with 225,000 delegates to something called COMDEX. Jackson Browne is playing New Year's at the Mandalay Bay. People are wondering what Mad Mike Tyson vs Lennox Lewis would be like. And how Don King will get a part of it.

Local heroes can save the world

31 December 1999

There's a dying cliché which should be put on the endangered species list before it leaves us entirely. It's the one where the old codger sits the grandchild on his knee and tells about the time, oh, when he was just about the age you are now, and he saw...

Well, take your pick what he saw. He was in Dalymount in that unholy crush when Brady made his debut and Givens scored his hat trick. He was in Croker when Foley saved from Ring. He was there again when Ali fought Al Blue Lewis. He was in Santry for the Morton Mile. Dammit, he was in Ebbet's Field when the Brooklyn Dodgers were more than a sentiment.

He sat on his Da's shoulders and Ring tossed him a *sliotar* or Ali gave him a wink or Brady signed a programme. Whatever. He was there and it mattered. He connected. Being there shaped the sporting prejudices of his lifetime and his sporting prejudices likely shaped lots of other prejudices.

That time is leaving us. Sport is making our senses redundant. It is merely a matter of visual gorging now, a function of the remote control, a matter of being on the right channel at the right time. We don't taste it, smell it, hear it, touch it in the way we used to. And we won't remember it and pass it on the way we once did either.

I used to think that you'd have to care about sport to know the tragedy of that passing. Ain't necessarily so. The denial of sport as a community experience will shrink us all. We don't have any other forums like it, any other places to go as real people where we can press against each other, shout and holler and express emotions without irony or reticence.

Back, way back, when this century was a toddler and organised sport was growing up, Jack Johnson was making himself rich. Looking back now, Johnson's story had all the wonder, lucre and scandal that would characterise the modern sporting tale.

His accession to the heavyweight boxing championship of the world was the wonder, the scandal of the age. A black champion! Without humility! It engaged people to the point of there being riots in cities across the US whenever he beat a white man.

Johnson, the son of Henry Johnson, a slave, finally lost to Jess Willard in Havana in 1915 and stayed away from the US for a further five years, returning one day to shake hands with the sheriff of Imperial County before crossing the border from Mexico into California, where he would begin a sentence of one year and a day under the Mann Act. He had been convicted in 1913 for taking white women as his lovers.

In Johnson's story you can find some trace of all aspects of the sports century that followed, but, most significantly perhaps, with the advent of Johnson came the arrival of his shadow. Tex Rickard, the promoter and dealmaker, was probably the first guy to see what sport could become.

Tex was the P.T. Barnum of sport. He saw percentages, ticket sales and deals where other people saw just sweat. He saw the market value of Jack Johnson, the man they loved to hate. And just as the people who set athletic records back then would gawp at the marks being set now, Rickard would be stunned at what his descendants have been able to sell us.

Sport, which has been a valve to society for so long, is scarcely recognisable from the form it had at the beginning of the twentieth century. It is sanitised, wrapped and perfumed. Trivialised. De-authenticated. For the benefit of television and sponsors, everything has been neatly whitewashed. No more sawdust.

The race to catch drug cheats is deliberately handicapped to favour the stars. You want to see how it works? Go back and read Gary O'Toole's writing on how RTÉ decided it would cover the swimming events in Atlanta in 1996. Imagine bigger stakes and greater money. Any wonder that what we get these days is often a facsimile of sport.

There is reason to fear that, if change continues at the same rate, sport as we have known it will either be lost to us entirely or we will be faced with having to re-invent it by the middle of the new century. That's OK.

I saw a discussion on TV the other night. A man was railing against the oppression of the computer age, wondering why it is that of all the educational tools available the computer was being imposed so relentlessly through classrooms. Was it big business perpetuating its own market?

Another man took issue with him. This man's seven-year-old had been asked to prepare a school paper about his Russian longhaired hamster. The child had been able to go to the Internet on his PC and access two sites dealing with the furry little rooskie rodent, sites crammed with detail and history. That, he said, is the value of the computer in the classroom.

And what, said the man, would have been the value to your seven-year-old of writing about what the hamster makes him feel, what he sees when he looks at it, what he has observed the hamster doing? What if he had written about those things, instead of regurgitating unverified Internet bumph?

And nobody had an answer for the man.

Sport has been roughed up in the past twenty years by men who came offering gifts of mirrors and beads. Sport has been turned into the whore of the marketplace.

More and more you can't see sport unless you pay. Lots. Yet you can still play for free. You can still dream for free.

When we wonder where sport will go in the next hundred years, we have some signposts with the onset of digital TV. Manchester United might cease to be a matter of emotions. How big-time sport felt and smelt and sounded might be reduced to a matter of schedules, access and price elasticity.

The latter stages of this century have been marked by the creation of a number of media behemoths ready to do battle in the new era. For News Corp or Viacom or Disney or Time Warner, sport is a battlefield.

Digital TV will hoover more disposable income out of the pockets of the middle classes and their leisure-rich bosses while leaving less and less sport for those who can't afford it.

Sport is being eaten away. Inside out and outside in. In England, Murdoch – not content with owning the rights to soccer – is relentlessly buying up shares of various top teams. In the US he already owns many of the pieces on the board.

So too do Disney Cablevision, Viacom, etc.

The question about the hamster might just as well be asked about sport.

Therein lies the best hope. It will be asked. Sky TV and Internet sites and replica jerseys are no substitute for the authenticity of being there, doing that.

If there is one thing better than owning a Manchester United jersey, it's working up a sweat in it. If there is one thing better than watching Jamesie O'Connor strike a *sliotar*, it is picking one up and striking it yourself.

The very nature of sport will save it at some level. Sport has generally been badly served by its leaders, but television and the great satan Rupert Murdoch must take a share of the blame. Taking advantage of the feeble-minded might be profitable, but it isn't honourable and may yet be its own punishment. In buying up every star and every league and every team, perhaps Murdoch, who understands sport less perfectly than he understands Swahili, has missed the point.

The best sport is local. The GAA, more gloriously than any other example imaginable, has learned that. The organisation survived in Dublin because, at the time of greatest need, Dublin produced a team of unforgettable charisma.

Hurling has flowered because the seeds sown at local level in places like Galway, Offaly and Clare have come through on summer days.

Sport changes the very air. I don't know how we would understand Meath or Kerry without their football teams. How we would see Tipp without hurling. There is no way of gauging it, but in your heart you know Clare is a happier, more confident place since 1995 and all that.

This has been a century when the communal experience of O'Hehir or Ó Muircheartaigh's voice punctuating the summer wind on a Sunday afternoon was our bond, when the communion of a Munster hurling final in Thurles was sacred, when the walk up the hill in Killarney to see Cork and Kerry play football was filled with anticipation, when even the rattling train to winter league games was a kind of excitement and the childhood penance of the Railway Cup on Paddy's Day would see you rewarded in the next life.

The crackling noise two computers make when they shake hands in telephonic greeting reminds me these days of reticent GAA men taking social co-ordinates.

What county man are ya? What club? By any chance do you know that hoor...?

Sport in Ireland, more than anywhere else I have seen, is the fabric of what is real.

Fortunately for us, sport works on two levels simultaneously. Entertainment and exercise. We can watch an Italia '90, a Sonia O'Sullivan, a Catriona McKiernan, a D.J. Carey and laugh or cry with them, but it is no substitute for the engagement of playing. It is just fuel for the daydreams we have doing it.

One of the few consolations of moving through the wreckage of urban America is the manner in which sports have adapted to the environment. Basketball hoops can hang from any wall, kids can still slam home runs with their own fantasy commentary track looping through their heads. In a world without opportunities, a kid can still have daydreams.

Dublin is losing that a little. Traffic is so relentless and green spaces so rare that the old games of soccer played between two sets of posts marked by piles of coats and punctuated by arguments of what exactly constitutes 'over the post' are dying out. Yet there is still the Saturday morning pleasure of seeing a field crammed with seven-year-olds learning how to swing hurleys, of watching kids knock themselves out having fun with a football.

We need the engagement which sport provides. Sport confronts us with fairground mirror reflections of our own prejudices. Hello again, Jack Johnson.

Hi to Jackie Robinson, Muhammad Ali. Hats off to Frank Barrett in Atlanta and to all the dark faces in familiar jerseys. Paul McGrath, Jayo, Sean Óg. Thanks for expanding our clammy notions of Irishness.

Sport has hard times ahead of it and great times behind it, but chances are people were saying that fifty years ago this week. They were right, and we will be right, but the core humanity of sports will outlive our pessimism. There's always another wonder, always another kid with a daydream.

Inner journey in the wilderness

4 March 2000

DeeDee Jonrowe lives in Willow, Alaska, with one husband, two cats, two labradors and eighty-six Siberian huskies. Willow lies between Big Lake and Sheep Creek, or more precisely in the middle of nowhere. Huskies outnumber people. It's a lifestyle, says DeeDee. But you'd guessed that already.

DeeDee's addiction. They call it the Iditarod, the Last Great Race, an adrenalin cocktail of tradition, history, extreme sports and pantheism. This old land of gold diggers, desperados, Jack London and Dangerous Dan McGrew keeps in touch with its own harsh and epic history through the Iditarod, a 1,100-mile sled race through the wilderness.

DeeDee Jonrowe is forty-seven, but the term middle aged is inapplicable to her. This morning she gets her twenty dogs hooked up on a street in Anchorage, faces northwards into the wild and sets off on her eighteenth Iditarod race.

In Anchorage, almost everybody looks as if they are a little down on their luck, as if they've run away from something. The wind howls from the Cook inlet, Mount McKinley stands ominous and distant, the broad streets have great scabs of ice skirting them half the year. It's a hard town which takes its stern nature from the great white land it serves as gateway to. Once a year the wilderness visits.

Fourth Avenue is a no-frills artery fringed by struggling tack shops and greasy-spoon cafés. At one end you can see the shark-teeth peaks of distant mountains. This morning, though, Fourth Avenue is the centre of the Alaskan imagination. From just outside Blondie's Café, 1,200 huskies yelp up the morning air, their brush tails wagging and ready for the trail, eager to be mushed off into the Alaskan interior.

You would call it lunacy if it weren't so austere. The mushers head into the great alone that is the Alaskan tundra, along frozen rivers, including the broad majestic Yukon, through two mountain ranges and along the windwhipped coast of the Bering Sea. The sleds bounce off snow berms, risk breaking on mogul fields.

One belligerent moose on the trail can end it all for a musher.

It is 1,100 lonely miles. They ride through the nights because it is too cold to stop. They snatch sleep in those hours when the sun spreads its watery light around. Mainly, though, they just keep on keeping on.

The place names are part of the sweet poem of the wilderness: Anchorage to Wasilla. Knik to Yentna to Skwentna to Finger Lake. Rainy Pass. Takotna. Cripple. Ruby. Galena. Shoktoolik. Golivin. White Mountain. Safety. Nome. And a lyrical necklace of little places in between.

The route from Anchorage to Nome is part historical, part whimsy. In 1925, when the Gold Rush was still swinging, the children of Nome became exposed to diphtheria. The only serum available in Alaska was in Anchorage. No planes were available, so the serum was sent to Nanana on the train and sped the rest of the way to Nome by a series of twenty mushers working in relay.

Before that the Iditarod trail had been a mail and supply route.

Iditarod itself is one of a number of entirely deserted mining towns along the sometimes eerie race route. The trail and the art of mushing was forgotten about until the Last Great Race was brought to life in 1973.

Today the Iditarod is a race, a supreme athletic challenge, a community festival and a central part of Alaskan culture. It unites newcomers and native Alaskan peoples in a love of an old art. It keeps people coming to Alaska for the same reason they always have, danger and adventure.

One day soon, DeeDee Jonrowe will win the Iditarod, the race she circles obsessively. She won't be the first woman to have done so. During the 1980s when Susan Butcher was at her peak they used to say that, in Alaska, men were men and women won the Iditarod, but when DeeDee wins the big one the cheering will rend the Aurora Borealis. She will be one of the most beloved winners the Last Great Race has known.

People come to Alaska and the Great Race for all kinds of reasons. Mike Nosko mushed through the wilderness as a catharsis after his six brothers died one after the other from alcohol-related deaths. Charlie Boulding just quit North Carolina to live a life of total self-sufficiency and sled dogs in an isolated cabin near Manley. Next year Chuck King is racing to stave off the Aids virus which has ravaged his body.

DeeDee Jonrowe came here, though, because her father was a military man and she had no choice. She came, stayed and became part of the landscape, part of the essential spirit of the Iditarod.

'We were nomads. I was born in Frankfurt, we lived in Athens for a while, I started school in Ethiopia, ended it in Okinawa, graduated from High School in Virginia and then came to Alaska in July of 1971 and went to college that fall in Fairbanks.'

How can DeeDee best describe Alaska, its wilderness and its

place in her soul? Perhaps by framing the picture within the parameters of deep personal loss. One night a few years ago, she and her husband and grandmother were driving home to Willow from a sled-dog symposium. On a dark Alaskan highway they collided head-on with another vehicle.

'My grandmother died in the seat next to me. My husband Mike was critically injured. So was I. I was the only one conscious. My labrador, who we had with us, died also. It was an extremely bad situation. Thirty below zero. Trapped in the car for an hour and half, one of those violent situations you have nightmares about. I had to deal with it, get a cellphone call for help.

So much pain and dysfunction surrounded their lives as a result. 'My husband Mike couldn't walk for many months afterwards, couldn't speak even. His mother and brother had died violent deaths and he'd almost joined them.

DeeDee ran the Iditarod race four months after the accident and came in fourth. It was something she had to do.

'I feel like my strength comes from being out there in the quiet. I'd had major abdominal surgery and lost six inches from my intestine so I was spooked about getting the handlebar in my stomach for eighteen hours a day for ten days or getting the dogs punching me in the stomach when they'd greet me. But the aloneness, the chance for that serenity and solitude and the chance to grieve properly after my grandmother's death and Mike's operations called me. I had to do it.

'I went off into the wilderness in tears wondering what I was doing there. It was a lot of stress, a lot of figuring out why this was important. It was about beginning to take charge of my life again, healing myself and getting back my time. I relate that to people now, people who come here in grief. This too will pass and the strength will come from living through each day.'

The race was the first time she had been separated from her husband since the accident. The sundering went hard on her. Through the miles her mind kept revisiting the fear that he wouldn't be there when she came back.

'But it humbles you and heals you, living as one with the animals, living in their rhythm, falling back on yourself and your thoughts, having to cope moving through the majesty of this world.'

That's what sled racing came to mean thousands of lonely miles down the trail. It started though with curiosity and a love of animals. Animals were a thread throughout DeeDee Jonrowe's wandering years and she fell for sled dogs as soon as she came to Alaska. Her first permanent home was in Bethel in Western Alaska and immediately she got herself a five-dog team and faced her first challenge. It was 1979 and the phenomenon of women who wanted to mush was unheard of.

'I bought a trained team of five dogs and they taught me. I ruined them in a way. I was soft and they got away with whatever I had to learn to convince them that we'd go the route I needed to go.'

Others needed convincing too. She began competing, with an entry into a little village race outside Bethel. Did okay. The race was run on the ice outside of Bethel rather than on an established trail like dogs run in the interior. DeeDee was the only woman in the race.

'They didn't think any woman would try to run, so they hadn't made any rule against it. It took them till the next year to make that rule.'

By then DeeDee had enough dogs to enter a twenty-dog team into the Iditarod.

Again Alaskans were gape-mouthed. Women didn't do such things.

'Once we got competitive, there was resistance. It's a bit better nowadays. It wasn't something they were real comfortable with.

Guys didn't appreciate it at all. They thought it might be a novelty, but, once you got competitive, they got more abrasive. Once you got competitive, it was too late for them to do anything about you being there too.'

The social environment she found was no surprise to her. She worked as a biologist for the state, driving boats hundreds of miles up and down the river, taking snowmobiles hundreds of miles into the interior just to count musk ox.

Alaskan men held no surprises for her. Anyway, her love affair was with the land and her dogs. All else was clutter.

Siberian huskies, her eternal companions, are very strong-willed sociable animals. 'Places to go, people to see, things to do,' is how DeeDee characterises them. 'They need each other and they need tasks and challenges.'

This year's is a key race for DeeDee. After a series of eleven top-ten finishes including two second places she had the unique experience of having her team quit on her last year when they were on the Yukon River. Her lead dog Commander became confused and overwhelmed by his task and just sat down. His despondency spread to the other dogs. They all sat down. Strike.

'That's a misnomer maybe,' she says. 'It wasn't a cumulative action. They stopped. Dogs will run themselves to death, they love it, but if dogs become confused and overwhelmed they stop.

'The lead dog just became overwhelmed. I couldn't convince him it was okay. In the end I just had to pull him off the river and take him home. He was out of his depth, competing at a level he wasn't mentally equipped for. He works with a recreational team at a bed and breakfast now and he is as happy as can be.'

On the marble-hard surface of the Yukon, the sense of desperation and struggle when a dog quits is unimaginable. DeeDee tried everything, including becoming lead dog herself.

'I even ran in front for a little while, but, whenever I had to quit, he'd quit too. There was also a 75 below wind-chill factor gale hitting him full in the face, so maybe it was natural that when I'd stop running in front of him he'd stop too. I tried switching dogs around. I turned him loose to play and rebuild his confidence. When he went back to a lower position in the pack he was happy to pull the sled, but by then none of the other dogs would take responsibility at the front point.'

Her first withdrawal in seventeen Iditarods hurt. Jonrowe spends as much as two years identifying those dogs who will lead the pack, moving them into different groups, putting them into different areas of development, moving them closer to dogs they are most talent-matched with, developing their personalities and bonding them to her.

She gets help from any quarter. This year she visited the horse whisperer Josh Lyons, learning how he works with the reinforcement of animals' natural instincts.

'I've learned about building the dog's confidence to the point where he thinks he is invincible, giving him tasks and challenges that he will always succeed at. I've taken the dogs all over Alaska getting them used to the mountains, the ice of the rivers, the wind chill from the Bering Sea, the storms, the endurance.'

And herself? Nothing is more vulnerable in the monstrous whiteness of Alaska than mere humans. Mushing is about courage and sense and survival.

'Yeah, I've been scared out there and I will be again,' she says. 'You are living off the edge, you are in over your head. It's Alaska.'

Her worst experience was a training run. Training runs leave you vulnerable because there is no race organisation backing you up. She was with a girlfriend and a pack of dogs in the Kuskokwim mountains when a storm descended.

'It came from nowhere. We had no survival gear, no food. We thought we were on a three-hour run. Alaskan storms can take away the visibility so bad that it's like finding your way through a jug of milk out there.'

The situation grew critical quickly. They had to turn the dogs loose, afraid of them getting snowed down too hard. The landscape was one white plain. Every option offered death. They sheltered behind a tree till they realised quickly that it offered no shelter. They dug a snow cave with their bare hands, but when it was built they realised they had no body warmth left and that they would die quickly, frozen solid and buried forever.

In the end they had to crawl. They were too weak and bowed to do anything else.

'We crawled three miles into the camp we'd set up. There was a break in the storm and my husband landed in a small plane. He took my friend out because she was in a bad condition, he got me warmed up in the tent and left me there.'

The ordeal wasn't over. The weather broke malevolently again and it was another twelve cold, hungry days before her husband could return.

'For me it seemed like the end, but the dogs stayed with me and they did just fine. Twelve days. The thoughts in my head. I thought he had crashed, maybe he's not going to get back. This was where I was going to die. It humbles you.'

This morning she leaves again. Her eighteenth Great Race, filled with adrenalin and nerves as usual. She thinks that youthful naivety was an asset. You can dwell too much on fears.

She has rebuilt the entire front end of her team, stocking it with new dogs.

Her foodstuffs have been deposited at the twenty-one checkpoints along the way. Ten days of solitude and cold await her. Her annual purge of the spirit.

'This is more than just a sport,' says DeeDee Jonrowe. 'This is a spiritual journey. This is why people came to Alaska in the beginning. To find what's out there.'

And what's inside.

The grown-up way of speaking

5 June 2000

One thing you notice about sports journalism in America is that the practitioners seem to think it a job, not just for grown-ups, but a career in which a person might grow old with some dignity. Weird. That notion is especially charming to those of us from the old world, accustomed as we are to the dysfunctional relationship which exists between athletes and the media. Where we come from, the guys with the notebooks play the role of unloved children and the people who sweat just play hard to get. And we've come to accept that that's how it is and how it shall always be.

There's a joke doing the rounds at the minute about the recently deceased Cardinal O'Connor of New York being expelled from heaven after the *Ard-Chomhairle* up there got sick of hearing just how it is that they do things in New York. At the risk of committing the same sin, let's just say that the relationship between hacks and jocks in America is a good deal healthier than we are accustomed to at home, and from that everyone benefits.

Before and after games in all major league sports all over America, dressing rooms are by mandate opened to the media. Hacks wander in and out holding conversations with articulate players who, in general, are happy to be jawing to somebody whose work will not only promote their image and their sport but will communicate to the paying audience something worthwhile about the game.

Just imagine!

There's the odd renegade, of course. People like Indiana college basketball coach Bobby Knight, whose oft-quoted view of the media is that 'most people learn to write in the first grade and then move on to other things'. For those of us still wielding a crayon though, the American way takes a little getting used to, especially when you've been reared on a strict diet of soccer-speak and the 'whatever you say lads, say nothing' culture of the GAA.

I was thinking yesterday of where I would be and what I would be doing were I at home, and one thing seemed certain: approaching five o'clock I would have been standing outside a dressing room somewhere with my tape recorder in my hot little hand waiting for some jobsworth from a county board to admit the media.

Things would have gone this way. After the final whistle, we, the wretched of the earth, would have evacuated our cramped press box and taken advantage of the traditional post-match pitch invasion to beat the players down to the dressing-room area.

There we would have formed a greeting line of exquisite sycophancy outside the winners' dressing room, bestowing on each arriving player the laurels of our biggest smiles and hoping that the sight of us being so pathetic would induce them to stop to talk.

Of course, while doing this we try to look like serious professionals, but frankly we look like nothing more than a kerbful of novelty hookers. Generally somebody will snare a player for a little yackedy-yak business, and we will crowd shamelessly around like flies on honey, chiming in by asking our own silly questions.

Then the gabby player will be summoned into the dressing room by some county board yahoo in a shiny suit who feels that speaking to the press is an occasion of sin which is likely to bring disease into his county. The yahoo will admit the player and tell us tersely by way of explanation that the manager wants to say a few words. Five minutes. Okay gentlemen?

We spend the next thirty minutes knocking on the door and cursing. Occasionally one of our number will wander up the corridor to the losing dressing room, wherein there is weeping, wailing and gnashing of mentors.

Losers shower and dress so astonishingly quickly that you just know they're not bringing two bottles into the shower – some of them can't even be bringing soap. Within minutes they are filing, heads down and mouths clamped, out the back door of their dressing room and the yahoo who guards the front door is still saying to us: 'Few minutes, lads, okay?'

We will be telling him in various stages of exasperation that, despite how things may look, we actually have a job to do. And he will be smiling back at us like a nightclub bouncer refusing a group of fifteen-year-olds.

His moment in the sun will come when he opens the door wide and says, 'There ye go, lads', and we walk inside to find the team physio and three waterbottles left to talk to.

This process holds true for most Irish sports, not just Gaelic games. The Irish soccer team have broken the spirit of many a young sapper with their reticence, and veterans will recall that even on that glorious day in 1994 when Italy were beaten in Giants Stadium, the Irish dressing room stayed locked for an eternity-and-a-half, with only TDs, clergy, blonde women and FAI council members being admitted, as Sunday paper hacks wept salty, post-deadline tears.

Meanwhile, the vanquished Italians were out in the corridor explaining patiently the deficiencies in their game and expansively discussing their tastes in modern architecture. By the time Ireland

got beaten by Holland, the boys who had spent months putting the
arm on newspapers for thousands of pounds in exchange for access
were refusing to speak at all.

Of course, there's variety in there, too. Some teams, like Meath in
football and Clare hurlers back in their heyday, are easy to deal with
whether they are winning or losing.

In fact, one of the great unlearned lessons about GAA management is that the teams who are more relaxed about the media
generally fare better. Sean Boylan's Meath teams are the leading
example, providing decent press nights and welcoming access to
dressing rooms with nobody getting hung up on avoiding us.

I was thinking about all this during the week when the New York
Knicks (having been assuredly tipped for glory in this column last
Monday) inevitably and spitefully went down in flames last Friday.
Within twenty minutes of that disaster, their traumatised players
were huddling with the media explaining their feelings.

It's easy to say that a hoopster like Patrick Ewing makes millions
while the hurler who sends his mammy to the phone every time it
rings during the summer is paid nothing; but the benefits of merely
having a grown-up relationship with the media must be visible to
most people and not just those of us who are growing too old and too
fat for cursing players every summer.

Number one in a world of his own

19 June 2000

It's Tiger Woods' world. We just live in it. On Friday evening they announced that it was too dark to play any more golf at Pebble Beach. Wishing, as he says, to finish up on a good note, Tiger Woods holed a simple thirty-five-foot putt for a birdie on the twelfth hole and called it a night, walking off the green looking tired. I was there at the time, feeling tired. Jesper Parnevik was there too, looking as if everything he knew was wrong.

Then Tiger put his face, his views, his logos on TV for a while and afterwards came to the press tent for a twenty-minute yakkety-yak with the intelligentsia, during which he discussed everything from Jack Nicklaus to the LA Lakers to his remarkable eight-under-par score after thirty holes of the US Open. I sat and listened and looked passably intelligent myself.

Then, at sometime after 10 pm, Tiger headed to his hotel, where he performed his ablutions and had something to eat. I headed to my hotel and did the same. I am Tiger Woods, I told myself.

Then at 4 am Tiger Woods got out of bed (perhaps by means of levitation, we just don't know), he performed even more ablutions, had some breakfast and headed to the driving range. He was working at the driving range at 5.15 am. He was on the putting green with Butch Harmon at 6 am. He finished the last six holes of his second round by 10 am. I know this because I saw the highlights on telly when I woke up at 10.30 am. I am not Tiger Woods.

Jesper got up early too. Finished the last six holes of his second round and caught the next bus to Palookaville. Look out for him running amok in a McDonalds or something. In all, Tiger Woods played twenty-four holes on Saturday. He finished up ten shots ahead of the bunch of losers who comprise the best golfers in the world, ranked two through to John Daly. Amidst crowds, bigger and richer than those which followed Moses, I watched as much of Tiger Woods as I could. I nearly finished up in intensive care. Give him this. The kid has got shots. The kid has got stamina.

At times in the past few days, watching Tiger Woods play the US Open at Pebble Beach was like watching a great maestro sing Puccini at La Scala. It elevated anyone who wasn't a pro golfer. It was the perfect confluence of talent, arena and challenge. Enough there to make us giddy but too much subtlety there at that exalted level of performance for most of us to understand.

Too much for Colin Montgomerie, anyway. Lordee but what a dreary old moanie minnie Mrs Doubtfire is. As if not attending the memorial ceremony for Payne Stewart (who was famously generous to the buxom Scot) wasn't embarrassment enough to heap upon himself, the old trout bumbles into the press tent on Saturday morning and announces that surely the gods do conspire against him in matters meteorological.

Then he goes out and partners Ernie Els for the afternoon. Els shoots the best round of the day whilst suffering the company of the hapless baboon from tropical, windless Troon. Either all weather is local or Monty ain't Tiger Woods either. Anyway, we came to praise young Caesar not to bury big Monty. We were talking about perfection.

On Saturday afternoon at 5.30 pm, Mr Woods finished the first nine holes of his third round. He pointed a sand wedge at the catering tents and turned all mineral water therein into wine before walking to the tenth.

Why not? He was nine shots ahead of the rest of the field at that point and the battle had become Tiger Woods vs Pebble Beach. The course, a great and beautiful warrior itself, had already whipped all comers. The average round for the day was 77.2 shots.

Woods went toe to toe though; his knowledge of the physics of golf truly makes this the sweet science. It took a mistake to put that in perspective. On Saturday morning, during his six-hole preamble to the day, Woods' drive on the eighteenth went for some surf-and-turf action and he filled the television screens of Mr and Mrs America with some salty curses. Alleluia! Cut him and he might bleed.

On Saturday Woods got through the first nine holes of his afternoon session in thirty-five strokes, or level par. Only Ernie Els and Padraig Harrington did better.

Woods' score was the more remarkable only because it contained a triple bogey and a bogey, the first punches which Pebble Beach had landed on Tiger Woods all week. His recovery from those misfortunes was so extraordinary that, in the press tent afterwards, we asked if we could put our hands where his wounds had been. Just to be sure.

There were times when he slapped Pebble Beach around as if it were a rented sparring partner. He stripped the old giant of its austere dignity at times. On Friday, the sheer temerity of a 205-yard seven iron from the rough on the sixth fairway to the elevated green ahead had to be seen to be believed.

From practice to trophy time, his week was filled with such jewels. The eighth at Pebble Beach is a wonder of the golfing world, a dogleg which breaks right, the gap being filled with the beckoning blue Pacific of Carmel Bay.

Jack Nicklaus, this old codger who used to be Tiger Woods, said once that, if he had one shot to play before death (or before dinner, who can remember all this stuff), one shot on any hole in the world, he'd pick the second shot at the eighth at Pebble Beach.

The hole calls for a little brinkmanship from the tee. Knock your drive towards the edge of the cliff and then whip your second courageously over the sea towards the stingy little green on the far cliff and you'll be fine. Of course, the ball should stick to the green the way a bad name sticks to a dog.

Woods devised something different, pushing his drive to the right, so perilously close to disaster that rescue services could do nothing. Then he'd whip it over the waves, trading the tougher lie for the simpler approach to the green and a birdie chance each time. Lots of ooohs as we follow his drive, lots of aaaahs as he sticks for his second.

In the end all of us followed him procession and homage. It was that kind of US Open – one man performing at a level that we could scarcely understand, one man planting the flag of Tigerworld on the highest summit at Pebble Beach. All bow.

One man. He Tiger Woods. He da man.

Back from the dead

1 July 2000

Each morning he wakes and lies awhile in bed just absorbing the sounds of the house. In those moments of fleeting serenity, everything is pleasantly amplified. Peach moving about downstairs, the crockery piling up, the dog padding around greeting the day, the cat scratching busily. The wan Texas sun lights his room. Beck Weathers thinks to himself that this is going to be a good day, another good day.

Maybe he has been dreaming. When he came home first he never had nightmares, but for the longest time he dreamt that he was climbing. Night after night he felt that sensation of putting one foot in front of the other, slowly leaving the earth behind him. Recently he has different dreams, escapes which cant him into bullet-proof mode.

Everything is possible. Sometimes in his reverie he looks down and he has two hands. Some part of his brain insists that this is dreamtime, but his voice just says 'Hey cool!'

Nothing fractures his contentment now. There is pleasure in every sunrise, he lives for the feel of wind on his face, for the pleasure of just contributing, he doesn't sweat the small stuff. Little aggravations don't matter.

He misses the sensation of touch, of course. People think that maybe he misses doing things he once did, that he yearns to recover some old function. Wrong. It's the fact of no longer having feeling coming through hands and fingers. A human gets forty per cent of sensory perception through the hands. You don't know what you've got till it's gone and being deprived of that is a cruel loss. It hurts relationships. People are tactile beings and having no hands makes an island of a man.

He thinks it a satisfactory trade, what he lost and what he gained. Even as they carried him down Everest with his two hands frozen solid in front of him he thought so. He remembers saying to Davie Breashears, upon whose shoulder his was leaning, 'Hey, Dave, before I came here they said it would cost an arm and a leg. I'm getting a bargain.'

Breashears shook his head. Minutes later, as the shuffle downhill continued, Weathers asked was it only him or did anyone else feel like singing. Then he started up with 'Chain of Fools' as they tramped along the worst terrain on earth.

Dying is easy. Comedy is hard.

Peach hated him just then. His own wife loved him and hated him. Beck Weathers was never an easy man to live with. Depression whipped him. Work and climbing obsessed him. He says it himself, he filched the life from his family.

As he came down the mountain, broken but singing, Peach Weathers wondered what to do with him. If he'd returned healthy, she'd planned to leave him. Now she decided to give her dismantled husband a year.

What he lost and what he gained. Beck Weathers speaks from a perspective that perhaps no other human being has. Man has walked on the moon, man has run four-minute miles, man has mapped the genetic code of the human body, but no man has come out of a hypothermic coma. Except Beck Weathers, the man who was left for dead, twice; Beck Weathers who has been to that place where a man has nothing left physically or emotionally.

He is frank to the point of nakedness. He stands in the warmth of the American summer four years later wearing a burgundy T-shirt with what's left of his arms hanging from the sleeves, his big red nose dipping down towards his loopy grin. He confronts you with his dismantled body, encourages you to deal with it.

'Being maimed,' he says, 'it's just something that is. Nothing I can do, nothing I worry about any longer.' He looks at you straight with his fierce brown eyes. This is not some rich goombah who went up a mountain and got into trouble. This is a labyrinth of a man.

Perhaps you know some of Beck Weathers's story. It's not the usual once-upon-a-time spiel from the summits. Big mountaineer gasps up big mountain because it's there and because he must. Big mountaineer contemplates life from the top. Big mountaineer comes down again.

One day in May 1996, Beck Weathers, running from depression, got to within 1,000 feet of the summit of Mount Everest. He could go no further and, while the rest of his party completed the ascent, he dawdled on the ridge below. By the time they were supposed to come back down, a storm had enveloped Everest.

Eventually, with a Japanese woman, Yasuko Namba, and five other climbers (four from another expedition), Weathers began the descent.

The storm worsened. The wind chill factor was 100 below, Weathers had lost his sight at altitude, but, with the blizzard whipping up, visibility was like 'looking out from the centre of a bottle of milk'.

It was a day of chaos and crisis on the mountain, a day when people found out who had iron in the soul. Noting that there was no morality at 26,000 feet, two Japanese climbers yomped past a couple of dying men on their way up and yomped past them again on the way down. A South African expedition refused to share oxygen with dying climbers. One expedition leader scooted down the mountain hours ahead of his clients, who had paid $65,000 a turn for his expertise. Eight people would die before the storm ended.

Coming back down the mountain, Beck Weathers's group strayed dangerously off course. Twenty-five more steps and they would have walked blind over a 7,000-foot drop. Sensing the danger, somehow they opted to stop and the three fittest from the group set off for high camp to get help. Duly alerted, Anatoli Boukreev, the Russian who had come down the mountain ahead of his party, climbed the mountain again, locating the ailing group at a critical time. He rescued the three who were members of his own expedition. Yasuko Namba and Weathers, both in a critical condition, were left to die.

And die they did. A cardiologist, Stuart Hutchison, and three sherpas came out later to find them. They found Namba and Beck Weathers lying beside each other buried in snow and ice. They were both frozen rigid, eyes dilated.

Hutchison had no choice but to leave them there.

It was a day of cruel, heartbreaking decisions, drastic errors, painful mistakes. One climber was misidentified crawling into camp and his family informed that he was back and safe, only to hear the next day that he had perished. Rob Hall, the leader of Beck Weathers's expedition, clung to the summit in the storm freezing to death despite the pleas of his friends to begin descending.

He made a final radio call to his wife. 'I love you. Sleep well, my sweetheart. Please don't worry too much.' And then all they could hear on the airwaves was his quiet sobbing. Yasuko Namba perished quickly. Beck Weathers wandered a little in a state of altitude delirium and passed from consciousness not long afterwards, slumping facedown on the ice of Everest, another body to be hidden until the light thaw of the following spring. His wife, Peach, and his two children Meg and Bub were informed of his death.

Peach thought that, in a way, Beck had willed his demise. Dogged by suffocating bouts of clinical depression since late adolescence, Beck had been suicidal to the extent of studying the different ways to end it all. One day, shaken by his own self-destructive instincts, he had cleared all the guns from his Dallas home, brought them to the police station and turned them in. His obsession with climbing and work had become his solution. It didn't take away the pain, but just left him too drained to notice it.

That was enough anaesthetic to keep him living, but, when death reached out its cold hand on Everest, Beck Weathers didn't decline the invitation.

Success had made a disaster area of their home. Weathers was an anatomical pathologist, an 11-hours-a-day workaholic who wedged workouts and large mountains into his spare time. He was a hero to everyone except those who knew him.

After fifteen hours of absence, he opened his eyes on Everest. He had been in the storm for twenty-two hours. He has no explanation for this miracle. His instincts are scientific rather than spiritual, but he has no rational way of explaining what happened. Nobody wakes up from hypothermic coma. Nobody. When he awoke, he saw in front of him his right hand, mottled, gloveless and frozen rock solid into a grotesque comic salute. And he also saw his family, their faces looming before him in stark and vivid focus. For the first time in his life it struck him that, between depression and obsession, he had never been there for them, that he owed them more than the news of his lonely death. He stood up and began to walk.

His Damascene epiphany was almost too late. When he finally came home, with his body ruined and crumbling, his wife Peach damned him for what he had done to her, to his kids. She gave him his year of probation, take it or leave it.

Pretty much from that day, he recognised the duty of the survivor was compatible with the task of the husband. Eight people were left behind dead on the mountain when Beck Weathers got off. Eight people dead, leaving behind them great concentric circles of grief. He owed them a good and decent life, a life not shrivelled by bitterness.

'I knew who to blame anyway. Me. My legs took me there and my decisions kept me there and finding somebody to blame for not saving my bacon is a waste of time. I came back and I made the very deliberate decision not to play the blame game. I didn't want that bile, not when I was trying to stop myself coming unglued. If you are building a shattered life, you have to focus.'

He returned to the world with a palpable sense of obligation, a need to find something of value. All his life he had measured himself against external goals, mountains, qualifications, income. He returned to work four months after he came off the mountain, looking to turn wounds into something positive.

'Dyin' ain't hard,' he says today in his southern drawl. 'If dyin' was hard, there'd be some Bubba stuck out in west Texas who'd live forever because he couldn't figure it out. Dying is easy. Living is hard.'

On the mountain he did the hard thing. He put one foot in front of the other and dragged himself back to the world. He was almost totally blind, but he deduced from the wind blowing into his face that he was going in roughly the right direction. An hour later he stumbled into camp.

Remarkable as Beck Weathers's resurrection was, it made little impression on those already there. They were each fighting for their own survival. Another expedition leader, Scott Fischer, was dead by then. They placed Weathers in Fischer's empty tent and left him there to die too.

'So, having been left for dead it turns out I'm the first person ever to come out of hypothermic coma and, after fifteen hours of lying face down in the snow in a wind chill of minus one hundred, I stand up and I stumble an hour later into camp. I haven't eaten in three days, I haven't drunk anything in two days. I'm hallucinating. Parts of my body are frozen solid, my hand is like a block of marble in front of me, my nose is about to fall off, my eyesight is totally gone, my suit is full of freezing piss, my wife's been told I'm dead... (pause) but, hey, I'm not discouraged.'

He might as well have been. He lay in the tent alone all night as the storm gathered its malevolence again and attempted to blow him off the mountain.

People steered clear of Beck Weathers's last lodging place, the deadman's tent.

By chance the next morning he was found out of his sleeping bag, tent flaps blowing in the breeze. He was frozen stiff. Still alive though.

Life doesn't unravel to any plan. The first months back at work were tough and frustrating. His partners imported a literal hired hand to do those things which Weathers could no longer do. More critically, nobody knew whether or not he had lost any brain function during his fifteen-hour outage.

'One of the things that is almost impossible to know is what you don't know. My partners had to be willing to look at everything I did for months to be certain that all the cognitive pathways were intact and there were no holes there. Fortunately, I may have lost a lot of neurons, but I could still work. That was so important.'

If Beck Weathers's story had finished with him dying in a tent on Everest, he would be no more than an interesting footnote in the mountain's dark history. He wasn't ready for that though. That vision of his family drove him.

Weathers was helped still further down the mountain. David Breashears, who was leading the IMAX Everest expedition, had abandoned filming plans and shared his crew's resources with ailing climbers all over the mountain. A Taiwanese army Colonel, Madan Khatri Chhetri, flew a helicopter up higher than any such machine has ever flown before, up and up into the thin air of Everest. Making two death-defying journeys, each using just seven minutes' worth of fuel, Madan plucked two dying men off the ice. Weathers was the second to go, having waved another climber on board before him.

'Character is what you do when you think nobody is looking,' he says. 'There were a lot of people who came through for me that day when nobody was really looking. For myself, I just didn't want to have a life of second-guessing myself if I had gone first and left a man to die.'

That's his story. The first half of it. He lost his nose and surgeons had to grow one back using skin from his neck and cartilage from his ear. They attached it first to his forehead where it fed off the blood supply till it grew upside down. Then they twisted it around and made a nose of it. He lost his right arm just below the elbow and lost a lot of his left. What remains is a massively swollen club of a hand with half a thumb that is moveable. Just sufficient to give him independence.

Unknowable things are hardest to fix, though. Depression beat him up worse than Everest did. Failing to find the right words to utter to Yasuko Namba's family when they came to see him still aches his heart. Putting his marriage back together was tougher than the eleven operations he suffered in reassembling his body.

And it would take more death and tears to make the catharsis complete. Howard Olsen was Peach's brother and all through her life he had filled in the gaps. Their father died when they were infants. Howard had to be more than a kid. When Peach married a man whose defining contribution to the marriage was his mental and physical absences, Howard filled the spaces left behind.

Eight months after Beck Weathers's return, Howard Olsen died of inoperable liver cancer. Howard had what Weathers describes with mordant southern wit as a 'die like a dog in the road' health insurance policy. Weathers spent the last four months of Olsen's life arguing with insurance companies, researching possible cures and supporting his wife, while fighting a raging rearguard battle against the cancer.

Beck gave the eulogy at the funeral. His daughter Meg sang 'Amazing Grace' and the recollection of her voice delivering the lines 'I once was lost, but now am found' still brings tears to Beck's eyes. Sometime during the depths of their grieving, Beck and Peach noticed that the blame and anger and recriminations had been sucked out of their lives. They were different people.

Beck Weathers didn't find that good oletime religion, although people told him that his survival was divine providence. He believes, though, that if he leads a good life and puts back more than he took out, he'll finish up ahead, even if there is nothing after death. That's enough for now, he says.

Whatever about the gods, his hours *in extremis* on Everest have given him a benign tolerance of humanity in all its porcelain frailty.

'I think people are mostly good. Given an opportunity, most people want to do the right thing, but the fact is some people are lions, and others are rabbits. Not everyone has the level of stamina or courage or even character to be what they hope they will be.

'You hope that when you are tested you will have a measure of honour and that you will conduct yourself with a sense of grace. One of the reasons you go there is to find that out and, if you had to ask the question, you know that at some level what you may discover is something about yourself that will be hard to live with afterwards. Maybe you could have been braver, but the fact that a person worries about that is a measure of their humanity. The person who doesn't have those feelings is probably the more cowardly soul.'

He awaits the return of that cowled old companion, depression. He has armed himself this time. Weathers grew up in a time which he describes as the John Wayne era: 'If somebody ripped your heart out and threw it across the room, well it's only a flesh wound, so a mental illness like depression was positively shameful.' Next time, he says, he'll be open, treat the depression as an organic illness.

In the meantime, life is about savouring the small things. Travel with Peach, a renewed interest in music, literally and metaphorically taking time to smell the roses. Joy is in the tiny quotidian things he never noticed before.

Happiness is opening new doors.

'I always thought of myself as a storyteller,' he says, 'but I was an anatomical pathologist and that doesn't make for much of a story. Now I have a story to tell, I wound up with a great story, not an adventure story, but a love story, a great love story.'

You ask him where he'll be in ten years' time, when he is no longer Beck Weathers the man who came back from the dead and walked off the mountain. He smiles and shakes his head. Targets don't matter. 'Me and Peach will be growing old together as comfortable as a pair of old shoes. That's all I know.'

And he says goodbye, offering the swollen trident that lives where once his left hand was. You grasp his reconstructed flesh and pump it. Dr Seaborn Beck Weathers, standing taller now than he ever did on Everest.

Sonia's sweetest medal of them all

26 September 2000

Did you leap out of the chair and roar or did you slip into the kitchen and cry? Were you whispering silent prayers or was your fist clenched and pumping as she came down the straight? This was the sweetest medal in our sporting history, a triumph, a redemption song, a perfect aria delivered by our greatest-ever athlete, the one we've been through the most with and known the longest. Sonia O'Sullivan, happy and brilliant again. Could you have been Irish and been unmoved?

She said afterwards it wasn't the hardest race she has ever run. Maybe so, but it was the bravest. Yesterday Sonia O'Sullivan claimed the Olympic moment she deserved in a race which compressed the agonies of the last few years into twelve and a half laps.

She came off the track and her face was shining and happy. She'd found a part of herself again.

This Olympic 5,000-metre final was one of the great races, an epic struggle to the finish line between two great rivals who won't like each other any better this morning but who respect each other a whole lot more. Gabriela Szabo of Romania did what we thought she couldn't do. She held off Sonia in a sprint.

This is what sport is about. This is what you came for. Afterwards you saw her stand in a little knot of love with her partner Nick and her daughter Ciara and the distance from Atlanta seemed incalculable. 'That was a nightmare,' she said, 'this was a dream.'

Gete Wami, the third-placed finisher, explained afterwards that the Ethiopians had planned to run as a team and 'then just before the race we decided it was wrong, not the fair thing to do'. For her grace, Wami was rewarded with bronze.

And for Sonia, silver. Fate owed her this at least. She'd wanted it all so badly that it almost destroyed her, back in 1996. She crumbled in front of us all.

'On the fourth lap, I felt like I was dropping off. It wasn't the pace, I don't know what it was. I was nearly gone. It was that voice in your head, "Do you want to go with this?"'

She did. She did. She survived by hanging on to Jo Pavey from Britain for a while and then getting between two Kenyans. 'Then I discovered I was so close to winning. I came off the bend. I was so shocked I almost stopped. I'm glad I didn't.'

And so she lived to fight her way down the straight, an epic slugging match right to the line. She glanced up, wasted but happy and saw the race times on the scoreboard. Two thoughts: So close. How did we run so fast?

She left finally to jog off into the cool Sydney night to warm down loyal muscles, to put order on a wild day, to think about running the 10,000 metres later in the week. She had a silver medal in her pocket, the Australian sky was inky blue and the torch was still burning. Does it get any better?

Burrows won't get helm off Hickey

8 January 2001

What's eating Richard Burrows? Does he not enjoy living? Can he not leave a blue sky unclouded, a smooth pond of contentment unrippled? Is there something lacking in his life that would make him consider taking up arms against Pat Hickey? People ask why it is that in horror movies pretty girls always dander into haunted houses, and I say, well, in real life rich guys keep going after Pat Hickey. Same thing. Listen up. Hickey has nice yachties like Richard Burrows for breakfast. Hickey doesn't just live in the warzone, he is the lord mayor.

Look behind him. Great and many have been the little Balbirnies who have picked up the sword and set off to slay the ogre. Quiet and unmarked are the graves.

You think nobody else wanted that IOC seat? You think nobody opposed Hickey as he rose through the ranks of the IOC? You think the Dublin International Sports Council needs to hire the Point Depot for its Christmas parties? You think Hickey ever saw a fight he didn't like the look of? Oh boys, boys, boys.

Hush! When the wind is right you can hear him licking his lips, sharpening his knife and fork. Eerie.

I first met Hickey eight years ago. We were in Monte Carlo covering the bid campaign which ended with Sydney winning the 2000 Games. Three of us wound up at a restaurant table. Two journalists and Hickey. Posh French restaurant. Three northsiders. Hickey looked around with boyish glee and pointed a finger at us in turn, then at himself. Kilbarrack! Finglas! Phibsboro! And here we all are!

Since then he has been the best show in Irish sport. Yup, he has done many things I can't begin to defend him for. He is suing or has sued most of the people I call friends; he gave accreditation in 1996 to a banned athlete and, like a lot of others, he kept his trap firmly shut when the Michelle de Bruin raft sailed clean over the falls; he has cultivated a Zelig-like ability to be wherever there is a sniff of Irish success, culminating in his triumphant RTÉ cameo as Sonia O'Sullivan's au pair on the morning after the silver was secured in Sydney.

He and I have more bones to pick than a couple of vultures hovering over a mass grave.

Yet something about that glee in being a northsider who made it big still makes him compulsive viewing and good company.

He is the original of the species in terms of much being said about him but little being proved. Sometimes the whispering campaigns against him could deafen you. He gave Eve the apple to pass to Adam and it's been downhill since. Yet nothing has ever firmed up. Could it be that he's just a guy who gets things done?

What's the story here? Last week the mullahs of canoeing, swimming and athletics announced they were going to Lausanne to complain about Pat Hickey. Swimming and athletics!!! These guys are our Neighbourhood Watch all of a sudden?

Beautiful!!! If you wanted to keep your butter unmelted, the first place you'd look to put it would be in the mouth of an Irish swimming or athletics official.

What else have we? Was it my imagination, or did not Petty Officer McDaid and John Treacy publicly demob Hickey and assume complete control of Irish sport some years back? All aspects of Irish sport – except the blame apparently.

They're both too dumbstruck to tell Bertie what a monstrous mistake the Bertie Bowl is, but, having assumed control, the Irish Sports Council is now stridently surveying athletes to find out what the OCI did wrong in Sydney.

Myles na gCopaleen, where are you in our time of need? What else? The IOC bribes scandals. Be honest. Hickey-watchers tipped forward their seats the better to hear the wireless breaking the news. Could it be our boy has done something rash? Not a whistle, not a murmur. Hickey gets mentioned passingly in a dispatch about being a guest at a golf match before he was an IOC member. Given that Dublin journalists systematically put the arm on golf clubs for free use of their facilities every day of the week, there was some quiet coughing and everyone went back to their desks and imagined Hickey cutting a swathe down a fairway. Later, a ten-year-old letter from Hickey to Tom Welch in Salt Lake City is uncovered. Hickey is warning Welch about bribes being paid by other campaigns. Drat!

Go watch Hickey work a room at IOC level. He's smooth and genial and has the ear of those more powerful than himself. He laid down a marker in Sydney during the elections for the IOC executive and would have finished stronger had Samaranch not intervened to insist that two seats be reserved, one for an athlete and one for a woman. Come next year in Moscow, Hickey will almost certainly be elected to the IOC executive level. That takes savvy and ability.

This column went on an advance trip to Sydney last summer to sample the preparations, and at every port of call Hickey's name was cited as an example of how to get things done. Like it or not, he is our most powerful sports administrator and will continue to be so, even if Richard Burrows drops him off the starboard side. That's the thing. Hickey won this battle long ago when he was elected to the IOC. He's got the power. The wise thing is to get on with him and harness his ability in a collective push for Irish sport.

Right now most of those standing ready to throw their pebbles are living in houses made of glass and urging another pretty girl to go into the big scary house. Drop the cudgels, lads, and go do something more constructive. And Pat, you go watch Ireland's smartest sports administrator, Liam Mulvihill, and see how mountains can be moved without use of noisy machinery.

Bugger rugger: Why I totally hate schools' rugby totally

30 January 2001

Rugby people. Can't live with them. Can't shoot them. Mainly can't live with them. Can't afford to live with them. Haven't the bloodlines to live with them. Haven't the patience to live with them. Haven't the language skills to live with them. Haven't the desire even. Rugby people have always been college scarves and jutting jaws and silly songs I don't know the words of.

C-A-N-N-O-T live with them.

Now, a quick word before we start. Every time I write one of my patented, bitter and twisted chip-on-the-shoulder social-cripple pieces about the rugby world, the same smug epistles hit the desk all the way from D4.

They tell me (surprise!) that I have a chip on my shoulder about rugby.

'You're like a little boy with his nose pressed up against the window – come on in and have a pinty for croying out loud.'

I know. I have a chip. Actually, I like having a chip on my shoulder about rugby. It is my inalienable right. I will not have a pinty. Thonks. I am happy as I am.

I don't like rugby and I work for *The Irish Times*. It's like being a day trader and working for Pravda.

Listen to this. I have tried. I have reached out to rugby. I have gone forth in a spirit of understanding and fellowship and attempted to break down the cultural barriers between rugby and myself.

For my troubles, I've had nothing but heartache and sorrow.

Let me tell you something I've never told anyone before. Once, and I am disappearing into a witness-protection programme after the next full stop, I played half a season of under-19 rugby with Suttonians.

Next time, I'd choose to do my time in jail, as my co-accused did. Despite being a Gaelic player, and therefore able to do some things most rugby people cannot do – i.e. catch a ball, kick a ball, run, etc. – I was press-ganged into being a second-row forward.

This is like choosing to do a heavy lifting job in your spare time. For a few months, I spent my time with my shoulder pushing the buttocks of other men and my arm reached up between their legs. Even after a lifetime in the Christian Brothers, I wasn't prepared for that.

My ears were always red and sore and my shoulders ached, but sometimes, to take my mind off all that, the opposing hooker would kindly give me a kick in the face.

That's how rugby people run the game and it's how they run the world.

I thrived only in line-outs, those strange masonic rituals wherein everybody uniformly mistimes their jump for some reason I couldn't initially understand.

Clarification wasn't long in coming.

After two clean catches, the person opposing you in the line-out would just reach across and pull your hair. Beats gravity every time. Hair-pulling wasn't a very manly thing to do, but neither was weeping: 'Ref! Ref! He's pulling my hair.' I learned to mistime my jump like everyone else.

For a while, I tried to bring several different coloured pairs of shorts to games in the hope that having the same coloured shorts as the opposition might save my testicles from being squeezed and twisted as we lay in panting heaps somewhere on top of the ball.

The biting and hair-pulling I could take. Ball-handling was a no no – even from teams we played regularly. (Note: In the GAA testicles don't actually exist – except as a metaphor for guts. If a *sliotar* should whicker *à toute vitesse* into your testicular area, causing the twenty-nine other players on the field to wince and you to double over squealing like a stuck pig, somebody will run onto the field, pour some water down your neck, slap your buttock and say: 'C'mon, son, you'll be grand in a minute.' This at a time when you need a general anaesthetic.)

Anyway it all finished between Suttonians and me one weekend when we played in a triangular tournament alongside the giants of the southside, Lansdowne and Blackrock.

Now most of the team I played with were actually quite good at rugby and had won the Harry Gale Cup (no less) the previous year. This didn't save us from being treated like bumpkins on our venture across the river.

It started with our kits, which were the same colours as Easons' bags, and it went on all afternoon, no matter who we played.

As luck would have it, on this Saturday morning we endured the sniggering of the Lansdowne chaps and beat them on the back pitch – in Lansdowne. This rightly fouled up the tournament.

The plan had been that we would lose to Lansdowne in the morning and then obligingly lose to Blackrock in the afternoon, ensuring a Lansdowne vs Blackrock play-off in Stradbrook the next day. Now, we yoiks would be going to Stradbrook.

The story has a sad end. We met at noon the next day under Clerys' clock. Maybe two of us weren't hungover. The others were pukey or giggly or both. The thought of perhaps beating Blackrock hadn't even kept them in for Saturday night.

Why would it? They didn't hate Blackrock the way normal people do.

They admired them. So we got pushed around Stradbrook for the afternoon and were beaten by a margin in the region of sixty points.

In the second row it felt as if we were going to have our scrawny necks snapped like royal pheasants.

For this, I had given up on a junior B football match with St Vincents? I was deeply ashamed. I never went back. Never told anybody except my spiritual adviser. He quit instantly.

I gave rugby one more chance. Arriving in UCD and not knowing a soul, I put my name down when some jut-jawed, scarf-wearing, acne-free, pinty-type, lady-killing bastard announced that there was to be a class rugby league 'to break the old ice, loike'.

I too would be an icebreaker! I filled out one of the little forms he gave out. I waited. The team sheets went up on the lecture theatre wall. I skipped across like a happy little puppy. No T.J. Humphries listed. My eyes welled up. My heart welled down.

I sought out the jut-jawed, scarf-wearing, acne-free, gout-ridden, Dublin 4, bestiality-is-best-boys, pinty-type, lady-killing bastard and explained my position. 'Shome mishtake shurley,' I said.

His brow furrowed. 'What's your name?' he asked. 'Tom Humphries,' I replied frankly. 'Where'd you go to school?' he asked. 'Fairview,' I said. 'Where's that?' he asked. I should point out that his geographical ignorance was no worse than mine. (I got off the bus at RTÉ on my first day in UCD.)

'Where the park is,' I said helpfully. The park was in the news regularly then for gay-bashing incidents. 'Well, that's it,' he said breezily.

'The teams have all the 'Rock guys together, the 'Nure guys with the Belvo' boys, 'Zaga in with Clongowes, Mero' with 'Knock and and so on. Roight? So sorry, but you lose out, Humpho.'

'Oh,' I said. I'd scarcely understood a word but realised I had come within an ace of being saddled with a dumb rugger nickname all my life. I went forth and never sinned against my class or my people again.

There were other sad days in rugby's spiteful jihad against me.

I lied about rugby to get into sports journalism, pretended I loved it, but soon got found out. I misidentified Brendan Foley as Moss Keane at an old-farts' charity game and didn't work again for three months.

I described King's Hospital, who haven't once won a small inbred provincial competition like the Leinster Senior Cup, as the 'whipping boys' of the event and the switchboards were jammed for a week by people who wanted to twist my testicles and pull my hair.

I was invited to a pre-match dinner for a fixture I was covering involving Lansdowne, but, when I turned up and they realised I wasn't quite what they'd been expecting, I was banished to a broom cupboard and given a hot beef roll.

I know these stories may be very upsetting for some sensitive readers, and perhaps there should have been an appropriate warning at the top of the piece, but I can only hope that any distress caused will serve as a warning to others.

There has been enough hurt already. Stay away from rugby. It is a plague, sent to us, like the potato famine, to undermine the fabric of our society. The depression-era justification for allowing rugby to prosper (i.e. it's the only way most of these oafs will ever get jobs) is no longer sustainable. The sport should be banned and driven underground.

Dark journey

Elias Nhlapo has had the same routine since he came to work at Bobby Locke's apartment building in 1995. He is the watchman, and, when he works, casting his eye over the sleeping complex and its tenants, he has learned to look for certain things. Security has become a problem since Locke died in 1987. The underground parking lot is a worry. Tenants sometimes arrive home drunk and clip their cars on the entrance. Thieves cruise by looking for an opportunity. Tenants forget to lock the gate at the top of the entry stairs, leaving it swinging on its hinges like an invitation.

Yeah, Bobby Locke lived here in his prime, when he was a match for any golfer alive, even Ben Hogan. This neighbourhood Elias now patrols was decidedly upscale then. Locke stayed in a two-bedroom cottage that still sits at the back of the building. The cottage has a heart-shaped swimming pool because his daughter Carolyn loved hearts. 'I have made more than a comfortable living,' Locke wrote in 1953, when in a moment lit by hubris he prefaced his autobiography. 'Frankly today at thirty-five I am glad to say that I am practically independent. One of the solid assets golf has enabled me to acquire is a block of flats in Johannesburg, with my own home adjoining, a home I named Sandwich in honour of my first Open victory.'

The building is old South Africa and was built with tiny rooms on the roof to house fourteen servants. Elias lives up there now and, to reach his room, you must cross the big ridge on the roof. Not many people have the nerve for it. At night, when electrical storms light up Johannesburg, Elias can sit up there and watch the rain hop on the roof. Tonight, though, he is working.

How good was Locke? They still tell stories of his early precocity and his lifelong cussedness. Arthur d'Arcy Locke – or Bobby as his black nanny tagged him – was born in 1917 in Germiston, outside Johannesburg. Grainy footage of him playing golf at the age of six ran in the Empire Exhibition at Wembley, London. By 1957 he had won his fourth British Open title, the final flourish of a career interrupted by World War II and later by a ban from the American circuit. There might have been more glory, much more. His seven tilts at the US Open yielded five top-five finishes.

So how good? Well, he minted the maxim about driving for show and putting for dough. About him Hogan once said, 'Everyone examines greens, but only he knows what he's looking for.'

Until Bruce Keyter defeated him by a stroke in 1955, Locke went twenty years without being beaten over seventy-two holes on South African soil. That took him from the era of the late Sid Brews to the early days of Gary Player.

He was this good. In 1946 a South African financier, Norbert Erleigh, paid Sam Snead to come to South Africa for a series of exhibition matches. Of sixteen, Locke won twelve. Snead two. They halved two. 'Everything he played was a hook,' says Snead today. 'I could beat him from tee to green fifteen times out of eighteen and still lose. He was the greatest putter I have ever seen. He'd hit a twenty-footer and, before the ball got halfway, he'd be tipping his hat to the crowd. He wore out his hats tipping them.'

There's a story the old South African pro Denis Hutchinson tells about the early days. Locke arrived in the US in 1947 and went straight to Augusta to play in the Masters, entering the old cathedral without so much as the genuflection of a practice round. He finished fourteenth and proceeded to North Carolina to play the Carolina's Open Tournament. He won that.

When he arrived for the Houston Open the following week, touring pro Clayton Heafner sniffed opportunity. Locke had what newspapers described as 'the worst swing ever seen' and he looked always as if he were getting set to drive the ball to some point well right of the fairway. Heafner pounced upon the little audience that he had assembled to watch Locke tee off.

'Boy'd better learn how to aim his shots,' said Lloyd Mangrum blithely.

'Well, if you want, we can have a little money ride on it, Lloyd,' said Heafner. 'I say he beats you this week.'

Jimmy Demaret volunteered that he'd like a bit of that, too. Heafner almost overegged the pudding.

'I'll make it interesting for you boys,' said Heafner. 'I'll let you both bet on Hogan against him. How's 'bout that?'

They bit hard on the hook and watched Locke sail the ball way out to the right and then watched as it came back and settled in the centre of the fairway.

Mangrum couldn't accept what he was seeing. He lost $500 that weekend and, by the time the tour got to Cedar Brook Country Club a fortnight later for the Philadelphia Inquirer Open, he was steaming. Locke won the tournament. Heafner took a Cadillac off Mangrum.

That season Demaret was the top earner on the tour, with $27,936. Locke, who popped over for the summer months, was only $3,600 behind. He'd won seven times, finished second twice and third once. Snead, Hogan, Mangrum and the boys brought up the rear.

So great was Locke's celebrity that, when he went to George May's Tam O'Shanter Tournament in Chicago, he received a $5,000 appearance fee, legal in those days. He beat Porky Oliver in a playoff and pocketed $7,000. Resentment festered.

Old Muffin Face, they called him. Also Droopy Chops and Vinegar Puss. He had an ample belly, and he walked with a funereal deliberation that made the world slow to his pace. Locke hove into sight again in 1948 and, although he was not quite as successful, he did win twice and finished second five times. The boys simmered some more.

Locke won his first British Open in 1949 and in the glorious aftermath cancelled his promised participation in a couple of tournaments in the US. That was sufficient excuse for the PGA to take action. George Schneiter, the association's tournament administrator, announced that Locke would no longer be considered a temporary summer visitor and that, given his recent breaches of contract, he was banned for life from all PGA events.

The motivation, thinly concealed, was that 'someone is afraid that Locke will pick up all the marbles,' wrote Arthur Daley in *The New York Times*. 'No other conclusion could be drawn even though [Locke's] personal popularity or lack of it undoubtedly enters into it.'

The ban was lifted early in 1950, but, with typical haughtiness, Locke made his way to the States only on the assurance of another hefty guarantee to appear at the Tam O'Shanter, which he won, beating the still unimpressed Mangrum in a playoff. 'You know, it's funny,' Locke said later. 'There are more horses' asses than there are horses.'

He came back from time to time, but America never had the same pull for him. If he was aware of the growing resentment among his hosts, he didn't show it. After one tournament in Maryland, he came to the podium to collect his cheque and produced his ukulele. To the tune of 'Sioux City Sue' he regaled the crowd with a ditty he called 'Sue Sammy Snead'. Pleased with the response, he performed an encore: 'Please Don't Talk about Me When I'm Gone'.

Elias has just begun his night's work. He does what he always does at the start of his shift – heads upstairs to call on the building's owners, the two ladies in flat 33, Locke's widow, Mary, and their daughter.

They are a curious pair, eighty years old and forty years old, respectively, but virtually of one mind. They have been living up here for twelve, maybe thirteen years, apart from a brief period when Carolyn was married to Elias's friend Mike Paledi.

They'd met at a party. Mike came from about as far on the other side of the tracks as is possible in South Africa. Zone 1, Diepkloof, Soweto, to be precise. Yet something clicked, and about eight months later they moved into the cottage behind the apartments. They had a ceremony in the Sandton Sun hotel in the posh northern suburbs. Not a wedding ceremony proper, because Mike still had obstacles from his first marriage, but enough of a do to make it seem like a wedding. Carolyn did nothing to detract from that impression. 'I never thought I'd marry, until I met this angel,' she told the journalists who showed up, and she wrapped her arms around Mike in a big hug.

The relationship was as brief and troubled as the doubters had predicted. Black guys don't marry white girls, they said. If Bobby were alive, there'd be a shooting.

While Carolyn and Mike occupied the cottage, her mother lived alone upstairs in flat 33, but, as Mike says now, 'It was like the two of them were married. That was what broke us up. The mother, the building, the way they were.' Mike went on his way in 1998.

Elias knocks at flat 33. Announces himself, and a shout comes to let himself in. It's early, but the women are already in bed, preparing to sleep. They could have lived in one of the apartments with two bedrooms or in the cottage which lies vacant out back, but they prefer it up here on the third floor with their two beds in the one bedroom. Elias goes into that room now and speaks to them, cracking jokes and making a fuss over them, just as he's done for the past couple of years. Nothing different tonight.

Mary Elizabeth Fenton had talent. The daughter of a judge, she was raised in Rutland, Vermont and educated at Wellesley. During World War II she served as a research analyst at the Office of Strategic Services. When she met the love of her life, she was working for the Central Vermont Public Services Corporation.

Locke had been married in 1943 to Hester Elizabeth (Lillian) Le Roux, with whom he had a daughter, Dianne, but he struck up a relationship with Mary as soon as he met her at an exhibition match in Burlington, Vermont. He told her to wait for him, and wait she did. Eleven years passed before they married in England in August 1958. The wedding caused a stir back in Johannesburg. Lillian Le Roux had divorced Bobby in 1953 on the grounds of desertion, but two years later the South African newspapers had reported that Locke had married a Sheila Sanford at a Magistrate's Court. Three years after that, with Mary Fenton on his arm, hot denials were issued. Nothing was ever heard of Sheila Sanford again.

In September 1958, Locke brought his bride back to South Africa and installed her in the cottage behind his apartments on Harley Street, in a section of Johannesburg known as Yeoville. Yeoville had a leafy swankiness to it back then, and it adjoined Hillbrow, where all the best parties were held. Briefly the Lockes enjoyed busy, glamour-soaked lives, hopping between continents. Money was easy, and nothing was hard.

Two years later, though, two events in the same week changed their lives. Carolyn was born on 16 February 1960. Three days later, Locke was nearly killed in an automobile crash. He was riding in a car driven by Morris Bodmer, the pro from Clovelly Country Club, after a day's golf. They came to a level crossing and waited for a train to pass before edging over the tracks. However, the train that had just passed obscured their view of the other direction, and their car was rammed by the 8:53 from Southfield. The vehicle was flung backward thirty yards down a bank, and Locke was tossed through the back window.

It was a couple of days before he came to, and a month before he could open his left eye. His head ached, he had double vision and he suffered from pain in both legs. Those ailments would keep him company forever. He had a list of prescribed medications longer than his arm and orders not to touch another beer. The second half of his life was beginning.

Outside and inside, the apartment building has changed over the years. After Locke's death, Carolyn got permission from the city to rename it. She held a bright little ceremony and christened it Bobby Locke Place. That was in 1988.

Yeoville and Hillbrow went downhill quickly. In the late '90s Mary and Carolyn's flat was broken into three times by men with guns. Almost weekly Mary would call Raal Nordin, the building manager, to tell him that she was frightened and depressed.

'Don't be silly,' he would say, 'the area is gone black, the country is black. What's wrong with that? We've got to live with it, make the most of it. It's a black country. What's so depressing?'

'Yes, Raal, you're right. We have to get our minds changed.'

Across the street a little shack appeared, grey-painted and low-slung, and people with no jobs came there to drink coffee and make calls on the public phone. Yeoville was suddenly full of people with no jobs. Full of Nigerians fleeing their own hell, full of South Africans living in theirs. First the problem was squatters, and then the squatters drove down the rents and the businesses left and the rents were so low that most landlords got out. Now people wander the streets all day, and at night nobody goes out because the crime rate is so high.

Raal and Mary had cat-and-dog fights about the tenants. Mary paid for a lift and a new boiler for the building. It cost her huge chunks of money, but the place was still in decline. She didn't want to spend any more. She didn't trust the tenants, even blamed them for wear and tear. Raal thought that a bit more money spent here and there would improve the place. He thought Mary and Carolyn should stop worrying and move to the suburbs.

'Look,' he would say, 'we can rent the cottage for you, and flat 33 and the one-room flat you store things in on the bottom floor. You'd get 4,500 rand [$563] a month. You can get a nice place out in Sandton for 3,000 rand a month.' And they would shake their heads and tell him that they could never leave. This was Daddy's place.

When Locke came to after the accident, he had suffered severe memory loss. He wasn't well and never would be again, but for Mary he had become root and sap. For Carolyn he was simply Daddy. Perhaps now he would have more time for them. Perhaps.

The medication exacted a price. Locke was a sociable man. He enjoyed his beer too much to obey doctors' orders, but now one beer hit him the way half a dozen might another man. Friends recall birthday parties that Mary planned for him, and he would turn up late and drunk. 'Never a thank you for her,' says Lorraine Korsen, an old friend.

Beer fertilised a mean side of his character. One night he drove

Mary to Parkview several miles away, dropped her there and let her walk home. He resented her having friends of her own or a life outside the cottage. In the '60s a group of American ex-patriots used to meet in the President Hotel in Johannesburg to talk about home. Mary, who missed Vermont, loved those meetings. Bobby grew resentful, so Mary stayed home.

With the drinking, his manners became diluted. Mary and Carolyn were often called to golf clubs to take old Bobby home. Outside he was a character. At home he was a nightmare.

'Mary was a saint,' says Korsen. 'She saw to everything. She saw to it that he had his tablets. She would drive him everywhere, fetch him from anywhere. She got a rotten deal.'

What had Mary Locke to live with? Some incidents from the life of Bobby Locke:

In May 1969 Bobby was arrested for drunken driving. The driver of the other car, a J.D. Van der Merwe, testified that he couldn't understand a word Locke said. Locke refused to let the police push his car from the road. He jumped in and attempted to drive it, but the back wheels were stuck. The police pushed the vehicle away with the old pro still inside it.

In 1985 in Southbroom, Natal, Locke was playing a four-ball with John Cockayne, a club pro. Early on, Locke felt that Cockayne was standing too close behind when he swung on the tee. By the third hole he started shouting at Cockayne. Finally, on the seventeenth, as Cockayne was addressing his ball, Locke stood right behind him and refused to move. Walking down the fairway, he hit Cockayne on the elbow with his club handle. In reply Cockayne swung his driver, hitting Locke three times on the back and shoulder.

Then there was the Big Boy Ndlovu business. The year was 1978. The apartment building needed a fresh coat of paint. Big Boy Ndlovu was contracted to do the job. When he had finished, there was a slight disagreement over the quality of the work. Ndlovu demanded 220 rand for his labours. Locke refused to pay. When the case came to court, Ndlovu testified, 'I walked away from him, and as I started down the stairs, I heard a gunshot. I felt a pain in my right shoulder and saw a little hole there.'

Locke testified, 'I thought there was going to be a drama. I returned to my cottage and fetched my gun. He was about to turn when I fired a shot. He was obviously coming back to make a contest.'

Why had Bobby fetched his gun?

'I am a golf professional and didn't want to damage my hands.'

Even in the old South Africa, the court had difficulty not seeing Ndlovu's wound. Locke was found guilty of attempted murder. He was fined 120 rand and had his gun licence suspended for six months.

Bobby Locke Place is a pretty building, three storeys tall, shaded by palm trees. Tracy Korsen, Lorraine's daughter, has a photo that she took in the cottage. Carolyn and her friend Jill Reeves are on a sofa. Both are young and beautiful. Their faces advertise the fact that they've just had a good night out. They are lying back, slumped, carefree and happy.

They could be wild, Carolyn and Jill. One blonde, one brunette. Crazy when they were together. But a few years ago Jill hired a car and drove out into the depths of Kruger National Park. She turned off the engine and took a massive overdose. 'That hit Carolyn hard,' Tracy says.

'You know that song,' says Nordin, '"Life Is a Rollercoaster" by Ronan Keating? Well, Carolyn loved that. I think of her whenever I hear it.'

'We called her K.C.,' says Jules Gordon of Carolyn, with whom he played in a band, Image, for more than 20 years – she on keyboards, he on vocals. They practised every Tuesday in the cottage. 'She would say to us, "Guys, this band is my life. What would I do without you?"'

It was the other way around, really. K.C. did the musical arrangements, schlepped the gear, kept the group going. Even later, in her roller-coaster years.

Elias asks Mary and Carolyn if they would like him to call back during the night or early in the morning. He can slip them fresh hot-water bottles and check to see if everything is OK. In the long nights of the South African winter, he did that often.

'No thanks, Elias,' they say, 'not tonight. Good night, Elias.'

Later, though, shortly after eight, Carolyn hollers for Elias. The women have a couple of lightbulbs that need changing, one in the dining room, one in the bedroom. Elias sets about his business, and Carolyn is fussing now, asking Elias if he still has the list of phone numbers she'd given him three months before.

'Yes, I have the numbers.'

'Are you sure?'

'Yes, I am sure.'

'Should I write them again? Just in case?'

'No.'

It is past nine when he is done.

'Can I switch off the kitchen light for you, Carolyn?'

'No. Don't switch it off. I need something to eat.'

'OK. Good-night, Carolyn.'

'Good-night, Elias.'

And that was it. For the rest of the night Elias stayed away from flat 33 and didn't think of its occupants again until the next morning when Miriam Magorosi, the maid, told him that she couldn't get into the apartment with her keys.

It was Monday morning, 24 September. Elias took the keys from

Miriam and strode upstairs. Tsk, tsk! Women! He would show her how to open a door.

In the cottage there is a room that the band used to call the post office. It was filled with junk and memorabilia. In 1993 Carolyn went to England, to Christie's, and auctioned off most of her father's trophies to see herself and her mother through a lean period. The four British Open medals alone fetched £82,800. The auction took in £178,089 in all. Still, though, the place was filled with memories and mementos that couldn't be discarded. There was a picture of Mary, Carolyn and Bobby coming down the steps of an old De Havilland airplane some time in the mid-'60s. They looked like royalty. Two pretty faces and old Bobby's solemn chops.

There were other pictures, too. Mary's eyes gaze out of a Polaroid, through a puffery of bruises and discoloration. Her jumper has blood on it. Bobby's fists had done that. She is an old woman in the picture, and she looks totally defeated. She asked Carolyn to take photographs of her when she still had anger left in her. 'She allowed abuse,' says Tracy Korsen.

'But Tracy,' says her mother, 'what could she do, who could she tell? Only me. He couldn't think straight. He wasn't rational anymore.'

Bobby Locke died of meningitis. His friends, those few who knew about the raging confusion of his final years, are reluctant to talk about his failings. 'I loved them all,' says Janette Makin, a friend of the family for almost fity years. 'I'd like to leave it like that.'

'I try to remember the good,' Lorraine Korsen says.

Really, it was the tidiest of endings. Mary and Carolyn picked up the four corners of their lives, folded them quietly in over their heads and evacuated this world. No fuss. Days before, Charlie, the snappy spaniel, had been taken to the vet with arrangements for his demise. Sylvia Sampson, the administrator of the women's estate, received a visit. They even went to the undertakers, spun a yarn about being afraid for their lives and picked out a psalm, 'Abide with Me'. Black farewell notes from two failed landladies.

They had their hair done and had a last lunch at Bennigan's. They took a call from Makin, during which they gave no hint of their plan. In all likelihood, after Elias left flat 33, nobody thought about Mary and Carolyn again till morning when Elias came to jiggle the key in the lock.

'I failed,' he says. 'The lock had been changed. I remembered the paper from three months before, all those numbers, and I started shaking. I knew their cars were still there. Where could they have gone? I ran to the police station. I ran. They came after an hour. They said they couldn't break the door. It would be like a burglary. I said I could break it while they were here watching me. They said yes.'

So Elias broke the door. Mary and Carolyn were in bed, holding each other's hands. Their faces were blackened from the drugs they'd taken. They had drunk half a bottle of champagne to wash down the sleeping pills they'd been hoarding for months. The last CD recorded by Carolyn's band was on the bed. One of Mary's eyes was open, fixed into a stare at her daughter. The police told Elias to fetch an ambulance to certify the deaths.

Four months later, on a sunny Monday morning in January, Elias still can't speak about their deaths without the shock registering in his voice. He has questions. Everyone has questions. Who influenced whom the most in those last months? What signs did everyone miss? Why such desperation when their estate reveals they were solvent?

Bobby was buried near his father in Westpark. In accordance with their wishes, Mary was interred in a different section of the same cemetery and Carolyn was cremated, her ashes scattered over her mother's grave.

All that survives is a broken link. Dianne, born to Bobby and his first wife, Lillian, teaches in a private school in Johannesburg. Tracked down, she is regretful. Too many years and too much distance. It wouldn't be appropriate to comment on such sadness, she says politely.

In the basement of Bobby Locke Place, Mary and Carolyn's cars are still parked side by side. Soon the bank will take them away in discharge of an old overdraft. And that will be that.

This self-inflicted wound will fester

14 April 2001

The most depressing aspect of the past seven days has been the reversion to peasant sleeveenism of those old accomplices, Fianna Fáil and the GAA. Like a pair of native rogues codding the Anglo folk in an episode from Somerville and Ross, they have made us endure the hammy lines of a pair of clumsy chancers.

When it was announced at GAA Congress in the Burlington last Friday night that the government had given £60 million to the GAA in order to take a few games away from Croke Park, that was all the signalling that was needed. The following day, forty-three delegates abstained on the biggest motion of the weekend. One leading exclusionist stood up and said quietly that not wanting to embarrass the government was a good reason to vote No. Three past presidents of the association spoke against the Roscommon motion. Peter Quinn, the past president who had first floated the possibility of Croke Park's expanded usage, spoke not at all. A probable future president left the hall on personal business as the vote was about to be taken.

They added a touch of Florida politics and a dash of Tammany Hall. The decision was made by a show of hands, a recount was asked for, a recount was denied. The trustees who counted the votes are evidently unimpeachable. Yet, when the presidential election comes around next year, independent auditors will be used to count the votes. So almost everyone went away whistling. The government announced that it was 'disappointed' the GAA wasn't offering a home to the very sports the government is so keen to offer a home to. The GAA announced that, well heck, it was close, and expressed bafflement at all the fuss. Both sides knew the vote had given Bertie Ahern a year with which to have his colossal vanity project set into contractual concrete. By midweek the heat hadn't quite gone away. Ahern, in best Flurry Knox mode, was telling people that, having failed to interest the GAA in the thin end of what they perceived to be a wedge, his main concern all along had been getting them to consume the whole wedge and share not just Croke Park but all their grounds. This is an insult to the intelligence of taxpayers.

Ahern knows that this will never happen (local GAA facilities have not just been built on sweat and blood and tears, but are overused as they stand), but it is a nice stick with which to muddy the waters.

In reality, Ahern, who made his grant to the FAI conditional on them abandoning Eircom Park and made his grant to the GAA conditional on them bringing fixtures to the Bertie Bowl, didn't attach any other conditions because he didn't want to. It would have been wrong to coerce the GAA into ground-sharing, but there were ways of leaving them to their own devices. He could have pushed the GAA a certain way by asking that, in all propriety, the announcement of the £60 million be delayed till after the vote. Instead, he gave a nod and a wink to the backwoodsmen. We need only examine the case of the Dublin vote to be assured that the Taoiseach got his way. The Dublin County Board had a meeting on the Monday night before Congress. The use to which Croke Park was to be put didn't figure largely in the discussions, but a board member raised it briefly late in the night. Some of the problems inherent with the motion were immediately evident when Finbarr Donovan, a Corkman attached to St Brigid's club, raised the matter. Donovan was surprised to find that one of the main voices suggesting the thin-end-of-the-wedge scenario was coming from a club colleague of his. It wasn't exactly brother against brother, but still...

Most of the speakers had questions about the financial implications of renting out Croke Park. It became clear a large majority of Dublin clubs were in favour of transforming Croke Park from a drain on vital resources into an asset.

It was agreed informally that the eleven Dublin delegates would support the Roscommon motion.

Most of the Dublin delegates met again on Tuesday, the following night, and in a run through the motions once again agreed to support the Roscommon motion.

That was how matters rested until Friday night at the Burlington, when the GAA announced that it had struck a gusher.

The following morning, the nature of the Dublin vote had changed radically. From being 11-0 in favour, the vote had become 7-4 in favour – a swing of eight votes. Con Roche, Sean O'Mahoney, Noel Murphy and an under-21 delegate from the Erin's Isle club all voted No.

There were cracks in the Limerick and Galway delegations also. The top table spent the longest time totting up the votes and, while the addition was being done, the feeling went around the hall that this was going to be one of those absurd, Kafkaesque GAA moments. So it proved.

In the aftermath, the peculiarly cackhanded opportunism exhibited by the Progressive Democrats missed the point as it conveniently rode the wave of festering resentments which the GAA decision stirred up. The junior government party continued to keep quiet about the proposed £1 billion being expended on the Bertie Bowl, despite complaints from the Department of Finance that the manner in which the Cabinet had approved the project had been a breach of procedures. As it stands, it is virtually impossible to get an accurate figure on the costing of one of the biggest capital projects ever undertaken by the State, let alone a decent rationale for proceeding with it.

A government presided over by a man who once boasted happily of his abilities to consume a gallon of Bass without impairment now speaks out of the corner of its mouth about drink culture in this country and the possibility of removing drinks sponsorship from sporting events. A billion pounds would build a lot of leisure centres in a lot of towns as an alternative to drink culture. A billion pounds, if spent wisely, could actually inject some life into that jaded catchphrase 'sport for all'.

That's the government's business, though, and, even if the PDs did pile in for the kicking, what happened at GAA Congress last weekend was almost unique among the litany of self-inflicted wounds which the association has administered to itself in the last decade or so. For once the GAA had arrived at a junction when the interests of the association precisely met those of the society it exists in. It was a time for graciousness and pragmatism. Both were spurned.

Instead, the decision taken grows more absurd the more it is examined. If the government is convinced (rightly) that it would be wrong to coerce an amateur body like the GAA into opening up its ground to rival professional sports, but is at the same time disappointed that it declines to do so, why dangle a £60 million solution on the eve of Congress? Why add to the costs of the great white elephant of Abbotstown by purchasing events with which to fill the thing? Those who study the economics of stadiums have long since noted that as businesses they are only productive when they make sports an export industry; i.e., if they attract outsiders, or if they prompt the sale of new rights in terms of broadcasting and merchandising. Stadium Ireland so precisely lacks what a major stadium needs for viability that it seems like a criminal misuse of funds.

Most of what will be spent in Stadium Ireland, on the rare occasions when it is full, is money which would have been spent anyway. Just less of it. The profit derived from GAA games played there will inevitably trickle down into the pockets of the government's private-sector partners in the business, rather than into the clubs and schools which built the GAA. Bertie Ahern should go and take a look at Toronto's ailing Skydome facility before he goes any further. In a city of 3.5 million people, with a professional baseball franchise which plays eighty-one Major League home games a year and with a serious Olympic bid behind them and a serious Olympic bid ahead of them, Toronto's twelve-year-old dome is a disaster.

The cost overruns which are inevitable with such a project led to the dome costing $600 million instead of the planned $150 million. After five years, private interests had to bail the government out.

So take a look at Toronto, or take a look even at the model for Abbotstown, Homebush Bay in Sydney. A suburban ghost town, struggling for viability.

Virtually none of the reliable revenue generators which a major stadium should have are present in Stadium Ireland. There are insufficient events there to attract big deals from food, beverage and merchandising concessions or car-parking operations. The infrastructure for Abbotstown in terms of the road network is disastrous. Imagine regular Wednesday evening traffic on the M50 with another 14,000 cars (the government estimate) added in heading to a soccer international. The facility merely replicates another one several miles away and brings nothing new in terms of franchise teams, historic resonance or a niche capacity.

Nor will the Bertie Bowl contribute an iota to urban development. Stadiums work best when set centrally in a pedestrian-friendly environment near restaurants, bars, hotels, parks, shops, etc. Visitors and fans spend more money, bring more life, and have a better quality of experience. The only modern rationale for the remote location of stadiums is to maximise parking and concession revenues. The Bertie Bowl doesn't have a fixture list strong enough for that. Ideally, Croke Park should be open for business now, and realistically such business would be minimal. Most international rugby games would fit into a 50,000-seat stadium if the government had a mind to build one. Ditto almost all Irish soccer fixtures. At most, Croke Park would be asked – at its convenience and usually out of season – to hold three or four extra fixtures a year. It would still have its £60 million. It would have cauterised a cash haemorrhage and turned it into a money-maker.

For this it would reap goodwill and positive exposure. Last week's decision brought opprobrium, division, a loss of income and credibility and, one assumes, a slew of questions from box holders bemused to see the GAA agreeing to strip fixtures out of Croke Park. Last weekend was a chance lost amidst a welter of embarrassing cutery and poor leadership. All week it has been easier to get Beverley Cooper-Flynn to see the funny side of lawyer jokes than it has been to get a figure of any weight in the GAA to come to the telephone. The GAA should expect more of itself, even if nobody else does. As for the man they went so willingly into cahoots with? Well, the populace may hiss, but when Bertie contemplates his Bowl, well, Bertie applauds himself.

No secret, love is at the heart of it

22 September 2001

There is no beginning.

At his ease, Sean Boylan walks you through his world. His little daughter, Doireann, tags after him while the sun makes his hair silver in the morning. Here he stores the herbs. And he pauses for a story. Here he dries the herbs. Another story. No, two. Here, well hold on till I tell you...

No beginning. His people have been here since 1798 practising this serene trade and before that they were in Tara doing the same thing. His life is a great ganglion of people and stories, each strand connected through Sean to something else, someone else.

His head is a cavernous store of unlikely links and odd anecdotes which he gathers together under the general heading 'Comical Scenes'. As in, I'll tell ya it was a comical scene there for a while.

Everest? When the lads went in 1993, Sean Boylan gave them a herb to make their tea with. It helped them cope with the altitude. 'Gas thing,' he says, 'a Vincentian priest brought me father the original plant from the Himalayas all the way to Dunboyne back in the '30s.'

The national struggle? His Father, General Sean Boylan, was

interned in Frongoch for six weeks longer than anyone else and was up for execution next in the queue behind Ceannt before John Dillon made his speech to parliament. Once, long ago in the 1960s, an interviewer called to Sean to talk about the herbs. Sean inquired where he was coming from. The man was on his way from Roscommon.

'I was doing a little piece on an old by-election down there.'

'Ah,' says Sean, 'North Roscommon 1917.'

'Yes,' says the man, 'how did you know that?'

'Sinn Féin's first seat,' said Sean. 'My father was the election agent.'

'I don't believe you.'

'Well, I'll tell you this then. Joe McGuinness (the original prisoner candidate 'put him in to get him out') was replaced by a man called Martin Conlon. His wife Peig was my godmother.'

'I don't believe you.'

And the interviewer walked the earth for a long time afterwards telling people that Sean Boylan was the most monosyllabic man he'd ever met.

'He didn't believe me,' says Sean now settling over his cup of tea. 'What did he expect? Aw, a comical scene.'

He is wantonly open to the wonder of the world around him. Famously, he is late for everything, reluctant to cut himself off from one experience to hurry himself to another. People and their stories always matter more than timetables and in Sean Boylan people and their stories converge like strands of a magic-realist novel.

His parents, to whose care he devoted much of the middle part of his life, are fondly remembered in many of the stories he tells. Which brings us to the eternal mystery of Sean Boylan. How can a man who drags around the epithet 'genial' like it were his birthmark – how can a manager with so little swash to his buckle turn out teams so backboned by steel. There is a toughness to Meath football and to Meath teams which doesn't merely spring from the character of the players, it is transfused into their blood.

Once, years ago, he recalls heading up to Armagh to Paddy Quinn's house. For a man fascinated by politics it was like an anthropologist's heaven up there. In the one family you had IRA, Sinn Féin, civil rights, People's Democracy, Republican Fianna Fáil. Everything.

'Halfway through the night,' he says casually, 'I knew I had pneumonia. I ended up in the Mater the next day. When I was in hospital I went unconscious and while I was out one of the radiators broke in the house here in Dunboyne and a fella arrived from the Veha factory to look after it. He knocked. And he said, "Is this General Sean Boylan's house?" Now my father never used the title in his life but he said, "It is."

"I'll tell you a great story," the man said, "remember we were picked up in Swords and we went on to Dunboyne and there were four Boylans to be taken away. The English army captain apologised to Mrs Boylan for having to take her four sons. Her answer was that she was only sorry she didn't have four more to worry him with."'

There were two people in Dunboyne village at the time not ashamed to be associated with the Boylans. Louis Magee's (the Irish triple-crown player) wife and Mrs Yeats, the great grandmother of Tina Yeats, whom Sean married. Funny thing about the Veha man's story. Sean's father died some time later and General Costello told the same story again on the night of the wake.

You stay with Sean when he is telling you a yarn because some other thought will crop up in his teeming brain and urgently campaign to be aired. Obligingly, he will loop back for it before picking up his original thread again.

All those years tending his father and then his mother should have

withered him. There's too much zest in him, though. As a young fella
he had his beloved hurling. Even in Belvedere College as a kid he'd
drag his hurl everywhere with him.

He had the dreams too. As a ten-year-old, he watched Meath win
the 1954 All Ireland and that was it. He wanted to wear the green
jersey. He wore it on hurling fields for over twenty years, dabbling in
football. Friends told him he was crazy. Good football teams were
being put together, trips to Australia could be had. Never cost him a
thought.

And he went out every night. His wife Tina says that Sean's
mother taught herself and every one of her friends how to drink and
smoke, but Sean himself was playing truant that week. Neither vice
interested him, yet he knew every club in Dublin. He'd leave the
house in Dunboyne close to pub closing time and be gone for hours
on end.

Then he drops a little surprise in.

Of course, there was the go-karting, too.

'What?'

Amidst all this serenity and intuition, there is an unquenchable
love for the roar of motor racing. He used go to hurling matches with
his go-kart strapped to the back of the car. He went on fire once in
Mondello, raced in Monasterboice, Askeaton, all the Irish road
circuits, internationally even.

And at night they'd boot around Dunboyne. One rule only, stick
to the left. Blessed that they weren't killed, he thinks. Blessed. Jim
Collier was the local guard and he had it bad too. He'd arrange for a
squad car to give the lads the lights on the road. And away they'd go
roaring between the hedgerows.

When Sean was a kid they had motorbike racing in Dunboyne.
Brian Naylor, who still holds the lap record, would leave his car in
the Boylan's garage and, while he practised and raced, the kids of

Dunboyne sampled the springs in his Maserati. Whatever was in that Maserati rubbed off.

Some of it anyway. Once, Sean went to Monte Carlo and left after the practice sessions, missing the race altogether. He had to get back home because Carnaross were opening their pitch and Meath were playing a challenge there. The lads denounced him as mad. Certifiably so.

But that's his life. Sample the flavour of everything. For a man whose family have lived in the one spot for over 200 years, he is remarkably open to new ideas. The variety and volume of ideas he has brought to the business of training the Meath team since 1982 are legendary. He says that much of it is intuition, an abstract which he relies upon faithfully.

'Sometimes, I'll look at the lads and I'll know what I planned for them is all wrong. I'll just tear it up in my head and start again.'

Another story. Some years ago he was seeing a woman. As life wore on after the deaths of his parents, he was conscious of the pure loneliness of having nobody to tell his day to in the evenings. He recalls the first Christmas Eve night after both his parents were gone, coming home, turning on a record. 'I cried like a child, but I was happy at home.'

Yet, some part of him was always resistant to company. 'As the fella says, I'd be only going steady when I'd have to break up.' But there was this woman, a lovely girl and he'd seen her a few times, and on Christmas Eve she called to the house and left in a present for him. A videotape. *Dead Poets Society*. It was a good and thoughtful gift, but Sean looked at it, knew the effect it would have on him and knew he wouldn't be able to watch it for months. He knew too that he couldn't see the woman anymore. Just knew it wasn't right for him.

Tina Yeats was home from the convent that year. Tina had come to the Boylans as a kid looking for summer work and, right through school, herself and seven friends whom Sean's family fondly nicknamed 'the choir' worked amid the herbs and the pleasant smells.

This Christmas, Sean ran into Tina's parents as they were going down to Caffrey's in Batterstown. They asked him to call down. He said he was going to town and he'd call in later. Duly he did and they had the chat and afterwards Tina, still a Daughter of Charity, came home to Dunboyne in his car. Nothing unusual there. Sean was twenty years older, but comfortable in the company of priests and nuns. They talked. They said goodbye.

That was Christmas. Tina left the convent in March. That August, Sean had two social engagements and invited Tina along. That night, he'd just asked her to marry him when the doorbell rang. It was two weeks before they got back to the subject.

By Christmas they were married, had the reception in a marquee on the worst night ever sent. Lights went, comical scene. Sure enough, when he watched *Dead Poets Society*, it had an over-whelming effect on him: the poetry, the loyalty, the very idea of people affecting people so powerfully.

This intuition… He told the team a long story before the third Westmeath game this summer about being abroad once years ago and feeling that the driver they had given him to get him to the airport on time was going to crash. Sure enough. This led him to his thoughts on the importance of being ready, stressing unusually the importance of being ready to play with fourteen men.

Afterwards, looking back on the match and the sending-off of Hank Traynor, some of the players remarked on this to Brian Smyth, who works with Sean almost as an interpreter for the benefit of players with questions, complaints, troubles, worries, etc.

Brian told them that the previous week he had been travelling with Sean to Gormanstown in the jeep, when suddenly, on a clear stretch of perfectly normal road, he saw Sean press his thumb to the windscreen. There were no loose stones on the road yet a half minute later a stone smashed against the windscreen!

Brian Smyth turned to his friend and asked why he'd placed his thumb on the screen. Sean said he just felt it would happen.

Once, he went to London to see a man in Westminster Hospital. The man's family asked him to go. Their son was dying of cancer, they said. They met Sean there and took him aside. 'Listen,' they said, 'he hasn't cancer, he has Aids.'

He remembers it was a Bank Holiday Monday and Tina and himself had just become engaged. He went into the ward. The man was in bed. Six stone gone off him in two months and a stare that told Sean that he didn't want him there.

Sean was easy with that. The man was a gifted musician and only for the intervention of his illness would at that time have been beginning life as the soloist for a major European orchestra. So he just stared at Sean balefully for fifteen, twenty minutes.

Meanwhile, Sean talked to the man's brother. The Chelsea Physic Gardens were down the road and Sean talked about them. 'It was like having to brag a little bit to let the man in the bed know I had something, some knowledge.'

The man had a racking cough. Finally, Sean asked if he'd mind if Sean placed his hand on his back. Another five, six, seven minutes passed. The man turned over. Sean placed his hand there. Fluid on the wall of the lung. Instantly, the man settled. He let out a big yawn and settled.

Sean rose to leave and, in the corridor, he met the man's parents. There was sugar coating it. He's going to die, but he's at peace, he said, now we're going down to the Abbey.

And off he went looking for Tina.

'I found her outside. She was talking to this old woman who was sitting on the wall. Tina introduced her as Bridie. This was a woman from Derry who had been in an enclosed order and left. She never went home again for the shame of it. She slept in doorways for twenty-three years afterwards and Tina had helped her when she was a nun in London. She'd give her breakfast and tea. She and Tina were standing there having a smoke.'

Bridie was talking about Mother Teresa and Cardinal Hume. Sean was enthralled. Finally, when they said goodbye, it was time to turn back towards the hospital. Sean spoke to Tina about Bridie, the wonder of her being asked to build a hospital by Cardinal Hume. And Tina said, 'Sure that's all in her dreams.'

'And you said nothing?'

'Sure isn't she happy?'

'I'll never forget that. This man upstairs who had everything and this poor woman below sitting in the doorway. Some lesson.'

That's the life which informs his football. The joke used to be that if he stuck around long enough the Meath team would make a manager of him. He made winners of them though and produced teams of such character that they define our whole view of the county they spring from.

Small beginnings. An O'Byrne Cup. The Centenary Cup. He remembers 1986 losing a league quarterfinal to Dublin by a point. Beforehand, Brian Mullins jokingly placed an arm around his shoulder and said, 'Sean, you'll win the league and we'll win Leinster.' Sean knew that day, in his blood he knew, that it would be the other way around.

Tomorrow, he goes looking for his fifth All Ireland as a manager. Dublin have won just two during his tenure.

He has learned lots, he says. Even about drink. 'There's an affinity between men who go out and have a drink together that people like me will never be part of,' he says. 'I used to talk to lads in the pub and they'd be complaining about something and I'd go away and get it fixed and I'd meet them again and say, "Hey, I got that fixed up" and they'd say "What?", looking at me as if I had ten heads. It was just talk, their chance to get things off their own chest. I was intruding.'

And it's not all moments from the Desiderata either. He is tough and resilient. He remembers on an All-Star tour in 1988 Kieran Duff of Dublin passing his table with a pint in his hand and nodding towards the stage of a pub in Boston. 'There's only one man can save that fella from himself,' said Duff, 'and that's you.'

Whooping it up on stage at that moment was one of the best footballers in the country. Jinksy! David Beggy. Meath were due to play Dublin in a National League replay two weeks later. Beggy was enjoying himself. It was 4.15 in the morning. People always said to Sean not to be so horrid hard on Jinksy, but now Sean said nothing. Not till they got to San Francisco late in the trip.

'You love the music, Dave,' said Boylan in a quiet moment.

'Yeah, I love the music and I love the oul' showing off,' said Jinksy, walking towards the propellors.

'What must it be like to play music in front of 20,000 or so people?' mused Sean. 'Imagine that feeling.'

'Must be amazing,' agreed Jinksy.

'Is it like that playing football in front of that many people, Dave?' asked Boylan.

'It is a bit, Sean, yeah,' said Jinksy, still walking.

'And do you think that you'll ever play in front of that big a crowd again?'

Silence. 'Oh lord Jesus,' Jinksy said.

End of story. And never another word.

Or take the spring of this year. Dublin played Meath in a

challenge in Santry on a foggy Saturday morning. Two teams putting the foot-and-mouth lay-off behind them. Some things can't be put behind anyone though and Vinny Murphy's brawn was soon the lingua franca of the game. Trevor Giles suffered a few heavy blows and the game was getting out of hand.

Suddenly and incredibly for the Dubs, who had never seen this before, Sean Boylan exploded. Popped like a geyser. Over the line, on the field, straight towards Murphy. They had to rush to hold him back.

'Yeah,' he says now. 'I felt that it was over the top. I lost the head completely. Nothing personal. If it was our own lads playing on their own, I would have lost it in the same way. We were both feeling our way back. It was not the place. Crazy scene. I apologised to the lads myself. We'd all gone so long without football. It was all pent up.'

You look for the key to the genius of Sean Boylan and perhaps it's his humility. Famously, a few years ago, a new Dublin coach told his team that he would be all things to all men. There would be no special coach, no dietician, no team facilitator, 'And if you have problems upstairs, I'm a bit of a headman too.'

Boylan surrounds himself with the best. His friend and confidant Denis Murtagh is a first line of defence. He has time for a quick Denis Murtagh yarn.

The 1999 final. Sean came up out of the tunnel, took the jumper off, threw it on the bench and it started.

'Go way, ya bollix.'

The Meath bench was in front of the Cork fans. One beauty.

Out on the field Sean went, out to talk to the lads. Comes back and the abuse is burning his ears. The only break is for the National Anthem and even at that Bigmouth can't wait for the finish.

The match is on. Phillip Clifford puts a ball over the sideline near Sean, who grabs the ball and throws it to Cormac Murphy. Apoplexy behind. So Denis Murtagh says to James Reilly, who was involved at the time, 'Next time your man starts at Sean, I want you to turn around and say this to him.' And James says, 'I couldn't possibly say that.' Denis says, 'Just say it.'

Seconds later, the abuse starts. James turns around. 'You! Shut your f***ing mouth.'

'Go way you, ya baldy c***,' says the man in the stand. And for the rest of the match he abused James Reilly.

He has two selectors, Eamon O'Brien and Colm Coyle. Then there is Brian Smyth, a sort of facilitator for team meetings, a confidant for players and manager alike, a buffer in times when people get tired of hearing the one voice.

And Denis Smyth, who tackles the logistics, from tickets to hotels. And Eoin Lynch would spend half an hour every evening making sure balls are right, gear is right. Pat Kelly looks after transport. Eoin Clarke and Michelle Lyons, the physios. Dorothy and Karen, the masseuses. All there performing labours of love.

Love is at the heart of it, the secret of keeping on, keeping on.

Last year, after they lost early in the summer, Sean was driving to the Chinese in Navan with Mochie Regan and his wife Susan, and with Tina. They were passing Dealgan Park and Tina caught Sean's wistful glance. She says: 'Do you want to go in and drive around Sean? You can get help for this, you know, for these withdrawal symptoms.'

And they laughed at the truth of it. A comical scene.

'It seems crazy. There are nights when snow might be coming down or sheets of rain or whatever and you'd wonder about it all, but I'd always be glad when I got there that I had gone. I'd get something out of it always.'

And there is no end.

Just for the record, Quinny's got something to celebrate today

---

6 October 2001

There is no book. There is no instructive text drawn from his thoughts. There is no literary finger which has been traced over his life. No anthology of the anecdotes. No album of bons mots. No record of the days.

Life of Quinny, it remains to be written. Here he is, delivering his twilight sonata, and we have no libretto.

'I'd have to tell too many lies,' he says with a grin.

There should be a book though. The *Disco Pants Years*. And it should be the primer for every kid who ever puts pen to paper at a big soccer club. Oh Lucky Man! Why? Well, in this bespoke world of swaddled millionaires where you are judged by the size of your wad and the cut of your pout, they should all be reading Quinny. Blessed in a football nation where young lads can nurse a grievance against the whole world for victimising them with money, success and fulfilment, there should be a book. *I've Been in Fortune's Kitchen and I've Licked Out All the Pots*.

'How's it goin', Niall?'

'Great,' he grins, 'very well indeed.'

He walks into a room and his smile hangs the sun above every-one. He's thirty-five today. Thirty-Bloody-Five! A man still leading the boy's dream life.

Unimaginable.

He's thirty-five today and, because dreams have always crystallised for him, he allowed himself this dream two years ago when he saw the fixture list: On the day he was thirty-five he might be playing in this fixture at Landsowne Road with the World Cup a possibility and with the chance to get the all-time Irish goal-scoring record for himself.

What a way to pass the half-way mark in your three score years and ten. That was the dream.

And here he is, fitter than he has felt in years, and the table is spread before him. Blow out the candles, ripple the net, accept the love. Just another perfect day strung onto a necklace of them.

You look at him in wonder. How come he's still here? This great lank whom we all went to see at Highbury in the bad old emigration days of the '80s. Never mind where he picked up all the skill and all the character, how has his unlikely body survived?

His knees were betraying him a few years ago. His back has a long-running industrial action against him.

Well, thank you for asking. His knees are obedient. His back feels good. As he told an audience recently, his back is behind him.

'I never gave the back a chance,' he says apologetically. 'Never took six weeks off or did the things that normal players did. Sunderland were always playing big games and I was saying, well, I mightn't be around to play another one of these next year. With Ireland I was trying to make the bigger games. I was getting treat-ment all week, hopping off the table to play on Saturday.

'Everything went down, performance, fitness confidence… Am I offering enough to justify being around?

'In the back of my mind, I said if I can still do it after six weeks off, I'll come back. I did that in the summer. Villa on a Sunday, Spurs on a Wednesday, Charlton on Saturday and another away from home last weekend. Four games like that. Three years ago I'd be hauled off. To get through them was great.'

Niall Quinn at thirty-five. Last man standing from the Euro 1988 adventure. The siren song of another World Cup calling him home to a retirement which he won't resent or resist. He's had the best time, enough of it to stretch to the moon and back.

So every day he stretches his muscles and thanks the silent heavens for his fortune.

He never thought he'd be here. In those coltish early days at Highbury when he was all legs and elbows he never dared look forward to a day when he would be a beloved old war horse.

He likes his old story about George Graham talking to the boys one day back in that time of big dreams and bigger hair. George was talking about lads getting a hold of themselves, about being fit and clean living and responsible.

And people like Tony Adams and Paul Merson were there gazing back at George, who looked around, and Niall can remember this perfectly, looked around and said:

'Do that and some of you, you'll play till you're thirty-five.'

Solemn nods. And then George, he added the rider: 'Well maybe not you, Quinny.'

So now, Quinny looks back and thinks: 'Hang on, I made it!' He pinches himself.

'I could never get upset about anything footballwise to be honest because it's been so good. I've been so blessed.'

You look at him and you think: Niall, Niall, Niall. Where did it all go wrong? Where did you learn to audit your blessings? How does a

top-class player wind up being a world-class human being, equipped
with things like perspective, gratitude and consideration.

Even rival fans love him. The downtrodden, browbeaten millionaires of the big leagues must resent the sheer amateurishness of his
gratitude.

And his perspective. They must loathe that.

Think back. At this stage of the World Cup campaign eight years
ago you travelled to Maine Road in the city of Manchester to talk to
Niall Quinn. He arrived late, drenching everyone in apologies. Not at
all, not at all, you said.

Ireland had one qualifying game left and Niall Quinn was a star.
He had started every match and would start that last one in Windsor
Park too. Along the way he'd scored a couple of goals, including the
equaliser against Denmark, which would prove vital. He spoke that
day in Maine Road about luck and taking care and the possibility that
perhaps, if he tended to both matters, he might end up playing in four
World Cups.

That bird fell from the sky. Famously he spent the 1994 World
Cup finals on the airless press bus. His season ended in injury and,
despite his best efforts and letters from surgeons, Manchester City
point-blank refused to permit him to play in the finals.

Eight years on exactly you ask him about this. Here surely was
something which he could allow fester into a grievance, into a full-
blown tumour of bitterness and victimhood. Now that he has another
World Cup within his reach, he should be showing us how he is still
twisted and convulsed by bitterness over it all. 'My Private Pain' is
what the headline will say. Nope. He hasn't the energy. Or the will.
Or the inclination.

'To be involved in making something good is something to be
proud of. I took a lot out of that in 1994, even though I missed out. I
started every qualifying game and scored the odd goal and I felt

content. As a professional you don't stop and stand still at a particular point.

'Roy will get to a cup final and United will win it and Roy will be thinking afterwards in the dressing room about mistakes and his head will be moving on to the next one. Even though I didn't play, I knew I had done what I had done. I was delighted for everyone to get there. Anyway I got to spend five weeks with Brendan O'Carroll (working for RTÉ). You couldn't feel sorry for yourself. We had a laugh. It was enjoyable.'

Enjoyment! Grandad, where do you get these notions from? Enjoyment!!! That's an *Antiques Roadshow* one. Next you'll tell us that it was cool and groovy. You endure success nowadays. You put up with it. It's worse than poverty. It's a blight.

The fellas have changed alright. Football is a different town now, a changed place. He notices it but doesn't mind. Everyone has more and enjoys it less. He doesn't judge them for it, but he remembers the old days with the music on the bus and the songs and the cards and the chatter. He misses that, but if you stay in the same game long enough things will change. That's the price. Living to one hundred ain't the same as getting to be twenty and staying that way for eighty years.

You have an old picture of him in your head. At Belfast airport in November 1993. Ireland have just got a point against the North in a night crackling with hatred. They are going to the World Cup, but for now the team is fleeing, flying back to Dublin. Hectic. And he is standing in a small queue of journalists and players at a public phone waiting to ring his wife.

Alan McLoughlin is in front talking to his own wife. As other journalists pass by, Niall is thanking them for various pieces that have appeared about him.

And you think: 'Thanking journalists?' Verily it was a time before mobile phones even. A good time too.

'We were naive before,' he says. 'Through that, there was a greater sense of fun – maybe that's too strong. There was a great sense of enjoyment though. Everything is regimented now. If you want to speak to somebody, well talk to my agent, there's his number. That used not exist. It was like the musketeers, all for one and one for all.

'We'd talk to anyone and if somebody wrote or said something wrong about one of us, twenty of us wouldn't talk to him. Now the agent is on the phone and says there's a cheque in it if you talk to him. Every dressing room has changed in that way.

'We used to speak more about football. Now on the bus the lads have earphones on and they are watching DVDs. You're looking around for somebody who still likes just having a conversation. Huge change.'

And the odd regret. The realisation that, when your number is up, it gets dark very quickly. People forget, brush you away like gossamer from their faces.

'Everyone remembers Paul McGrath, say, because Paul was outstanding. But there were others. Ray Houghton was world class. Absolutely. You wonder if the guys I play with realise how good he was. We know Roy is a world-class player, because he does what he does, but I sometimes wonder how quickly we forget guys. Even Roy. That's a bit sentimental, but that's why I like playing. When you cross that line, you are forgotten about. The show goes on.'

These days he rooms with Kevin Kilbane all the time. Somebody said to him that Kilbane is the type of bloke you'd like your daughter to marry. He hasn't mentioned it to young Aisling Quinn, but generally Niall agrees.

'I enjoy him because he is so sincere. He came in today in City

West. Our room has a double bed and a single bed and he got there
before me. He's got to the stage where he's nearly going to take the
double bed. He's thinking about it.

He's put his bag on it but when I came in he took his bag off and
went to the other one. He's starting to come good. Before he
wouldn't even have put the bag there. That's Kevin. When he gets
his full confidence, he'll be a huge player for Ireland and
Sunderland.'

For now, though, young Kilbane can just bask in the sun. He can
watch Niall Quinn get ready and wonder if he'll tell his own kids
about the time Quinny broke the record.

The last Niall Quinn goal for Ireland, the twentieth, was a while
back in Giants Stadium, New Jersey, the winner in a three-goal
divvy-up with South Africa. That was June 2000. Can it really be
true that we haven't seen him score a home goal since twelve months
before that? June 1999 against Macedonia?

He approaches the twenty-one-goal milestone with humility. He
tells stories about baggage handlers at Dublin airport pulling his tail
about the record, about his friends bursting into spontaneous chant:
'You'll Never Get the Record! You'll Never Get the Record!'

Humility and respect and a bit of fun. It's Frank Stapleton's
record mainly. And before that Don Givens. You tread softly on
memories like that. You pay your dues.

'I've stumbled across twenty goals really. I'm not a natural
goalscorer. I've been a player who's had to show and lay it off. I
never saw myself as threatening the record even, but I've been in a
successful team. Frank only had that at the tail end.'

Don? Look at what he got. Less time and less space even.

'Yeah. Frank leads you to Don. For me anyway. How great was
Don Givens to have the old record, nineteen goals, with twenty
games less than Frank, playing in a team which, with respect, had

moral victories as their aims. People who played with him, they all say he was a sublime, elegant footballer. If Don played with the team-mates I had, he'd have got double.'

It's about respect. It's about memory. The family of Irish soccer. Passing it down, hand to hand, hero to hero. Don's hat trick against Russia on the day that Liam Brady made his debut? Where were you? Niall Quinn has a pure memory of it.

He was there in the sway of grimy old Dalymount inhaling the delirium.

'Yeah I was. I was at the match. In Manortown we'd get tickets and some coaches would bring the kids, we'd clamour to go to the Wednesday afternoon games to get off school. It was brilliant. That hat trick. Don was a hero for me and then, later, watching the Cup finals in the late '70s, Frank replaced him. From about thirteen or so, Frank was a big hero.'

God, how long ago was all that? Funny, he only had *Match of the Day* (vs Gaybo) and *The Big Match* (Sunday lunchtime). Now football is force-fed seven days a week, but, tell you something, the kids know less.

'We knew everything. We talked about who did what, how they did it. We wrote away to find out how to get stuff, we got programmes, we had football cards. Everything.'

Now sometimes at Sunderland the coach, Bobby Saxton (there's a name from the days), will start soccer quizzes on the bus, mainly with the other coaching staff and the older guys who aren't playing with the DVDs. And Niall will draw down an answer from the recesses and they scratch their heads and ask: 'So, Niall, just how old are you?' And he'll explain. 'Growing up. We knew all that stuff. All of us.'

Frank? The joke used to be that he got up every morning and smiled at himself in the mirror just to get smiling done with for the

day. Yet when Niall Quinn arrived in Arsenal in the early '80s, Frank
had just left and his reputation for hard work was like a useful
residue about the place.

Quinny had a suspicion that he might be out of his depth. He
arrived in the hush of the marble halls and noted that his new
employers had acquired the services of the youth international centre
forwards from England, Scotland and Wales. They were confident
and perfect. They had been coached and polished and buffed. Told
tenderly that they would be stars, told this for four or five years.
They knew all the drills in training. Niall Quinn had come from the
Dublin minor hurling team and he hadn't played soccer in five
months or so.

'I felt inadequate. I really felt, well, at least I'll have the few bob
for a while, and I can always go home.'

But Frank still haunted Highbury.

'Frank was what they spoke about. Frank had gone to United.
They'd take me aside and say: "Listen. I promise you Frank hadn't
half your ability. He had to work really hard. You'll have to put the
work in."'

Niall thought they were only having him on. Making sport for
themselves. But they never said anything like that to the other lads,
so he took them at their word. They saw something there maybe.
They'd bring him to parts of the gymnasium. They'd say, Frank used
to keep the ball up here 100 times with each foot and Niall would say
that he'd be doing that by end of the week or whatever.

And next time Terry Neill or somebody would pass through, he'd
show them. No pats on the head. They'd find something else for him
to do, something else that Frank had done.

Now years and years later he's on the threshold of doing
something that Frank never did. Scoring twenty-one for Ireland. A
little symmetry.

'I never met Frank till I got on the senior squad. I was in awe of him. If I was ever going to be good, it was through being like him. We played in Iceland in 1986 in that famous tournament. I'd never spoken a word to him. First session I went for a ball with him and scraped him because I hadn't cut my nails. He gave me a hammering. I'd never said hello to him up till then. I was thinking "Oh no, I've upset Frank Stapleton". The lads were winding me up saying, you know, he's really grumpy. He'll do this now, and that, but in fairness he was a big help. Not the sort of fella who put his arm around you, but he'd point out one or two little things and I'd put them to good use.'

And in case it's getting too maudlin, the big man laughs.

'I remember thinking recently about Frank's twentieth, when I got near the record. For Frank's record I passed to Andy and Andy clipped it and Frank shot in. Ten years later I wouldn't have passed it – as much as I was in awe of Frank. Now, I'd really, really love to do it. I maybe didn't want it badly enough at the start, but thinking of the buzz of the World Cup, etc., I'd love to get it.'

Today, one of designated celebration, would be the perfect day. Naturally he looks back for perspective rather than forward for glory.

'I suppose I feel blessed. I look back to the group of lads I went over with. I got tall and strong. And it was a time when they wanted tall and strong centre forwards. By the time that had changed, I'd learned how to hold it up.'

He's thinking back again on those early days at Highbury, in the big smoke and small streets of north London. Who was there? Who went where?

There was John Woods. He went to a club in Wales and went non-league. Hasn't seen him in fifteen years. And John Purdy. Went to Wolverhampton Wanderers, played a bit during all the furore when big Derek Dougan was in charge. Dropped out and played for Corby. Some lads made it. Paul Merson started then. Martin Hayes…

Players would come every year. New ones and better ones. They brought John Bacon over from Ireland and thought he would be the new Norman Whiteside. John got homesick. Went again. And Kwame Ampadu. Remember him? Whoa! Big Niall saw him coming over from Dublin and, no kidding, Kwame could do things with a football none of the first team lads could do. He was a conjuror.

Niall bumped into Kwame recently. Sunderland played Exeter in a pre-season friendly. Kwame played for Exeter. Kwame's earned a living, but, when Niall looks at the talent that he had coming over compared to what Niall had, 'Well, it's immoral that I actually made it and had the career I've had. It really is. It should be the other way around.'

So, for all that much, thanks, he says. For moments like the one he may be about to receive sometime this evening, much thanks. For the good times, the never-ending good times, muchos gracias.

'Naturally it's going to end. You love it so much, it becomes twice as valuable as you get older. You enjoy it twice as much. Nobody has loved it like I have. I've been blessed. No, I didn't get to play in 1994, but I played in 1990. Had me day and it was incredible. I'd love to be fit enough and give Mick everything I have left in the locker next summer. It would be a wonderful place to finish up. It would be the perfect ending, but I'll be realistic about it too.'

Enough time for that Niall. Blow out those candles first.

Caught in a sleep that doeth me head in

12 November 2001

Saturday night. 1.00 am: I lie awake, naked, sweating and writhing on the sheets (oh, come come ladies, don't pretend you haven't imagined it). The latest nightmare is retreating slowly. As usual it concerns the football team. This business with Iran and the conditions met by the visiting journalists.

A stadium, all old and ramshackle and higgledy-piggedly. The soccer people say it doesn't belong to them, what can they do? The mobiles don't work here.

The press box is primitive, no TV monitors, no phone lines, no electrical sockets. Downstairs there is an intimidating press bunker where all the domestic hacks crowd in to natter in the local lingo. A couple of hours after the match finishes, everything will shut down, whether the journalists are finished working or not. Deadlines are pressing. Nobody cares.

I cry out. What is this place? 'Welcome to Lansdowne Road,' says a chirpy voice, 'home of the Republic of Ireland. Sponsored by Eircom.' Take me now, Lawd, take me now.

2.45 am: My Dream of Mick. We are in the bandroom in the

corner of Lansdowne Road. We have just beaten Iran by two goals to nil, Hartey and Keane the scorers. We are sweating over deadlines. Mick McCarthy is taking an inordinately long time to arrive.

Suddenly the lights in the bandroom go out. Those of us who work for this paper instinctively reach into our pockets for 50p to put in the meter, but suddenly a soft light appears and Mr Chirpy of the Lansdowne PA voice says:

'Show your appreciation please, ladies and gentlemen, for the king of croon, Mick McCarthy. Sponsored by Eircom.'

Slowly Mick hoves into view on a revolving stage. He's wearing a top hat with white tux and tails. He's seated at a Steinway grand sponsored by Eircom. He has sparkly rocks on his fingers. He gazes down at us, winks, turns back to the piano and, looking like Liberace but sounding like George Formby, he begins:

'There May Be Trouble Ahead.'

We write down every word. Then I notice the figure in the background. He's naked except for his cane, his ermine posing pouch and his nipple rings. He's performing an immaculate soft shoe shuffle. Mick Byrne, you never lost it. 3.17 am: Awake again. Make some cocoa. Suck up a little crack cocaine and fall asleep on the sofa, braced for what dreams may come. The horror that follows makes me fear sleep.

I am in a lime-green leotard. I am jogging. Or jiggling, depending on how mean you want to be about the fuller-bosomed man. Let's say I am joggling. I am joggling around Lansdowne. Everywhere I jog, two red dots, like laser beams, follow me. If I don't keep just ahead of the dots, they settle on my skin and burn my flesh. When this happens the crowd roars. Oh, it's a regular laugh riot.

I flee the dots, running faster and faster as the rabble fall into a hypnotic chant.

Finally a man wearing a floppy Mr Motivator hat over yellow

vest and shorts stands up and acknowledges their applause with a razor-thin smile. The chant just grows greater. 'Keano! Keano! Keano!' Roy Keane turns his eyes down from full glare to default glare and the red dots disappear. I fall to the ground in a heap. I can hear the spectators. 'Roy this. Roy that.'

'Who was the other poor guy?' one of them asks.

'I think it was Richard Dunne,' says his friend.

'Slower than he looks.'

3.58 am: Have a quick draft of laudanum, and a stiff brandy. Drift off again.

Suddenly we are in Tehran. The game begins and the Iranians fly about like characters from Harry Potter playing Quidditch. After three minutes they score.

Mistake in our defence. 2–1 on aggregate. Mick McCarthy comes out of the dugout to roar, but all that comes out of his mouth are pretty bubbles and some butterflies.

Iran continue to swarm us. The game lasts forever. Finally just a minute left, thirty seconds, fifteen seconds. The Iranians launch a high, hopeful ball. The defender who gifted the first goal, he who shall henceforth be known to Iranians as The Great Santa, strides out, slices it woefully. Bagheri heads home.

4.56 am: Gossamered in cold sweat. Try several opiates. Find sleep. We are in Tehran again. Trailing by three goals with half-an-hour left. Roy Keane pulls one back. They score again. Two minutes left. Roy makes a crunching tackle near his own penalty area. Pop! A large spaghetti of ligaments, cartilage and general debris explodes from his knee, yet he gets up and chases the ball, his cruciate ligament trailing behind him now. Iranians are trying to stamp on it, a cocker spaniel is chasing it. He beats one, beats two, beats them all before slotting it home. He turns to his team, his subjects, with his arms raised. He is looking a bit pale but otherwise fine for a man who has just lost four pints of blood and half his leg. Mark Kinsella respectfully hands something to Roy. His kneecap.

And lo, as the angels sing we realise that verily it was as the herald had it. Roy Keane has sacrificed his knee and his career that the Irish nation might go to the World Cup and sing merry songs about itself. *Tá an* Celtic Tiger *ar ais arís*. *Olé* x 3. We are once again the greatest little nation on earth.

Roy holds his busted patella aloft. The Azadi stadium is silent now as he surveys his trusty kneecap. With a rueful smile Roy crumbles his knee in his hand and scatters the dust on the Tehran wind. 120,000 Iranians fall to their knees chanting 'Ayatollah Keano!' At home, people weep into their beer. Pete Saint John, now known as Mustapha Ali, composes a hit song, 'The Knee He Loved So Well'.

6.45 am: The merciful dawn discloses a cold, crisp day, but stark headlines on the paper which hits the screen door early. Staunton, Quinn and (say it ain't so, Roy, say it ain't so) Keane, all casualties of war.

Shivering, I turn in the bed to face Juanita, my Mexican serving girl, and ask her in my rustic Spanish to pinch me. I must awake and put an end to these infernal nightmares.

Days in a different world

17 November 2001

1. Think of it as opera and it makes sense. Think of something out of Verdi, some grand and strange last act. Think again of the Azadi, the bruised sky of dusk and every hand raised to the skies, every voice chanting answer to the imam's call to prayer.

Think of the final lines, the stage disappearing under belches of smoke, flames burning all over the ground. Think of all the portents, the ghosts, the auguries, the warnings. It was opera. Not football.

Mick McCarthy as hero. His destiny, of course, to be decided in this strange place. All the ghosts which came to him on Thursday night. An echo of previous tragedy. The game almost done. A corner. A sweeper comes up field like a fireman after a three-bell alarm. Meaty header. Goal. For an instant we could have been on that field in Macedonia again. History plays out twice. First time as tragedy, second time as Farsi.

And the press conference that followed. We haven't seen such chaos since the first Macedonian disaster. Irish journalists having to fight their way in. So little said. McCarthy's mood not yet fully formed.

Just realising that character is, in fact, fate.

And Banquo's ghost. How many battles have Roy Keane and Mick McCarthy fought shoulder to shoulder?

They know the price of each other's absence now. What a touch by the gods, giving us Keane to guide us up the mountain, then withdrawing him when, quite literally, the air was thinnest. Without Keane in the breach, the unbeaten record went, the Iranians pressed us into retreat. We were boys.

The record went and the professional heart was dented. No doubt. When the hugging was done and they made their way back to the dressing room it was big Ian Evans who burst in and shouted it out.

'We've lost the bollocking unbeaten record.'

There was a silence. Then. 'For fuck sake, Taff.' And after that Mick Byrne couldn't be stopped singing. It ain't over till the physio sings.

It was opera, this qualification campaign. In twelve acts. One man marching towards his destiny. His disciples around him. And the stage for the last act was dressed perfectly.

An opera in twelve parts. A story lived but not yet told. Little pieces of it just beginning to coalesce.

2. We poured out of the Esteghlal hotel like a rabble. It had been one long week. Fascinated by the culture, challenged by the logistics, amazed by the traffic, charmed by the people.

Mainly, though, it was a wait, a long chronicling of anticipation.

Love the place, love the place, we said, but, if you do yourself just one favour today, take a dump before you leave for the match. Those holes in the ground. You don't want to know.

3. He's sitting alone here in the airport. Long legs stretched out, Roddy Doyle book in his hand, smile never off his lips. Eight years ago he had a night like this, twelve years ago too, but…

'I was younger then. I was jumping around, slapping everyone, kissing everyone. Now I'm just sitting back enjoying things. I'm so pleased for the young lads, for Mick. This buries the ghost of the old team, this buries it. We move on now, Irish football will be great now for many years to come.

'I'm just sitting here looking back, thinking how lucky I am to have lived through a perfect time in Irish football. It's a great thing.'

Niall Quinn made his deal early and kept quiet about it. Every day a medical report on the big man's condition found its way into the press. By Wednesday, when the team trained in the Azadi for the first time, the signs seemed bad.

Niall was wearing his pained face. The back was no better. We bought it.

But the fix was in, the deal was done. Quinn himself knew four days before the first game in Lansdowne Road that the Azadi wasn't a place where he would be starting. The deal was ninety minutes in Lansdowne and if the team takes a lead away with it you sit on the bench. Run the battery down. And if we can get twenty out of you in Tehran, we'll do it. If not, no worries. You have served and served well.

Things changed a little. Roy went out and there was talk about an experience deficit. But Mick McCarthy came on Tuesday and said no, the deal was still good.

If the team need a dig-out with a target man at the end, well be ready.

Otherwise you'll be sitting on the bench beside Alan Kelly and the two of you will be talking your way through the longest game you've ever seen.

'Peter Reid [his manager at Sunderland] was brilliant. He rang me in Dublin on Sunday night. I hadn't answered the phone all day just in case, but he caught me and he said: "I know what you are like, do what you have to do. See you when you get back." That's class.'

4. All week long they spoke about him. Even when consciously trying not to. Roy Keane. Roy. Keano. He is the framing device for all achievements. This will be an achievement without Roy. All the greater, then.

There are rumours too. Roy is getting a hard time in the papers at home. The players will refuse to publicly discuss Roy. The PLC at Manchester United leaned on Roy. Roy never bothered to apply for an Iranian visa. Roy didn't fancy the trip.

So on. Nobody ever tires of talking about Roy Keane.

Yet it is worthwhile. This team hardly makes it onto Roy's Christmas-card list. He is so solitary that one wonders if he has any such list. Yet his will runs right through this team. They fear him, love him, loathe him, mainly they voyage around him.

Next summer they'll get to spend four or five weeks with him.

5. The first hint of what life can be like here. We are stopped in our coach at a gateway outside the Azadi Stadium. It is three hours or more till kickoff and it looks just now as if we will be spending it all here. The men in uniforms aren't interested in our laminated media badges, our VIP coach pass, our Iranian guide. They just aren't interested in letting our coach in. No reasons given.

We sit and sit. Outside the bus, there are angry exchanges. The uniforms just shrug. Finally our guide gets off. He is mortified, embarrassed in front of new friends. He starts demanding their names. One by one, you and you and you.

Writing them down. It's fascinating.

You think of the team hotel, which backs onto a massive prison. A wall runs up the mountain in a great forbidding loop defining the outer limits of the prison.

Most of the prisoners are kept underground. Their crimes are sometimes inexplicable.

Being at war with God. Depraved dancing. Non-Muslim thought.

Mick McCarthy and Ian Evans were driven around here by a luxuriantly-moustached man whom they christened Des Lynam. Des spent a week underground in the prison next door. Just a week, but when he came out he wasn't a professor anymore, he was a taxi driver. Just one argument with the wrong person.

We look out at our bespectacled guide arguing on the dusty concrete. Hope he knows what he's doing.

Minutes later the bus pulls away. We're in.

6. 'Yeah. Mick, he came to me and he said I was going on. He wanted me to run around, he wanted me to keep going, he said for me to work my bollocks off. So that's what I did.'

Your grandparents lived in Garristown. Never gave them a lot of thought. Once you played in an FA Youth Cup game for Crystal Palace and a little guy with a keen eye came to see you. Brian Kerr he was called. A few words. Planted a seed.

Still, you are an English kid, maybe they'll come calling too.

Now you are Clinton Morrison, Irish international and you are sitting in Tehran looking at a grandfather singing. You're singing too, because this song filched from the kiddies programme that grandpops watches with the lights of his life has become the unofficial signature tune. Every time you see Mick Byrne, the grandfather in question, it starts 'Welcome, welcome, to the big blue house'.

And Mick has a little shuffling dance like the bear in the big blue house and the two of you do it together.

Were you nervous tonight? Never. Not with Mick Byrne starting the jokes and the singing. Not with the lads. You've fitted in here like a foot into an old boot.

'I'm just so glad,' you are saying. 'I'm going to go back to Palace and soak it up and have a laugh at anyone who's not going to the World Cup. Good to be Irish, innit?'

7. Look at these faces. Look at them in repose sitting around the gleaming lobby of Tehran Airport waiting to go home. You will never see them like this again. You may never see them together again.

Look at the quiet ones. Steve Finnan on his own. Richard Dunne, thoughtful. Gareth Farrelly, Andy O'Brien, Rory Delap. Faces which beam back at Mick McCarthy's but whose eyes carry clouds of wonder.

Take a piece of paper. Play Fantasy Mick McCarthy. You love these kids. Seldom have you met a player you didn't like. Something in your blood. They do it for you, you want to be there for them. Now on your piece of paper you can write twenty-three names. The first three will be Given, Kiely and Kelly. You have twenty left.

Be conventional. Take four strikers, eight midfielders and eight defenders, conscious, of course, that some guys can switch. Strikers are easy, you have them around you now. Niall Quinn, Clinton Morrison, Robbie Keane and Dave Connolly.

Midfield. You'll be handing tickets to Roy Keane, Jason McAteer, Mark Kinsella, Matt Holland, Kevin Kilbane, Damien Duff, that's six certainties.

We'll come back.

In defence you have so many names. Kenny Cunningham, Steve Staunton, Steve Carr, Ian Harte, Gary Breen, Gary Kelly, and probably Steve Finnan, are all certainties.

Now you have the hard choices. Two midfield places to fill, one defender wanted. Look over at Rory Delap, all the trips he's made and never played a minute. Could you do it to him? Leave him behind?

Young Steven Reid, left sided, most promising player in Division

One, he's the future. Do you go over and tell him that you hope he'll get another chance?

Mark Kennedy is on the phone. You took him under your wing when he was a kid straight over from Dublin. You love the kid to bits, but he's harum scarum and, well, you have Lee Carsley to consider, consummate professional, reminds you of yourself a little bit, squeezing everything out of himself. And there's Stephen McPhail, so long blossoming, but if he could just be given the space and time, his creativity would change games.

Leave it, move onto defence. One name. Gary Doherty you can use at either end and with Big Niall suffering with his back that could be his ticket. But tell Richard Dunne thanks for Lisbon and Amsterdam and all that and enjoy watching it on the box? And what about Andy O'Brien, every review from Newcastle just raves more about the guy. By May, if you leave him out you'll be crucified.

Look at these faces. This is the best moment, the purest moment, perhaps. They've qualified. Tomorrow they begin a new game and some of these faces will be showing nothing but disappointment next summer.

8. In the dressing room beforehand things were quiet. Everyone with their own thoughts. Weird room. Three park benches stuck in the middle. School corridor lockers all around. Space enough to hear yourself think, though.

Arriving at the ground had been a boneshaker. Even the barracking of the night before hadn't prepared one adequately. The firecrackers and apple butts and other bric-a-brac which hit the pitch during warm-up time. Do you want to go out there now?

Really? Mick McCarthy speaks. He talks of the campaign, the team, sticking together, tonight is their night, having come so far.

Ian Evans speaks. His loud voice almost echoing. Thoughts about the match.

Logistics. Do this. Do that.

Don't forget the other.

Then Stan. In his Dundalk/Liverpool accent he talks about the game. You look at him. How many years have you known Stan? How many trips have you been on with him? How many laughs, tears, etc. And here he is, top of his game again, telling it like it is, captain of Ireland in Tehran tonight.

You say a few words yourself. You speak about all the time you've played, about going to the 1988 European champions and to Italia '90 and how it made you as a person. If you go out there tonight, you say, if you go out there and get the job done, your lives will never be the same again. Even people like Robbie sitting there, whatever you have achieved in the game, to qualify and go to a World Cup, it changes your life. This will be the dividing line.

Silence returns.

'Thanks, Niall,' somebody says.

9. In the tunnel leading into the stadium the riot gear is all laid out neatly and the policemen have brought their lunches with them in those little khaki-coloured canvas bags we all used for bringing our things to school in the 1970s. It is almost three hours till kickoff; the noise inside the stadium is incredible.

We come up through the tunnel and the place erupts. Western journalists! We are marched halfway round the pitch as the crowd sink into loud dementia. When we reach the stairs that lead to the press room, it looks like a thick bramble of hands. They reach through the railings on each side, patting your back, shaking your hand, but mainly predicting a three-nil victory. Out of loyalty to the team, we nod eagerly and say 'three-zero, yeah yeah'. What we want to say is 'yeah, put a tenner on it'.

10. They are a different bunch this Irish team, younger, richer and more remote. A team that doesn't like eye contact. A team that hasn't opened itself up yet. They seem at odds with the world. They hang together and hang tough with everyone else.

On away trips, they don't mill about the lobby drinking coffee and chatting like their predecessors did, they are holed up in their rooms playing with their gameboys, working their remote controls. Collectively they radiate surliness, whereas their predecessors gave off a sense of excitement and easy glamour.

Hopefully the adventure of a World Cup will bring out the wide-eyed innocence in them.

'I didn't enjoy it,' says Jason McAteer, 'not at all. We had a chef with us but there was only so much he could do. I couldn't sleep at nights. I was with Kenny [Cunningham] and get him talking and you'll nod off quick enough but this time I couldn't. Nerves. Boredom. That feeling of responsibility that you didn't used to get. Couldn't hack it.'

'I just waited and waited for training every day,' says Steve Finnan. 'Sat in the room. Chatted. Read. Just killing time all week. It was long. We're footballers and we're not really used to weeks like this.'

Joe Walsh knows what's what. Creating home from home is about knowing what's important. Kettle. Tea bags. Fig Rolls. On Tuesday evening in Tehran, Joe was entertaining seventeen for tea and biscuits.

It ain't all about hanging tough.

11. The final whistle. All hell and all heaven break lose. The Iranians have a huge banner at one end of the ground, it is almost as wide as

the pitch and it reads simply 3–0. This banner is on fire now, swoosh, up it goes.

Hundreds of smaller fires are all around, riot police are everywhere, players are hugging, things are being thrown at them. Time to work.

The Azadi isn't communications heaven, but they do more for us than Lansdowne Road ever does. They have Internet machines and e-mail facilities and a custom-built press conference room. Some of us have to literally fight our way into the press conference, but that's another story.

We compare quotes from players and management. Everything is for sharing on these trips. We work as a big co-operative and there are heroes of the filing and heroes of the technology and no room for rivalry.

Ray Treacy rounds us onto the media bus like a narky collie. We speed away. The road to the airport is covered in ice. Ice on such a pleasant night? No, it's glass. Miles and miles of fragmented glass. The driver explains that the post-match traffic through here was slow and the disappointed hordes ran through in groups smashing every piece of glass in every car. And now there are miles of glass and we are peering out the windows, noses pressed dumbly to the glass, wondering when the first stone will come or when we'll hear the first gush from our shredded tyres.

Wouldn't be a bad little story if there was a place to file from at the airport. Not bad at all.

12. Sport is about the next thing, about moving on. There's the World Cup draw, the warm-up programme, the worry over where the team will be based, what the squad will be. You don't look back.

Yet there is something about Iran this last week that it is hard to leave behind, just a wistful thought that, for a people who awoke one morning to revolution and went to bed that night under a dark fundamentalist sky, to a people who lost a generation in the war with Iraq, who have had their turn being used, demonised and sanctioned by the world, to a new generation of Iranians trying to express themselves and liberate themselves, well perhaps the fun and fiesta and pride of the World Cup would have been a freshening breeze.

They crave outside contact, friendship, communication, change. In a taxi in Tehran, stuck in traffic down a sidestreet, two young women talk. They are laughing infectiously. Suddenly one lifts the cloth from her head and for a split second you see her hair. It's dyed vivid red. And the veil is back in place and, as we inch forward, all that's left is the trail of their laughter.

Another day, another car and across the road in front of us walks a girl, twentyish but her garb stops short of her ankles and there, shockingly, is an inch of female flesh running down to where the leather of her shoe begins. Every male eye follows her. She walks with the style of a Parisian model.

Sport is about moving on, though. The ticket to the big dance is in our greasy palms. It's our greasy till to fumble in. Another World Cup bookends the fat old Celtic Tiger years and boys reared in the time of plenty go off to represent us. The Irish team will moan about all those who didn't believe in them and they'll grow fat at the corporate pork barrel suddenly prised open for them.

Yet we'll crank up the machine again, doling out the hype and the superlatives until sometime next summer on a faraway field a moment of wonder will bring the old passion flooding back and we'll see these kids as giants and this past week as just their causeway.

Bowl not needed in bad times or good

26 November 2001

Mick McCarthy's boys are in for a change of environment. Mick has always divided the world into those who are inside the tent urinating out and those outside the tent pointing in the opposite direction. Success can make a crowded squatter camp of your home, though, and no sooner had the lads returned from Tehran than the queue formed to get inside the tent and join the lads peeing outwards.

Chief among them were those mind slaves of Emperor Bertie who used the occasion to co-opt the national football team into the cheerleading sector for the Bertie Bowl.

T'would, we were told, be the cheek-reddening shame of this great little nation, the equivalent of a great hole in the seat of the national britches, were we to go off to the World Cup without a spiffing Bertie Bowl to call home.

The erection of a Bertie Bowl would be the crowning glory for our sporting achievements.

(Readers of advanced years will of course remember the cruel mockery which pursued the team and the greatest supporters in the world at previous major tournaments back in the last century. Jibes

like 'Your Roof Isn't Retractable' or 'What's It Like to Have no
Executive Box?' Insults which withered a nation.)

Of course with a chary independent report coming down the
pipeline and the government preparing to slip the national hairshirt
back on the national back, the Bertie Bowl needs all the ra ra
treatment it can get. The idea looked liked a self-aggrandising folly
back in the time when the national mood was keyed to such things.
In harder times, it looks like an election loser.

Times have changed quickly. The Celtic Tiger business is done
with and, apart from the social necessity of a shiny metal spike for
O'Connell Street, it's hard to think just what we'll tell the
grandchildren we did with all the money.

There's a pile of blueprints and those tribunal investigations into
memory loss, coincidence and careless filing. And there'll be a neat
anthology of arrogant quotes about how we can't take all our oul'
dough with us, how we can afford to fix health, education and build a
Bertie Bowl with trimmings. The good times will be remembered
mainly for bragging and vulgarity.

So for the lean times, the pinch-cheeked era ahead, what should
we do? Well, in the past six weeks or so, one venue has reasserted its
claims for a facelift and reminded us that, when it comes to stadiums,
location is everything. The soccer games against Holland, Cyprus
and Iran, the rugby match with New Zealand were great occasions,
not just on the pitch but in the preamble and aftermath.

The stroll, the eating, the drinking, the chat, those things are part
of what Irish sport is. Lansdowne Road offers them. So does Croke
Park. These are things accountants can't measure and shouldn't
try to.

The proposed location of the Bertie Bowl and its grandiose side
palaces has never made sense. Not in terms of traffic, or centrality or
social considerations. Do you want to spend three hours in traffic

before being shoehorned into the Bertie Bowl still quivering with road rage, there to have your allotted diversion before rejoining the treacle-flow of traffic? Will the rugby fans who come here in such numbers from Britain during the season be queuing up for that experience?

Now the whispers have it that everything is to be shorn from the Emperor's Palace and we are just to have the naked Bertie Bowl shivering in splendid windswept isolation out in Blanchardstown. What a comical testimony to our stupidity that will be. On match nights, we will sit in our recently NCT'd cars in the endless M50 traffic and wonder why there can't be a stadiums tribunal.

The entire social aspect of attending a big sporting event in Dublin will have evaporated.

Lansdowne Road is easy to make fun of. After all, it wouldn't get done so frequently in this column if it was hard. Still, the old place has a lot going for it. The walk out there, the history, the way the area quickly absorbs a large crowd and disgorges it back into the city.

The time has come surely to blow the dust off the old plans for turning Lansdowne around (so that the current West Stand lies behind a goal) and turning the place into a modern 45,000–50,000 stadium. The government should pay for this, compensate the IRFU accordingly, and encourage the GAA to permit the occasional playing of rugby or soccer games that require a bigger crowd at Croke Park. One imagines that a well-reasoned motion to that effect would have few problems at Congress next spring.

After all, how many times is Croker (or a Bertie Bowl of the originally proposed capacity) likely to be needed under those circumstances? Once, twice a year? Maybe this year the Holland game in soccer and the England game in rugby would have demanded a bigger venue. Next year soccer has nothing but friendlies until after the World Cup, then we go into the European qualifiers as number one seeds in a five-team group, which is most welcome but it means we won't be having the Hollands and the Portugals coming to play here.

In fact, we'll be playing just four competitive home games between now and the summer of 2004.

There are good arguments for the GAA keeping Croke Park to itself – having built the place is a remarkable achievement for an amateur organisation, etc. – yet, realistically speaking, the extra usage involved in opening up is small and the rewards are attractive.

It's time surely to get realistic about the paucity of big sporting events we have in this country. GAA is a summer spread. Everything else is an occasional treat, the enjoyment of which would be severely impaired by having to travel to a concrete Siberia.

Time surely to consign the Bertie Bowl to the same grave as Eircom Park. We can look back at the blueprints in years to come and have a laugh about it all.

A velodrome! We need a decent indoor stadium built downtown/ dockside and a couple of stadiums the size of Croke Park and Lansdowne, and we need to put millions of punts to better use.

Why take another piece of colour and life out of the city? We need to preserve that aspect of what makes big occasions in Irish sport great.

Words to the wise on World Cup build-up

3 December 2001

May I suggest:

1. A ban on World Cup blather on *Questions & Answers*. It is as yucky as your grandmother slipping her tongue in when she kisses you goodnight.

The whole ghastly business is usually triggered by some obligingly gormless prole who throws the politicians a footie question like a kid being allowed toss fish to dolphins. Big smile. 'What does the panel think of the draw for the World Cup?!!' The panel have all been interested in Manchester United for, oh, three or four years now, so they are just the people to ask.

As one, the wretches push their snouts to the surface and the water comes over all oily while they clap their flippers and swallow the sardines and remind us politicians are almost like humans. Of course we wish Mick and the boys all the best. Tremendously exciting.

Great spectacle in prospect. Quite a wonderful achievement. Like France '98 all over again, I certainly remember the excitement of that one. I'm sure they'll do us all proud and, heh heh, give us the boost we all need after four-and-a-half years of this government. May I just say, John, that we'll be looking for our own little result before that.

Ah, stop.

2. That there needs to be a fatwah declared on the people who produce those dreary World Cup anthropology columns. Self-regulation won't do for these big-footed daytrippers who drop by to the sportsnation every few years to kindly explain to us all exactly what it all means to us all. Listen, lads, some of us work that patch in the dark days between World Cups. We have to explain what it all means when we lose to Macedonia. We've had to explain the meaning of Keith O'Neill. We've had to decipher the Tao of David Connolly. We've been in confined spaces with the greatest supporters in the world. We have presumed to explain the meaning of sportslife to the few hundred who stand like sodden herons on baldy terraces on winter days. Keep out of the garden now, the going is good.

3. Ditto politicians. No turning up at airports. No laps of honour. No huggies with Mick. No squeezing into the team photo. No Bertie Bowl guff.

4. Ditto rich geezers having a wonderful time in Japan. No pictures of Eddie Jordan and Denis O'Brien whooping it up with each other.

5. To be tried as witches is too good for the commissioning editors of fluffy feature articles on 'what women will do when all the football is on'. Listen. Most women will go to the pub and watch the football when it is on. They shall understand that, when the little green men put the little roundy thing into the funny net thing, an Irish goal has been scored and there will be hugging, spilling of beer and refloating

of the economy. If you are a woman who actually feels panicked and confused by a disruption to TV schedules in the summer, well, get thee to a nunnery.

5. Sorry, but this column calls for the garrotting of those who peddle po-faced columns explaining that it is a mark of our national immaturity to gather in public houses to cheer against England.

Hey! I bare my immature Irish buttocks to whichever parsons shall climb into the pulpit armed with that little homily. I stick my fingers in my ears and dance from foot to foot singing *la-la-loo – I'm not listening to you*. England are in the Group of Death and I'm loving it. So there.

I'm mature enough to get over the 800 years of *cos ar bolg* and dismiss it as a misunderstanding, but John Motson's jingoism I can't get over. Tony Blair being Emperor of the World I can't get over. Three Lions on a Bloody Shirt I can't get over. Germany 1 England 5 I can't get over.

Let us not forget the tradition which most of us were reared on; to wit, the comedy that is English footballing tragedy. Mexico 1970, when hubris undid them; Wembley 1974, when Jan Tomacescki undid them; and so many handballs and dastardly Johnny Foreigners ever since.

They are the fat man. The World Cup is their banana skin. And what makes us a great nation is the ability to laugh at the misfortunes of others.

6. Which brings us to: the patronising English quality newspaper article. Normally headlined 'The Irish, Aren't They Great?', or 'Scorn Not Their Simplicity', these atrocities are traditionally associated with Cheltenham week, but an Irish qualification for a major football tournament can cause unseasonal outbreaks:

'Irish eyes were smiling in Busan and beyond last night as Mick

McCarthy's happy-go-lucky band of merry men enjoyed a barrel or three of the black stuff after all their Hail Marys came through in Saturday's draw. While bookies' favourites England were handed a real job of work, Sven Goran Eriksson could hear the lilt of Irish laughter as the jolly green men cranked up the sort of year-long Irish party we have come to expect of a team who like nothing better than an old fashioned singsong as they go to work on a wing and a prayer.

'The bleary-eyed Irish contingent were thanking their lucky shamrocks for the kindest of draws. "Faith, shure it could have been worse," winked one of their moonfaced officials over a pint of local brew, "shure everyone knows God came from Co. Mayo."'

7. Which leads us to the topic of patronising articles about Cameroon. Please place on the table the only things we know about Cameroon: nearly beat England in 1990. Roger Milla once tried to organise a tournament for dwarves in Yaounde. (Yes, the takings were small.)

They drop successful managers the way the IRFU do. Yes, their players will have a row over money before next June because this is the only time they have leverage. Yes, they have only two stadiums with grass pitches. Yes, when Olympic Mvolye failed for five years to win promotion from the central province second division, despite the backing of a local millionaire, it was widely felt that witchcraft was at work.

And what might Cameroonians know about us quaint folk who nearly beat England in 1990? We have no national soccer stadium. We run a mickey-mouse league where the takings are small. We have a squad of millionaire players who will make out like bandits from their players' pool. We'll be having a party and a singsong after we say our prayers and kiss our miraculous medals tonight.

Let's be careful out there.

Pile-up gifts Australia its first gold as Ohno comes up short

18 February 2002

Apolo Ohno is the sort of person you don't expect to like. Too much dude in him. Long hair and a little smig which looks like it's been stolen from somebody's genitalia.

Better looking than anyone with talent has a right to be. Then there's that kooky celestial name plus a biography that kind of gets under your skin. Afraid to travel anywhere after 9/11 when, of course, we all feared for the safety of short-track speed skaters.

Totally cracked under pressure at the US Olympic trials four years ago. Accused, wrongly it turned out, last December of being involved in a race-fixing scam. All that and a poster boy for the raucous American media who beat the drum all the way to Salt Lake City talking up Apolo's drive for four golds. No thanks.

So, on Saturday night, as we watched the men's 1,000-metre short-track final in a state of sublime ignorance, all we knew (well okay, all I knew) was that it would be pretty amusing if Apolo the raging favourite were to be beaten and everybody had to shut up about him.

And lo it came to pass in circumstances so dramatic that it will be popping up on the 'What Happened Next?' segment of sports-quiz programmes for decades to come.

The five-man field came around the last bend with Apolo Ohno in front, holding off Li Jiajun of China and with Mathieu Turcotte of Canada and South Korea's Kim Dong-Sung in pursuit. Steve Bradbury of Australia was dead last, skating a different race apparently.

Then Li Jiajun took a tumble. And the front four fell like dominoes. Swoosh! Scrape! Slide! The crowd was in sudden uproar. With a big sheepish grin on his face Steve Bradbury slid unmolested over the finish line and won Australia's first ever winter Olympics gold medal.

Well here goes, we thought, setting our tape machines to long play for the beginning of the sort of double album, gatefold sleeve, whine which Mary Decker Slaney produced when Zola Budd tripped her up back in 1984. Hit us with your moaniest shot pretty boy.

As we waited for word from Apolo we looked at the slow motion tapes of the race which NBC were showing over and over again. The crowd in the Ice Centre booed solidly, encouraged perhaps by the new Olympic tendency to hand gold medals out to crowd favourites.

Looking at the replays you had to admit that the kid did pretty well to bounce off the wall with a six-inch gash in his leg and stick his skate out for a silver medal, but the sight of him being tended to and pampered by half the American Olympic community afterwards rubbed that generous thought out.

'Apolo is in a wheelchair,' they said. 'Give us a break,' we said. He may be able to manage with crutches they said. 'Oh, boo hoo,' we said. And damnit the kid came and he spoke and he conquered and he reminded a few of us just what the Olympics are supposed to be all about. 'Is this a scandal or is it just the sport?' he was asked.

'Hey, it's just the sport,' he said. And the rest of his words were an outburst of generosity and decency which we thought had no place in modern Olympics anymore. Turns out that Steve Bradbury, the bleach-haired Aussie who found the gold dropping into his lap, makes Apolo's skates. The pair of them had been e-mailing each other best wishes on the night before the race.

'Yeah, it's a wonderful opportunity for Steve and I congratulate him. He's the guy that makes my skates. Last night he sent me an e-mail saying: 'Apolo, if you win tomorrow be sure to give a shout out.' And on he went happy as a lark as we picked away for a little piece of bitterness.

'Whose fault was it?'

'I have no idea. I still have got to look at the tape. This is short track. It was out of my control.'

'What about those four gold medals?'

'My quest, my journey, is not about winning four golds. It's about coming to the Olympics and experiencing it and enjoying it and performing my best regardless of the medal outcome. In fact, I thought it was one of the best efforts of my life. I was definitely happy with the performance, regardless of what medal I have.'

Bradbury, one of speed skating's journeymen, has a CV filled with lower rankings and was thrilled to have made the final. In fact, he was thrilled to be alive. In 1994, after an accident, he lost four litres of blood. Two years ago, in another accident, he broke his neck.

Those are the second and third most strange anecdotes he will be telling his grandchildren. He got through the quarterfinal stage when two of the skaters in front of him went down. In the semifinals, same story. In the finals? Ditto!

'Obviously,' he said with a grin, 'I'm not the fastest skater, but those were my tactics. Luck was on my side. I won't take the medal for the minute and a half of a race that I won.

'I'll take it and think of it as something for the last decade of hard slog. I was the weakest guy in that field. Everyone went down and I'm the winner. That's just unbelievable to have everybody to down like that. But I'll take it. It's good but it doesn't feel right you know. I wasn't as strong as the other guys. I consider myself the luckiest man. God smiles on you some days and this is my day.'

And off they all went. Apolo Ohno, wheeled out, but vowing he'd be alright for the next three medal attempts. Steve Turcotte, the third-placed Canadian with a cut on his backside, grinning and saying he'd be back too; and Bradbury, the man who won the lottery.

Made fans out of us again, so it did.

Fathead liberals shalt be crucified

4 March 2002

I am indebted (as they already know) to the soothsaying community for their dire warnings and auguries as to the consequences of the GAA permitting several games of soccer to be played in Croke Park. Furthermore, I agree that these consequences have hitherto been unforeseen by 'fathead liberals' such as myself.

Indeed we in the fathead liberal community now acknowledge ourselves to be a caste who 'have nothing better to do all day' than sit around making snide comments about things we know nothing about. Blessed not are the snide.

I now accept that, in the event of the GAA deleting Rule 42 of Holy Writ, the snakes which St Patrick once thoughtfully banished from this isle shall return in abundance, and truly they shalt thrive (and perhaps look) like lawyers in a lengthy tribunal.

It is my understanding now that, in the event of the wanton deletion of Rule 42, there shalt be a most of it and a least of it. The return of the snakes shalt definitely be the least of it. The following, which represents the most of it, is also inevitable:

That the infidel soccer team which represents the hyphenated

nation of Enger-land shalt play at Croke Park whenever it suits them.
Big matches.

Friendlies. Garden fêtes. Bloody liberties shalt be taken by the
great Satan. In their perfidy, the fans of Satan shalt wave Union
Jacks on Hill 16 and people like me will be forced to 'see how we
like it then'.

There shalt be no room in the calendar for the practice of the
Gaelic pastimes of football, hurling and camogie. In fact, following
the pogroms of Irish speakers by this column's West Brit friends (we
reject the soothsaying community's crude allegation of greater
intimacy with West Brit friends), there shalt be further pogroms, and
again this column shalt be forced to see how he likes that. Verily, he
shalt like it less than he would like a pointy stick in the eye.

There shalt be a general razing of the dominion which we now
know as the northside. As areas go, it shalt be no go. A no go area.
Would you want to go?

No. Thank you, but no. When the Union Jack-waving fanatics
from the great Satan are done with it, shalt the northside still be a
resort area? No.

Even the near southside shalt be affected and a bijou hut of mud
and wattles near Rathgar selling for 75 million will linger on the *IT*
property pages for more than a fortnight.

There shalt be floodlights. They shalt be erected upon pylons
which grow like beanstalks from the doomed, cracked earth. The
floodlights shalt beam like pagan suns to suit the 'bloody soccer
crowd'. To the Gael they shalt be too dazzling to be gazed at with the
naked eye and all good men and women who do so gaze shalt be
struck blind. They shall wander the northside bumping into each
other.

Thus the fabric of society shalt come undone quicker than a fat
man's Lenten fast.

There shalt be no virgins and all young women will take on the wall-eyed appearance of herrings. Roll mop shalt be considered a fashionable look. Mackerel shalt be deemed sluttish. That shall not be a bad thing.

The soccer crowd shalt have 'first call' on all facilities belonging to the Gael. The rental from all such arrangements shalt be capped at 'thirty pieces of silver'. How many days' luck shalt the GAA have with these thirty washers? Not one.

Clubhouses shalt be desecrated by the staging of orgies, pagan ceremonies and hurley-burning events. Yes, verily there shalt be a great hurley burny throughout the land. Only collaborators like this column shalt be invited to the orgies. Verily it is written that they shall contract 'the pox' and the 'knob rot'. After that, no mackerel will touch them.

Speaking of which, a slap in the face with a knob-rotting slut of a mackerel shalt be the sensation enjoyed by the long-suffering Croke Park residents. How much more can they take? When they came to view the house, the estate agents hid the huge stadium behind a painting of some dogs playing billiards and smoking cigars. The long-suffering residents fell for it, to the extent that they now think they were there before the stadium was. Fair enough, but now this: Brits with floodlights! Cloven-footed, Union Jack-tattooed storm-troopers of darkness defecating all over the place! Great and yet poignant will be the whirring noises from the graves of the dead patriots. Living patriots will wish they were whirring. Learned men shall meet in catacombs and discuss whether the anguished dead spin in the manner of compact disks or rotate quickly like chickens on a spit.

There shalt be no saints or scholars. No saints. Just Pat Dolan's SuperSaints, who will bestride our world like a colossus up whose shorts we can peek. No scholars. Damian Duff's educated left foot shalt receive a doctorate and enjoy a lucrative life as a speaker in US universities. It shalt be invited onto the telly to debate with The Wolfe Tones on matters of national importance.

The GAA will grab every penny? Of course they will. Or else they shalt be too smart. Soccer is a Trojan horse. The GAA is wary of geeks bearing gifts. The GAA weren't born today nor yesterday. When did they arrive? Not in the last shower, certainly. Not down the Liffey in a bubble. Perhaps overnight, when the Croke Park residents weren't looking. Anyway. The soothsaying community seems divided on this acquisitiveness business.

All agree on this.

There is a whirlwind. Will it be reaped? Wasn't that a Neil Young song? Only Frank of the Holy Combover can save the earth. Frank should wear his underpants outside his slacks in the manner of the superhero. Holy Modernities! To the Batmobile, Frank! In the event of Frank putting his holy finger in the leaky dyke, shalt the soccer crowd cease and desist from the promotion of their evil lifestyle? Of course they shall, and great (*agus as Gaeilge*) will be the rejoicing. Shalt they spend their money elsewhere? Not at all, they willst to impoverished hurley makers give it. Will Sky Sport continue to pollute the blessed airwaves? No. It shalt be all Michael, all the time. With breaks for the *Angelus* and reruns of four-hour speeches from Frank of the Holy Combover.

How shall we like that? The soothsayers care not how we shall like that.

Late goal keeps dream alive

6 June 2002

It's a walk on the wild side. In perfectly ordered Japan, this Irish World Cup adventure is a riot, a sun dance, an anarchic subversion of football logic.

It defies analysis.

Ninety-two minutes gone and old Niall Quinn shakes off his decrepitude.

Robbie Keane, that impertinent whippersnapper, does the rest and suddenly the final whistle has gone and the Irish are doing the cancan in the Ibaraki night when minutes previously they'd lain dead in a narrow grave.

The Germans can watch only through the cracks in their fingers. Daft.

And so it goes on, this tale of the unexpected. Cameroon soundly drawn with. Germany the latest world power to be slaughtered one apiece. On to Yokohama next Tuesday, the inept Saudis in our way. And after that, on to who knows where?

All that's certain is that their troubles have galvanised this team to the extent they are blood brothers and, for all the wonder he provided us with, perhaps no contribution from Roy Keane to his team was as great as his having left it when he was too unhappy to stay.

We conceded a goal early last night, a careless gift of a goal which left us with the old familiar hill to climb. Steeper perhaps. Germany, three times world champions, and masters of the percentage game against our furious passion?

Surely the Germans would swat us like wanton boys. The last fifteen minutes of the first half offered some hope of salvation. Keane tried his luck with a bicycle kick under the disdainful eye of the imperious German keeper, Kahn. Then once or twice Duff dribbled like quicksilver and made believers of us again. And lo! A cross or two arrived without homing in on Kahn's gloves. Had we been given the option, we would have worked through the tea break.

Half-time in the Irish dressing room was some kind of wonderful. The best-laid plans being unravelled and recast in a cacophony of voices.

'We're an emotional lot,' said Gary Breen afterwards. 'We all had some kind of say.' And they came back out and took up where they left off with the huffing and the puffing. The Kashima stadium burned with excitement as the Irish attacked the end behind which their fans were massed. The chances came and, if they weren't spurned, they were snatched away by Kahn. And the clock rolled on, impervious.

The longer the Irish besieged the Germans, the more romantic and heroic the failure we seemed destined for. High in the stands, we scribblers prepared our solemn obituaries. Honour in defeat, died as they had lived, etc., etc.

Mick McCarthy was seeing a different ending though. He was going for a tall tale. Namely Niall Quinn. The long string of charm from Crumlin has been with us on practically every great Irish football occasion back to the time when crowds wore cloth caps and carried rattlers, but never has his impact been more concentrated or significant.

Old glory. Quinn's arrival set off a three-siren alarm in the German defence. The Irish didn't abandon principle but they abandoned caution, playing three players in attack, young Duff and Keane feeding parasitically off what Quinn pulled out of the air. And still the clock went about its business, not dawdling for even a curious second. Ninety minutes, ninety-one minutes… The ending needs no retelling really. Quinn's flick. Keane's bloody-minded persistence. The ball bouncing off Kahn and shuddering his net. Keane's trademark flip and then his disappearance under a heave of Irish bodies.

In the morning comes the reckoning. Cameroon play Saudi Arabia today. Assuming they win, the shakedown will be simple. Cameroon and Germany will play each other on Tuesday. They will have four points each. We will play Saudi Arabia and, at start of play, we will have two points. If the other game is a draw, we need to score more goals against the Saudis than Cameroon do. If Germany beat Cameroon, or if Cameroon beat Germany and we win, then we go through.

The odds have tilted in our favour. Summer gets dizzier. 'Dunphy, Only A Game', said one banner in the Kashima last night. Only a game to make grown men cry.

El Tel and the seventh circle of Hell

29 July 2002

I know that in the next life things will be good. I know that I shall be reincarnated as something good and useful. I'll be Alice Munro's pen. Venus Lunny's violin. Julianne Moore's loofah. Michael Kennedy will represent me in negotiations. I know because, in this life, fate has decreed I be a Leeds United fan. I am an untouchable. I walk with the wretched of the earth, and the wretched of the earth laugh at me behind my back. Sure. Into each life some rain must fall, but enough is enough. In the next life, I'm owed. Big style.

The latest deluge comes in the form of the oleaginous but legitimate businessman Terry Venables, who has replaced Uncle Dave in the manager's swivel chair at Elland Road. Say what you like about Uncle Dave (and we did, we did), at least he wasn't a spiv, at least you didn't have to count your fingers after he shook your hand. Dave wanted to hump your leg. Dave wanted you to love him, and at least when he swaddled you in his gentle thoughts you just knew that Uncle Dave was too sweet to be wholesome but there were worse things he could be.

Me and Tel go back a long ways. Once, when we were young and fashionably freelance, myself and the esteemed football correspondent of this paper went along to White Hart Lane one Saturday afternoon to watch Spurs play Everton. We went as boys. We left as men.

Ironically, we had no legitimate business there at all. We were in London. We had finagled accreditations. We went along to see some footie for free and to eat all the pies in the press room (well, we were freelance and poor as church mice) and afterwards, well sated too, we waddled down to the press conference being conducted by the small but perfectly tanned El Tel. Free theatre.

At the time the poor misfortunate we now know as the Major League Soccerballer Paul Gascoigne was being lured and wooed by the politically incorrect Italian outfit, Lazio. This seemed to be a sore point at Spurs, but for the longest while you couldn't tell.

Venables shared his thoughts on all other matters in a separate series of little sessions. He did the Sunday boys first, the daily boys next, any feature stuff then, and he kept the chaps laughing. Terry's bonhomie rendered them all invertebrates.

All was happy and Gazza was never mentioned, until one crazy poor soul from the London listings magazine *Time Out* blurted out the question which would haunt him forever. 'Terry,' he said, 'what's the story with Paul Gascoigne?'

Now, myself and the football corr were as innocent as the *Time Out* man, but we sensed immediately that something was wrong. We were as blameless as any of the citizens pouring out of the Biograph Theatre in Chicago behind John Dillinger on the day he was mown down by the Feds. We were feckless, pie-thieving, freeloading bystanders, but we sensed what we were about to see would scar us.

Mr *Time Out* had a death wish.

'Who are you and where are you from?' said El Tel coldly.

All chatter in the press room stopped. The hacks shrank away. Outside the skies grew dark and a raven landed on the sill. We wondered if somebody would inform the *Time Out* man of his rights. Too late. 'I'm Johnny Hapless from *Time Out* magazine,' he said brightly.

And for the next five minutes, in view of us all, El Tel told Mr Hapless what he thought of him, his magazine, his question, his presence in the north London area, his existence in general. El Tel wasn't impressed by any of it.

I wasn't present for Roy Keane's celebrated Saipan speech to Mick McCarthy, but, when I imagine it, I assume that Roy was using the Venables template. Cold, chilling words delivered with a quiet, serial-killer intensity. A verbal kicking to death, but with little picador stabs in between, the sort of thing that freezes and transfixes all onlookers and makes them wonder afterwards why they didn't intervene.

Since then I have never liked Terry Venables. To be honest I never liked him before that anyway, but since then it's been personal.

Now Tel is manager of Leeds United, a club decaying at the core, a club run by the impossibly slippery Peter Ridsdale, a club which seldom seems happy or wholesome.

A few years ago, I was among the many who fell to their knees before Ridsdale's pearly smile and hailed him as the saviour. He marketed himself as a decent sort. He was interested in performing the unlikely alchemy which would turn Leeds into a club full of decent sorts.

He talked a good game. Having come on heavily to Martin O'Neill, he finally gave Uncle Dave the Leeds job and made it seem as if he'd had a lucky escape from that shallow, flirty jezebel O'Neill. Uncle Dave was the sort that any chairman should be looking to settle down with.

I never admired Ridsdale more than when he said prior to the Woodgate/Bowyer trial that, if either was found guilty, the heaviest sanctions would be thrown at them. What an example, I thought, if Leeds were to place principle over profit and just get rid of them and the stain they might leave.

Bowyer got off, his reputation not escaping further blemish in the process.

Woodgate got the millionaire's sentence of community service. Bowyer declined to pay a club fine weeks later. Leeds transfer listed him, but backed down. A couple of weeks ago, Bowyer travelled to Liverpool for talks. Gerard Houllier decided that Lee Bowyer wasn't his type. Leeds will have to employ him a while longer.

The Woodgate situation is sadder. In the wake of the disastrous sale of the Rio Ferdinand, Ridsdale displayed all the cowardice of his convictions by stating publicly that Woodgate could be the future of the club. I'm all for rehabilitation and am happy for Woodgate to have a career and make his millions, but Leeds should have more pride. Leeds and Woodgate both need a clean start.

But no starting again. No clean sheet. Leeds go forward as before, only spivier, smaller, even less likeable. Ridsdale has moved Uncle Dave out of his lovely job, not because Uncle Dave wrote a distasteful book (along with Dave Walker, another director at the club), which Ridsdale claims took him by surprise, but because at the end of the season the money thing didn't add up.

I don't think Uncle Dave was ever going to lift the Champions League trophy; in fact, I would be surprised if somebody could tell me hand on heart that Uncle Dave had the respect of his dressing room by the end of last season. But for every time Uncle Dave spoke with forked tongue, so too did Peter Ridsdale.

Now we move into the era of El Tel, the man whose pressing business in the Seychelles kept him away from his players for the last few weeks. Soon Leeds will lose a couple of points of light in

Gary Kelly and Robbie Keane. It will be the club of Woodgate, Bowyer, Alan Smith, Danny Mills. How ugly is that?

Three hopes. That Steve McPhail's flashy passing might be El Tel's cup of Darjeeling. That the El Tel era be brief. That all this is forgotten about come reincarnation time.

Time heals but some wounds remain

31 August 2002

If you would like to get up and leave now, that's fine. Roy Keane will understand. If you've had enough. If it galls you. If you're tired. If you don't want to come along for the ride. He can live with it. He knows. There's been a lot of Roy Keane this summer and maybe you've had enough. He has.

He opened the Sunday papers last week and there on the front was the blood feud between Eamon Dunphy and John Giles. Old friends falling out. And he thought to himself that everything had gone far enough, when Giles and Dunphy are rowing over Roy Keane and newspapers have nothing better to fill their front pages with.

He's coming to Ireland next week to do some signings and he's supposed to appear on Pat Kenny next Friday night, but he thinks now he'll give it a miss. He doesn't need to do it, he says, and anyway he thinks RTÉ have had their dealing trick out of him by now. Sitting down with Pat would only stir it up again, and anyway people like Pat and Jack Charlton had their little say during the summer.

'So I don't think I want to give them the satisfaction of their twenty minutes or twelve minutes of me. I'm thinking they can take a run and jump. I'll give it a miss. Time to put all this to bed.'

It's still OK if you want to leave now. The doors aren't locked. Unbuckle your seatbelt, walk up the aisle, and disembark. He understands. Four paragraphs down the runway and Roy Keane is telling Pat Kenny to go and take a run and jump. Same old Roy Keane, you say.

But he can laugh. He still has that cutting wit. Last Sunday he watched Cork's bad-tempered exit from the All-Ireland football championship.

'I was sitting there watching the second half and I thought, well, at least I know where I get it from.'

If you want to poke his chest and say to him that, hey, it was Roy Keane who walked out in Saipan and it was Roy Keane who brought out the book, he can see where you are coming from. He thinks the reaction to his book has been a little over the top, but nothing surprises him these days and, if you want to sit and listen, he'll give his side to it all. It'll be bumpy and turbulent and you can leave now if you like, but he promises a gentle landing.

And then he's happy to sit and listen. He knows what's coming. The great tsunami of backlash. The great drop from the sky. A winter in the stockades. Fair enough.

'I'm having my say. I'm nearly done having my say. And then Mick will have his, and other people. I'm sure Mick will say I was a right prick to deal with. In time he will. He'll have his say and I'll have to accept that. I'm happy to put it to bed now and let Mick and the players get on with it. I'll get on with my career.'

He's mellow today. He arrives as usual without any bouquet of PR posers, no battalion of media flunkies, just walks in and sits down and starts talking about anything you want him to talk about. He's selling a book, of course, but he doesn't have to sell it. Every print run will vanish quicker than the trees can be chopped to print them on. He's talking because he wants to explain.

Q. Don't you regret that you'll never be thirty again, going to the World Cup as one of the great players?

A. 'Honestly I feel relaxed about it now. Sometimes I think I should feel that way, but I had come to the end of my tether. There's things in the book and things I've said regarding all the different things that were bothering me. They sound small if you take them in isolation, but it boiled down to the fact that it wasn't working for me. I couldn't go on. I'm sure Mick would say the same. It just wasn't happening for us. People say I should have stayed for the sake of the country. It's different, though, when you're dealing with somebody every day. I wasn't on the same wavelength.

'We just weren't heading the right direction. We pretended. Mick tried hard. To manage is hard and you are not going to please everybody, but it just wasn't happening. Even going back to the days when we were playing. We tried. He tried as hard as me. And I did try. It was just coming to a head. It was the timing, on the eve of the World Cup, that made it all so bad.'

He has mellowed about it but aspects still hurt him. Players coming out and having a slice of him should know that it's not appreciated. Tony Cascarino and Denis Irwin have had a lot to say. It's not their business, he says, they should keep their mouths shut. Touch certain points and he's still bruised. Touch other areas and his claws come out.

Q. Was it just Mick? You've given the impression that Ian Evans wasn't a favourite either?

A. 'Taff hasn't been mentioned much. I can't remember ever enjoying a training session with him. That's not sour grapes. I mean it. That's why I used to come over as late as I could, apart from the fact that I'd be getting what I considered proper treatment over in

Manchester and, to be fair, Mick was understanding about that, especially when we had the free weekends and he would get the lads in quite early.

'The times I spoke to Taff, he never spoke to me. The only time he'd speak to me was when he was looking for autographs. I'd say you're allowed have a conversation with me, but it was always either getting the autograph or making snide comments. He didn't help. Even in the room in Saipan when I was having my blowout with Mick, he was in the background and I'm looking at him thinking you're fucking next. It never got around to that though.'

Q. And the friendships?

A. 'Friendships. Yeah. They're not really regrets, but on the other hand I had good times with those lads, Niall, Stan, Kells. I wouldn't try to blame them for anything. The problem was me and Mick, and probably Ian Evans too, but in my gut I still feel they shouldn't have gone to that press conference. I feel they shouldn't have done that to me. They are entitled to their opinion. I understand they had to stick by Mick, but I don't think they had to go and sit there, especially Stan and his "disbelief".

'You didn't have to go there, lads. Again, though, I want to put that to bed. I've had some good times with them and they are pretty decent lads, but I still remember that like yesterday. And I remember the next morning when they were leaving too. Listen, before you say I brought all this on myself, I know that. I'm responsible for my own actions.

'I'm responsible for my part, but I know if it was the other way around, I know what I would do for a player. I remember with Sparky (Mark Kennedy) and Babbsy (Phil Babb) when they got put out. That's where team-mates defend a player. That morning when they left Saipan, I remember sitting there thinking they mustn't think that highly of me if not one of them came to knock on my door, nobody could come and say "see ya, Roy, all the best, have a safe trip or have a long trip". I'm sure I would have done it for somebody else.

'Mick Byrne knocked. That's all. I know Johnny Fallon, the kitman, for years, Tony, the security man. Packie. I could hear it all out in the corridor. I was in the second last room along. Things like that hurt you. You come home and say this was the issue or that was the issue, but these other things confirm for you that there is no going back.'

Surprisingly, he feels that there was a way back in the twelve hours after the disastrous meeting. He still insists he was set up. Several times he noticed Mick McCarthy and Ian Evans watching him when he was on the beach that day and, when the team sat down for their meal at 6.30 pm, there were no staff members present. Since the time when he was an under-15 player for Ireland, he says, he can't remember that happening. They dangled the carrot, he says, and he ate their hand off.

Q. When you left the room, was that the end for you? Was there a way back?

A. 'If Mick had knocked on the door that night or next morning, yeah, probably there was a way back. Just to say that things got messy, we all made mistakes here. I know it took two to tango. I'm not going to say Mick is one hundred per cent to blame. It's easy for me to sit here and say the set-up was crap, I understand that a lot of it was done through the FAI, I'm just saying the manager has to get the ball rolling. If he had come, I'm sure there would have been a way. It was a long night. It was long for me. It must have been long for him. There was a cooling-off period before they left. It's not like we had the row at half-seven and they left at eight.

'The press conference threw everything, though. I couldn't understand, time-wise, how they had it even. By the time they had it and some players came to my room, they'd had a press conference. That shocked me.'

That morning, when the team left Saipan, the longest day of his life began.

His flight off the island wasn't till half-four in the afternoon. The morning dragged horribly. He rang the front desk of the Saipan Hyatt at noon and asked if he could book a taxi for about 2.30 pm. The hotel manager told him that there was a handful of media camped out waiting for him.

He thought that he might as well face them, they weren't going to go away, but the manager sent up chicken and chips and said he'd organise a lift to the airport. A credit-card machine was sent up to help him pay his massive phone bill. When Roy Keane finally went downstairs, he thought maybe he'd speak to the press, but the hotel had a car waiting out the back.

He gave all his Irish Umbro gear to the cleaners. His World Cup suit. Tons of Umbro T-shirts.

'I said to them to take them. I left quite a bit there. No point in bringing them back. Left my shoes there with the Irish flag on the back. I'd say somebody is playing football in them, only there's no football pitches in Saipan.'

Michael Kennedy met him in the British Midland lounge at Heathrow when he got back. Keane was waiting for the half-seven morning shuttle. Kennedy said he'd come up to Manchester with him. He said there was a lot of press up there. So Keane said, 'Michael, what are you going to do, make them disappear?'

Kennedy told Keane there had been gossip on the Internet about his private life. A woman had been ringing Theresa, Keane's wife. So he rang Theresa straight away and she said it was nothing, everything was fine.

'You're not going back to the World Cup, are you?' said Michael Kennedy.

'I don't think so,' said Keane.

Kennedy told Keane he needed to maybe say something.

'I hadn't really understood how big it was. He said I should give my side and then [laughs], the way Michael works he got a deal out of the *Daily Mail*. He said it was to make up for what I was losing out on in the World Cup through Diadora, etc. That wasn't the issue, but that's the way he works. He always looks after me.'

The Tommie Gorman interview on RTÉ he dismisses as a red herring overfed with hype. Michael Kennedy was keen for him to do a television piece explaining his side of things. RTÉ were chosen.

Rumours ran around Izumo and other parts that Keane was going on television to apologise, that some deal had been brokered, and as soon as the words fell from his mouth he would be whisked away and put on to a plane on his way to a happy reunion.

Q. How close did you come to turning around and going back to Japan?

A. 'I don't think I was ever really going back. I think, looking back, that was a waste of everyone's time. Michael said "Go on television and let people know how you feel," but getting interviewed is artificial. It's thirty-six minutes long and they were saying "Can we cut this bit out?" They thought I shouldn't say that stuff about Niall Quinn, or whatever, I said "Use it all".

'Nah, there was never anything going to happen from the interview. I think he [Tommie Gorman] was desperate for me to go back. He was talking about the troubles in the North and all that. I don't know if they were trying to instigate an apology or to open a door. It never got to that stage. It was never going to. I wasn't going to be apologising for anything.'

The small things which weighed on him needed explaining then.

He feels now it's harder and harder to articulate them. The rumours that the *News of the World* was about to stitch him up with a story about his private life was, he says, among the least of his problems. He thinks he might have confused the issue by saying to Mick McCarthy in Saipan that his discontent was down to personal problems.

'I just said that because Mick wanted to know what to tell the press. He's obsessed with the press. I should have just said "I've had enough" and faced the music from that side.'

He has cooled a little on the subject of Mick McCarthy, but, when he lets his mind wander back, when he starts thinking about it, the same old irritants crop up. They were never a mix, never a match. The time together in Saipan just confirmed each man's view of the other.

Keane, as a senior player and captain of Manchester United, expected to be consulted on an almost daily basis on matters to do with the team. He felt ignored and slighted, mostly. He's sure Mick McCarthy just viewed him as a thorny bastard. That's fine. There was little love, so there is little hurt.

He confirms the detail of a little-circulated story about one night in the airport hotel when a row broke out between some friends of Gary Breen and a party being entertained by Roy Keane.

'If I went into detail about every incident like that, there'd be no book left.'

Q. But when McCarthy came out into the corridor, you told him to go back into his room?

'Yeah, yeah. I did, to be fair, and I apologised the next time. The next match was against Wales. I apologised. There was drink involved. Not that drink is an excuse.'

Q. What was it about the relationship that meant you couldn't stick it a few more weeks?

A. 'I remember Mick getting up on the stage at the barbecue in Saipan and he gave the lad who was hosting it a bit of stick about wearing a wig and I was just thinking, I cannot imagine any other international manager in the world doing that. Thanks for the night and then an insult about his hair.

'I saw him one night on *I Think It's All Over* with Gary Lineker and I'm not trying to run anyone's life here, but he's on about eating hairy burgers and all this, and I'm shaking my head, "Mick, Mick, Mick. You're the Irish manager."

'People think I'm an awkward customer. I played with Rockmount for nine years and never had a problem with anybody at Rockmount. I had a year at Cobh, no problem. Nottingham Forest. Brian Clough, who is fairly strict, he and I had our moments, but ask Liam O'Kane, Archie Gemmill and, hopefully, they'll say I was never a problem training. To Manchester United. Kiddo, Steve McClaren, all these people. It's just the Irish set-up. I'm actually not the awkward bastard people think I am.

'I was hoping that Mick and Ian Evans would pull something out of the bag in Saipan, that they'd do something which would make it more enjoyable or more interesting. The first training session, we did this shooting routine with Ian Evans, like we always do. And you were getting a shot every fifteen minutes. Normal coaches would have four goals to halve the time. I'd love to know where they got their coaching badges and close it down.

'I always thought the whole system was wrong. I'd come in on the Monday evening for midweek games and the lads would be going to the pictures on the Monday night. They'd be saying "Hey, you missed a good one yesterday, two and a half hours of a session we did." They'd have played on Saturday and the day after should be a day of loosening and stretching and a Jacuzzi, or something. It was the same with flying to Saipan the day after the Nigeria game.

Twenty-three hours, three different planes, after playing an international match.

'When I think of that stuff, it's all confirmed it to me. I'd come in on the Monday and enjoy the picture and the diet coke and the pop-corn and the Minstrels. That was the highlight of my international weeks under Mick. And the games. I enjoyed the games. I'll miss the games. I'll miss next week. Not the travelling and that chaos. Probably I'll watch it.

'I won't miss being treated like a child. I used to come over on a Monday night and, as I say, we'd go to the pictures every Monday. I enjoy the pictures, they were the highlight of my international week. But this one night I was knackered. I told Mick Byrne I was knackered. "Okay," he says. Two minutes later he came back. Mick McCarthy is upstairs, he says all the players have to go, everyone is on the bus. I'm feeling apologetic all of a sudden. Two minutes later Mick Byrne is back. "If you don't go to the pictures, nobody is allowed go." I had to go. In my late twenties and not allowed to decide if I'm tired or not.'

Through his account of the whole affair, it strikes one that, given the failings of the two central characters, some buffer, some authoritative figure who could act as a court of appeal or a go-between, was needed on hand. The FAI? The FAI he describes as 'just a shambles'. Since he was involved with Irish teams from under-15s, 16s, youth, under-21s and senior, he hasn't found a better word for them. Shambles.

In the matter of Saipan and what happened afterwards, he found them so irrelevant as to be part of a different, unexplored galaxy. He is surprised even to be asked if they had any part in things. Being honest, he doesn't even know any of their names.

They are a vague, gassy blur somewhere off in the distance. 'I know people in League of Ireland clubs and they say the same. They are shocking. They have a chief executive now, I think, but it's amateurs trying to run professionals. I haven't had any personal contact with them since the meeting in Saipan. Not one. They might have rung Michael to find out what was happening, I don't know. They weren't part of it.

'I don't expect for us to get what England players get, they have hundreds of millions, I appreciate that, but it's not the team's fault that the FAI are blowing six or seven million on a study for a stadium that'll never be built. We are punished in daft little ways. They wouldn't bring our wives to the World Cup. Eventually we got four free tickets after an argument. Football has made me a wealthy man, I'm not bitching over the money, I'm just talking about doing it properly.

'It's just crazy. I've seen them boozing up with players in Cyprus. I've seen them all over the world sitting in the first-class seats. An FAI official came to my room in Dublin before an important game and he was pissed, asking for an autograph. Eleven at night. I won't give his name, but he was steaming. Is that acceptable? Tell me I'm wrong if it is.'

Still with us? There's the drink to be dealt with. He feels, too, that he has been misrepresented in terms of his views of other players' drinking habits.

When he could do it, he was as guilty as anyone, he says. Under Jack, he'd come in on a Sunday night and just get wrecked. He'd be out on the town and he'd arrive in at half-past six or seven in the morning. Train in the afternoon on Monday. Sleep most of the day Tuesday and play on Wednesday. Usually get something out of it.

That was years ago, though. Times have to change, he thinks. He gave up because his injuries couldn't bear the burning which was being done at both ends of the candle. And he couldn't bear the trouble he was getting into. He misses it like a hole in the head, he says.

The drinking in Saipan didn't bother him, though. 'People would say I'm a fine one to talk. The next day at training in the heat, the lads were dying. I got a laugh out of that, the stories and the hangovers. That wasn't a problem.' Nor did it ever cross his mind not to go to Saipan, to just skip it and join the team later. He thinks that, because he'd had leeway over the years, he felt he should go to Saipan. He knew that the leeway he got on other issues must have played on the other players' minds. They'd have the odd laugh, the odd tease about it, but he knew it was there. The resentment about him coming in on a Monday for a Wednesday game. He decided it was out of the question to be coming a week late for the World Cup.

'I wanted us all to go together. I thought fundamentally it would all be sound. We got there, the pitch, the gear, it all snowballed.'

And he appreciates that perhaps there were other people besides him feeling an undercurrent from the Niall Quinn testimonial incident. Of all the fallout, the disagreement with other players seems to bother him the most and hurt him the most.

Q. Do you regret saying what you did about some players?

A. 'In hindsight, I've had a few harsh words to say about Stan and Quinny and Kells. It must have been hard for them, to be fair.'

Q. Do you regret calling them cowards?

A. 'No. I think they were. They should have said to Mick that the problem was between him and me. Nothing to do with players. Steve Staunton shaking his head like Stan's never given anyone dog's abuse?'

Q. So what do you regret?

A. 'Ah, I suppose I do regret it. I think it was unfair for the players to get involved. I just don't think they should have. Life goes on.'

Q. You play against Niall Quinn today. Steve Staunton in a few weeks. Will you talk to them?

A. 'Probably not. I'm sure they won't want to talk to me. It doesn't mean that I've got a problem with them. It all got really messy, didn't it? From everyone's point of view. They hurt me. They really did hurt me. I felt hurt after it. I still do.

'Afterwards, that statement that went out, even though it wasn't supposed to, but it did go out. I'm at home watching Sky and the players have signed the statement. I genuinely believe that's what they wanted. I felt that they might have been better off without me and I have to accept that.'

Q. Does it make a difference that they'd talked Mick around?

A. 'It was as confusing for me as it was for anyone else. It was a shambles. The whole lot of it was a shambles. The time difference didn't help. I'm getting this and that back. I couldn't go back. Not after the injury accusation. They were saying if I apologised. I couldn't get my head round that. I wouldn't go back on that basis. If we'd said let bygones be bygones, maybe.

'And all the stuff after I left. I turn on the telly and Quinny is on giving his press conference. He's telling everyone what a week he has had. I'm at home now and I'm saying to the telly, "What a week you've had, Quinny?" He says he shouted at Gillian and then he wiped his face and said he was shattered. He's been staring at the ceiling. And Damien Duff said [adopts slow mournful voice] "Is This What the World Cup Is About?"

'Well, I'm at home, there's stuff about my personal life on the Internet, I'm supposedly sleeping with more women than I could dream of, I've got dozens of women pregnant, apparently, in Dublin of all places! I have to be careful there at the best of times! I couldn't leave the house. My Mam and Dad were in a caravan we have. They were in hiding, but some of the local media scumbags got there, banging on my mother's caravan. "Right, Mossie, can you come out and say something?"

'And Quinny was having a hard time because he had a go at Gillian? Mick said it was the most difficult week in his career. It was a walk in the park compared to what I had to put up with. Not just for one week. For the whole summer. It's calmed down a bit now, but there's still that booing at matches, which [laughs], okay, they'd do anyway, but, lads, it was no walk in the park.'

He watched the World Cup in distracted, fitful moments. He is reluctant to criticise the on-the-pitch performances, partly because he saw so little of them, and partly out of loyalty. The team played nice football. He feels, though, that the celebration in the park must have been an embarrassment for some of his old colleagues when they analysed it in terms of results.

Q. Was it hard to look at the World Cup?

A. 'The games? I watched the penalty shoot-out against Spain thinking I should be there. As a player, you like to think you would have helped, ask any player, they think they could give that bit extra to the team. I think I could have and would have.

'The biggest relief, in a funny sense, was the team getting knocked out. There wasn't any satisfaction in it, I was sorry for the lads, but every game the press were outside. I'd pass and they'd say, "What's it like for them to have qualified without you?"

'I bit my tongue. The morning of the Spain match there was a big crowd of them. I went out and got back for about the last twenty minutes of normal time. Say the extra time and the penalties. I came out later that afternoon to walk the dog and it was amazing, the street was dead. No story any more. The story was that they were doing well without me, and they were, to be fair. Then it was finished.

'It was like that scene from *The General* when Martin Cahill comes out on the morning he was shot and there's absolutely nobody there. I'm looking around wondering if there's somebody in the bushes, waiting for me. There's a part of me saying "Thank God that's over". I was upset for some of the players because we were so close. On the other hand, we should have won. They were gone when I saw it, gone mentally, usual Spanish scenario. They were a shambles, they were there for the taking, ten men for half an hour. Go kill the game.'

So life goes on. He hopes it will return to some form of tranquillity soon.

He's happy that his kids are too young to understand it all and the rest of his family has got through it. He's made mistakes, he thinks, and as the heat goes out of the situation he sees them more clearly.

He'll miss stuff. When he thinks about what he'll miss, it sets him off again.

'The atmosphere for a big game in Lansdowne is the best I've ever played in. Better than the World Cup, better than big nights at Old Trafford, big European nights, it's just brilliant. Holland and Portugal. Those games were better than any other matches I've ever played in. Are we asking too much to repay the fans by doing things right?'

The aftermath will linger, of course. Other books to come. The FA and possible legal cases hanging over him in England. He's found a strange calm in the middle of it.

'If I have to answer the FA, I will. If I have to go to court, I will. My attitude is, like, "relax everybody". Myself first of all. It's only a book.'

You ask about Alf Inge Haaland. He says it's with Michael Kennedy. He has confidence there. He reminds you that Haaland played on that day, that his other leg has kept him out of football. There's a difference between hurting and injuring, he says. A difference that every footballer knows.

'Listen, I'm playing Sunderland this weekend. I want to hit them hard. They want to hit me hard. There's a difference between that and wanting to injure them.

'I've played professionally for thirteen years now. I've been involved in two tackles where players have been injured and taken off. Once, at Forest, against Nigel Winterburn. I got the free. Once, for United, against Dennis Wise. He jumped in late. I got the free again. I get hurt every week. I play in the middle of the park as a ball-winner. People want to hurt me. I want to hurt them. It's not the same as wanting to injure them or end their career. People need to chill out.'

And Roy Keane. Is he chilled at last?

'Listen,' he says, 'it's all done now. Everyone has to take their blame right along the line. Me. Mick. The FAI. Maybe it would be unfair to blame the players, but the rest of us have to stand up.'

He's done. No foam around the mouth. No vein throbbing in his temple. That wasn't too frightening, was it? Glad you stayed?

'Gotta go,' he says, and flashes a rueful smile full of hard-earned wisdom.

Kilkenny perfection

9 September 2002

For the great teams, excellence supplies its own narrative. There are no stepping stones from contention to achievement, no guff about having to lose one to win one. There's just the game and the pursuit of perfection.

Kilkenny brushed Clare aside yesterday in an All-Ireland final that was about introversion and obsession. As D.J. Carey said afterwards, they had nothing against Clare, virtually no history with them. This was about a journey within the game. This was about Kilkenny being as good as they can be.

Last summer, in the popular imagination at least, Kilkenny threatened perfection as they cut through Leinster. They came to Croke Park for an All-Ireland semifinal with Galway and were widely advertised as possessing a full-forward line that was the eighth wonder of the world. They lost.

The time since then hasn't been spent sticking pins through maroon-coloured voodoo dolls.

It's been a movement towards the type of performance which Kilkenny gave yesterday. Two goals and twenty points scored. Three wides over the seventy minutes.

Sublime contributions from all parts of the pitch. McGarry. Kavanagh. Barry. Shefflin. Carey. All wondrous. Just about everyone else outstanding.

And when Kilkenny began introducing their subs, two of them – McEvoy and Carter – hit wonder points just for fun.

Few teams have done what Kilkenny have this year in winning both league and championship. They have maintained a standard that is impressive even within the context of their own history and, in the latter stages of the All-Ireland series, they have handed in two performances which were sublime. Could they be as good yesterday as they were against Tipperary some weeks ago, we wondered?

They answered emphatically.

For Clare, the achievement was in keeping the crowd from seeping out of the ground. They played with the heat and the passion which is their modern hallmark, but the winning of twenty-seven All-Ireland titles means that hurling craft is congenital in Kilkenny and acquired in Clare. That's a lot to overcome. Their pride was their defiance.

'We were beaten by seven points today,' said Cyril Lyons, their manager. 'I don't know if we were seven points the lesser team, but it doesn't matter now anyway. They were always ahead by five or six and when the score is that way you can try things and they come off.'

They come off because excellence makes its own rules too. The world must bend to accommodate its prodigies. Nobody who heard that D.J. Carey intended coming back to the black and amber of Kilkenny when the spadework of the provincial championships had been done could have demurred.

If he had left it until yesterday to step from the stands and declare himself available again, there could have been no objections. What would be the point of building a cathedral like Croke Park if D.J. Carey were not to soar within it.

The joy of the game and the thrill of yesterday was seeing D.J.'s genius unfold again under the command of his will. D.J. came back to the game eight weeks ago.

He won his fourth All Ireland yesterday and one suspects that the two games he played all year will be enough to secure him a ninth All Star. He brushes it all away. Even his goal, another chunky contribution to the cause he has served, was played down until it assumed the significance of a man removing lint from his pocket.

'Ah, I took the chance and put the hurl up and flicked it in the net. Just one of those things.'

And his resurrection? His journey back from being hurling's most talked about retiree to the Croke Park pastures?

'It's been worthwhile. You dream when you are a youngster of this. It's occasions like this that matter. I didn't do as much this year as the rest of the lads, but today is fantastic. We knew that Clare would come at us in the second half.

'They got points. And we hoped we'd tack on a point or two when they did. They came back to within three points and then Henry got a great point and we got it back to six.'

His mind wanders off into the mechanics of the game he loves. Shefflin. He wishes he had ten years left playing with Shefflin. Charlie Carter, his old confederate, how Charlie can still illuminate Croke Park when he walks on stage.

D.J. was at the Leinster Final this summer and he had that edginess within himself, that little insistence that he was gone before he was ready to go.

'I felt disappointed that my year was gone. Watching in the stand that day, I was very passionate. I've never been a spectator. I knew then. At this stage I have the heart to go on some more... it's all about the legs next year, though.'

He went out and trained and lifted weights on his own. He trained when the panel he had rejoined were still resting. And he found the sessions had changed. Every session was like an All Ireland. Brian Cody had marked out a pitch the precise size of Croke Park. Training on that every night makes lead of a man's legs.

Fortunately, Kilkenny's hunger for excellence matched his own. When their paths intersected, a September afternoon like this was inevitable. The team he rejoined was making its own journey. They were convincing champions this summer and will start next season as favourites to repeat.

In the Kilkenny dressing room, with the Liam McCarthy Cup lying on his kitbag, Andy Comerford stands on the bench and speaks to the players he has captained all year. This is the soul of the GAA we are prying on, those moments when an ordinary man expands his horizons and seizes the respect of others. He speaks passionately.

'You can all hold your heads high, lads. Thirty men got us here and every one of them was needed. I'll say one thing, lads, respect yourselves and respect your families. Celebrate for sure, but Kilkenny were always men that were humble.

'Always remember that you're Kilkenny hurlers. Whatever way you celebrate, do it with dignity and do it with pride. Be proud of what you achieved. Respect the jersey. Always remember that you are Kilkenny hurlers.'

He stands down with the roar of applause coming towards him. Kilkenny hurlers. All-Ireland champions.

The jersey. The dignity. The pride. That's the story of the season. That's the narrative of one team's excellence.

Stick on Freddie, Mick, and mellow out

21 October 2002

This won't mean a lot to you, in fact I don't know why I bring it up, but I met Freddie White once. It was the cursed late 1980s and myself and some associates had gone skinny broke from trying to promote music, comedy and anything else which needed our suffocating touch. If you wanted proof that the brightest and the best had all emigrated we were it. With petrol in one hand and matches in the other we couldn't have promoted the use of a fire door.

I knew Freddie White would work, though, because less than a decade earlier, if you could get a woman into your mildewed bedsit in Ranelagh, you would woo her sideways with a little Freddie White. Freddie made you interesting by proxy. He sent out the message that you were an heroically melancholic soul concerned with so much more than, well, just the usual thing. And if she went home before the usual thing, sure you had the carry-out and Freddie's voice and some roll-up to get you through the night.

Then there were the gigs, one light shining on this man in a denim shirt, this guy who knew songs from places and people you didn't know existed. He knew people called Fats and Hoagy and Randy and he looked like he'd lived twenty lives already.

So I signed Freddie up for (bizarrely) a lunchtime college gig because, well, that guitar, that voice, that jutted stance, those songs, Ranelagh, he was a hero. Three people turned up. I lacked the touch when it came to promoting.

So, red-faced and broke, I stared at Freddie White across a not very crowded room above a bar off Mountjoy Square. He stared back and shook his head. I could only assume he'd met some chancers in his day and he'd met some gobshites too, but he'd never met the whole package before.

And then Freddie White took out his guitar and played for three people and some staff for seventy minutes, during which time we experienced phenomena like hair standing up on the backs of our necks and lumps invading our throats and eyes welling.

That type of thing.

Finally Freddie White took from me the twelve quid I'd taken at the door and took also from me a cheque with which he could have played squash. He put the twelve quid behind the bar, barter for a bottle of Smirnoff. Then he and I sat on high stools till the bottle was empty. By then I'd heard many good yarns and he'd heard several bad excuses. I'd seen him play live a hundred times in every sort of place. After that, I never saw him again. It wasn't his time anymore.

Still that voice and those songs of his have more clarity than old photos. To hear Freddie White brings me right back to the summer when myself and Sean K were so flat broke that we shoplifted tins of sardines and packets of sausages for two months just to live. I hear Freddie White and I'm belching John West.

Few things in life have that redolence. For some people it is scents. Or places. For me it is voices. I hear Mick McCarthy's voice and I think of 1990.

Not just that mad summer, but the innocent build-up which preceded it, the impossibly dull friendlies of that spring. What was the sound that you could hear all over Lansdowne Road? Mick McCarthy's voice. Foghorn Leghorn at the back. That bluntness, a second blade of it behind Charlton's, it seemed indicative of our proud defiance.

I was just trying my hand at being a sports journalist back then. Not long before, I'd gone to droll Mr Bank Manager and whined for a loan of £1,000 because I was going to sign off the dole and dive wholesale into the world of sports hackery. Mr Bank Manager made a good and cautionary point: last time you came in here it was to be a promoter, he said, and now it's to be a hack. I'll tell you now, because it's the next thing, I don't lend money to pimps or pushers.

For me, McCarthy always seemed stapled to that good and happy time. A big, reliable man with the dopey Captain Fantastic tag wrapped around his neck like a St Bernard's brandy barrel. I could never have imagined that in this lifetime I would hear him booed in Lansdowne Road or that I would be scribbling pieces suggesting that he leave his job as Irish manager. Not three months after seeing him lead us in a World Cup.

The booing in Lansdowne last Wednesday night was ugly and the onslaught on Mick McCarthy this weekend was bloody. There's great sadness in it because you know that Mick McCarthy loved the good days in Lansdowne Road as much as another man loved playing a guitar in front of an audience. But when you put yourself out there on the highwire of public life, you take the risk that you might never hear applause at all or that one day, shockingly, it might stop. It just won't be your time anymore but what you'll be left with is the game you loved or the music you loved and the memories you stored.

Mick McCarthy had that summer of 1990 as a player and, in a

more complicated way, he had the summer of 2002 as a manager. That's a whole lot of good times. To see him losing his grip and his perspective, to see his proper place in the affections of the football public vanishing is hard, but it's the flip side of the adulation.

Only Mick McCarthy can deal with it. He has earned the right, I think, not to be sacked, but he has an obligation to himself and the national team he serves to take himself out of the way if the atmosphere around him is being poisoned by his situation. He has made big mistakes and, stubbornly, he stands over them. The stubborness more than the mistakes is the current difficulty.

In years to come, I think that if Mick McCarthy gets granted perspective and serenity he'll see that he made a lot of lousy decisions this year. Those decisions aren't the point here though. The point is that he should get out with the good things he has got, let the best days speak for him again.

About two months ago, feeling the big boulder of middle age being levered onto me from behind, I started looking around for Freddie White's first two albums. Some guys get red sports cars, flashy mistresses or Seamanesque ponytails. I get music that makes me sentimental for other days. (Yes, that's how deep and interesting I am, gals.) I still had the old vinyl copies, but owned nothing to play them, on so I haunted the record shops and searched the net and asked around and everywhere felt like that poor old man looking for his fly-fishing book in the old Golden Pages ads.

Then last Wednesday I found those two albums reissued, remastered and freshly corralled into one handsome gatefold sleeve. No explanation for this good deed. None needed. Just a lot of people out there with boulders rolling over them, I imagine. I'm no expert but be assured that the sparse and haunting *Live on Tour* – Freddie White's 1979 album – is still among the greatest Irish albums of all time. *Do You Do* swings and struts just as profoundly. Imagine those two little cuts of vinyl made two decades ago, they still stand as perfection, the high point of an epic career.

And that's the message for Mick McCarthy. All things pass. Don't battle it.

Take a high stool, take a bottle of vodka, stick on Freddie at the start. Then get yourself lost down in all the mellow that follows. Your time comes and your time goes but what you did is what you did; what you achieved is immutable. Two great moments. Enjoy that. Let the affection come back.

Move on. Stay sane. Get happy.

Grounds for complaining about the cold

28 October 2002

Out our way it's been a leaf storm all week long. The wind roughs up the trees, the rain pins the golden leaves to the ground, we pad around on this slippery new carpet. Of course, it's relentless too. Never a little snap storm and then a return to blue winter skies. Just this eternal grey and the rain blowing so hard that when it's only drizzling it starts to feel tropical.

Great little country. I still haven't got the warmth back into my body since the second International Rules Test. Whatever happened to the great promise of global warming? Do we need to go to the top deck in Croker and simultaneously point our aerosols at the ozone? If it has to be done then it has to be done.

Weather like this reminds me of being a kid. Most of you will remember that, with the exception of two sunny days, and a lot of bitter frost, the weather was exactly like this from about 1969 to the early '90s when I got a job, thus inadvertently ending my epic childhood. Those of us who walked to school suffered frostbite, hypothermia, mugging and the narkiness of stray huskies. On arrival, we assembled our anoraks into a steaming heap on top of the ancient radiator and moved like cows in a parlour until we could get some part of our buttock area pressed against that same radiator. There we'd stay until such time as the teacher would stride in and request *duine éigin* to open the window.

Wednesday was a big day in our lives back then. The GAA fixtures for the weekend would appear in the evening papers on that day, a thrillingly comprehensive service which even delved into the murky world of B-grade football and hurling. Wednesday was also the day Dublin Corporation would begin decreeing whether its pitches would be playable for the weekend.

The second half of the week was therefore a race against the elements.

Generally, the urine of an incontinent cat was sufficient disaster for a pitch to be dramatically declared 'waterlogged' and for all fixtures to be called off.

Actual rain at any time in the first half of the week made the Corpo look dubiously at the prospect of any games being played anywhere. On Thursday or Friday, ominous little notices would begin to appear on the back of the *Evening Press*. 'The following Corporation pitches unplayable this weekend', or 'All Corporation pitches unplayable this weekend'.

In those days, little postcards used to arrive in the school or home informing the recipient that his selection had somehow occurred for the under-15 F game against Erin's Isle and that his presence was required at the corner of Griffith Avenue on Saturday at lunchtime. The desire to get a game was so great that often we fooled ourselves into thinking these postcards overrode the power of the Corporation and some of us would trudge to Griffith Avenue despite having seen the Corpo notices. We'd arrive and huddle hoping the Erin's Isle pitch would be available or that we could sneak a game in some-where else or there had been some mistake.

It seems like a small, perverse pleasure now, but the greatest joy was when it would stay fine(ish) until about teatime on Friday and then start bucketing down. We'd head off to Sillogue or Saint Anne's or some such oasis of charm and get dressed under the scant cover of open car boots and then play a game in the driving rain and wind, getting so cold we had to have our boots removed by surgeons or fire brigade men afterwards.

The territory stretching out beyond the small square would be a quagmire, the like of which they left after they fought battles in World War I. Never mind losing a *sliotar* in that mud, you could lose a small corner forward. All that guff you hear about how speed tells on a hard surface, it's all theory. For years we thought a mentor was just a man with an umbrella.

Win or lose you could go home feeling as hardy as any generation that went before you. Your legs, from ankle to upper thigh, would be encased in mud. You'd slip your drainpipe jeans on over this new skin and, all the way home, as it cracked, it felt like you were having your legs waxed very slowly. When we'd get home, most of us washed at least an acre's worth of Corporation land down the plugholes of our baths.

In this manner we'd get up to half a dozen games played during the winter and then all competition would be suspended to make way for the allegation of summer. Oftentimes, in those far off days, we'd wonder would a Strategic Review Committee ever be established to look into this situation and somehow move summer to the wintertime so that actual competitions could be played.

Once, by mistake, I played rugby for a winter. The Corpo were so assiduous about cancelling matches that you could have alternative careers as a rugby player and a Russian cosmonaut going on in the winter months and nobody would notice. Anyway, the rugby didn't depend on the Corporation and the colder and more mucky it got the better it seemed to be for the rugby fellas.

I knew I wasn't going to be making a career of it when they brought us to Greystones and introduced us to the concept of the wind-chill factor. I was standing there shivering when one of them gave me the ball and the rest then fell on top of me, where they remained in a gasping heap until such time as my head had completely adhered to the muddy surface.

I could see the trade-off. You got to share body heat, which seemed sensible, but you had to surrender all the oxygen in your lungs, becoming so impaired that you enjoyed the post-match rugby songs. I got out before it was too late.

I've always wondered though (fabulous example of unimpaired intellect coming up) why as a nation we don't entice other similarly blighted countries into joining us in an Olympiad of games to be played in miserable weather. Not Winter Olympics, which is just clean snow, but games to be played in rain, wind and mud on public pitches. We'd excel.

You could see it last week at Croke Park. Tall, tanned, fit professionals should have minced us. But they didn't. The sort of weather you wouldn't put a cat out in was our ally. As I sat shivering I tried to think which was the coldest most miserable GAA ground in the country to stand in on a winter's day.

I gave it to Ballinascreen, outside Draperstown, just ahead of Fintra where Killybegs play. Fintra at least looks beautiful.

Anthony Rainbow, who was playing last Sunday, once had to be treated for hypothermia after a game in Ballinascreen and many are the tales of players stepping into the showers in their gear.

There are other pitches around the place which are surely more miserable and ugly, but I've never been anywhere colder than Ballinascreen on a cold day. And as regular readers will know, my experience of misery is considerable. I was in Clones for that Ulster final in the early 1990s when it rained for forty days beforehand and forty days afterwards. The Ulster Council were just beginning to refurbish the ground and they stuck the poor media on a lorry trailer on a bank.

In the torrential rain, a Down minor broke his leg slipping on the surface and the bank on which the trailer was placed began to disintegrate and slip. We made our escape and stood precariously on chairs as the rain drove down.

I've been miserable in Casement Park and in Bruff. Soaked in Fraher Field and Ballybofey. Shivered in Mullingar. Once in Longford it was so cold the county secretary went to the pub and came back and handed two bottles of whiskey into the press box. As for Brrrrrr in Offaly…

You are wondering, of course, what's the point of all this. Well, 'Locker Room' has moved house and has no central heating as yet. He is cold and fell to wondering about the coldest venues. Profound but sharing. Thanks for your time.

Many skeletons in Locker Room's closet

23 December 2002

The Sports Editor picked a little scab of eggnog from the teeming undergrowth of his dense and manly moustache and, deeming the eggnog to be inedible, he flicked it in the general direction of 'Locker Room'.

Old habits die hard and out of instinct 'Locker Room' dived to the floor to save the morsel. 'Grushee!' yelled the Sports Editor, delighted with his subordinate's hairtrigger response. 'Locker Room' got up from the floor and dusted himself down gingerly.

'Time was…' he said ruefully. 'Yeah,' said the Sports Editor, suddenly, and uncharacteristically, reflective. His brows knitted together.

Both men knew it had been all too few Christmases since the little piece of eggnog, or one like it, would have formed the centrepiece of the 'Locker Room' Christmas table. Indeed it had only been a few Christmases before that when the Sports Editor couldn't have afforded to give a piece of eggnog away just like that. Changed times indeed.

'It's been a long, hard year here in the workhouse,' said the Sports

Editor, 'but once again "Locker Room", you and I have managed
to stay two steps ahead of the workstudy police, we've fooled the
efficiency experts, we've dodged the grim reaper of voluntary redun-
dancy, escaped the scythe of unemployment. For that I raise a glass
to you, "Locker Room".'

And he did just that. Draining it in several gulps as 'Locker
Room' stood with his hands in his pockets, beginning to wonder why
he had been summoned.

'Now listen, "Locker Room",' continued the Sports Editor, but
not before he'd let out a long and satisfied belch which carried on its
tail the smell of meths.

'Now listen, I want you to make like I'm somebody that is
interested and tell me the highlights of your year. Tell me about the
lows and the not quite so lows. The regrets and those other things
that you didn't get found out about.'

'Eh, why the sudden interest?' asked 'Locker Room', 'you've
never talked about my work before. That's the deal. I don't tell
anyone about your Freddie Mercury complex. You don't talk about
my work.'

'Enough with the questions,' said the Sports Editor enigmatically.
'I move in mysterious ways. All will become clear. For now let's talk
about you. What was the high point of the year for you? I know high
point is the wrong word for what has been a long plateau of failure,
but humour me. Was it the Winter Olympics?'

'Why do you say that?'

'Well, at a time when the paper was going down the toilet, we all
liked your style in Salt Lake. Totally out of your depth on the skating
scandal. Then missing the Irish story of the Games.'

'Refresh my memory.'

'Oh just the simple matter of a geezer called Lord Clifton
Wrottesley coming fourth in a death-defying event called the

Skeleton. Never mind. I think you gave us a dull colour piece on curling that day, complete with a pun about clean sweeps. You da Man!'

An uneasy silence descended like a rain-cloud over the two men. Nothing good would come of this. 'Locker Room' was uneasy. He could sense there was more.

'Or was it the following week?' continued the Sports Editor, twirling so quickly now in his twirly chair that 'Locker Room' began feeling nauseous. 'February still, I believe, when you went to California for World Matchplay golf and sent back a series of columns bellyaching about your shuttle-bus driver.'

'But,' began 'Locker Room', keen to get in a point about the Matchplay final having been between Scott McCarron and Kevin Sutherland, neither of whom had previously known that golf was played on Saturdays and Sundays.

'Hush,' said the Sports Editor, 'hush now. Let's hear all the nominations before we choose a moment above all the other moments. We're only at February. For March I think your failure to get a Paula Radcliffe interview stands out. Plus your reassurance that she never does anything.' He tapped his nose. 'Instinct, eh?'

'Locker Room' shifted his weight to his other buttock. 'I think he's forgotten me not being at the Masters,' he thought happily. 'Maybe we can get through this.' 'Moving along,' said the Sports Editor, 'if you can keep up. We've never spoken about how happy you were with the end result of your huge piece on the Ireland vs Italy game in New York in 1994, the one where you were going to speak to all the Irish players and piece that day together again forensically as if it were the Kennedy assassination.

'Personally I was surprised to see it shrank into a Phil Babb/Jason McAteer piece, but what do I know about, ehm, your art?'

'Well,' began 'Locker Room', eager to make a point about the

phone being off that week. 'Ah we're only getting going here,' came
the interruption. 'This is the small stuff. I bet your part in screwing
up the whole World Cup for the whole country must be up there on
the top shelf in your little memory bank. Couldn't bring yourself to
make Roy seem a little happier in your little interview? Couldn't ask
him to say something nice for the folks back home? Couldn't slap
him across the cheek and say "Pull yourself together, man"?
Couldn't pretend your tape recorder was broken?'

'Ah now Jaysus…' 'Locker Room' began.

'But having kept you out there for your own safety, when does
your big colour piece on the phenomenon of the South Korean fans
come through to us? On the night they get knocked out!'

It was late now. The cleaning staff had begun their night shift,
many of their faces familiar from the days when they worked in the
news room. 'Locker Room' was suddenly stung with guilt. No, fear.
He was stung with fear.

'Where are we going with this?' he asked. 'Well let's just see
where it takes us. We'll forget about the fact you stand up and pass
water any time somebody mentions rugby to you. We won't mention
you falling sick the night before the European Athletic Championships and not being there at all. We'll fast forward to the Ryder Cup.
Great event. Great win. Key Irish input. You denounce it all as the
most evil fraud ever perpetrated on mankind.'

'Well there was good stuff too, wasn't there?' said 'Locker
Room', coming back off the ropes. 'Not talking about that are you?'

'Well there was the "humorous" column mocking Cork people.
There was the plague on all their houses piece about sports administrators that was so good it drew a letter of complaint from one of the
most comical sports administrators in the country. You picked Sonia
for the New York marathon. You bleated on about your little camogie
team till they threatened to sue. You "got an interview" with Tommy

Lyons when the only valid journalistic achievement this year would have been keeping interviews with Tommy out of the paper. Your biggest expense claim of the year, by the way, was mileage for a trip to Kerry to interview Páidí Ó Sé in depth. How did that go then?'

'Okay, Okay. What's the bottom line here?' asked 'Locker Room', pale and shaken now.

'I'd bring that piece of eggnog home to the family if I were you,' said the Sports Editor, lighting a stogie. 'This has been your very own Genesis report. Goodbye, good luck and season's greetings.'

Sorry saga finds a fitting end

15 February 2003

First of all and last of all. Roy Keane is not a traitor. Roy Keane is not a comic-book superhero. Roy Keane is something in between. Roy Keane is a footballer who found himself in a difficult situation at work. A man. That's all.

The entire saga from Saipan to Scotland has been about the human frailty which we don't allow sportspeople to have. It has been about what happens when the people we make gods of kick each other with their feet of clay. Everyone has lost.

That's a human way to end things.

If there is a sense of national disappointment that Keane won't be playing for Ireland again, you can be sure that Roy Keane shares it. If there is a sense of relief within the Irish side that they won't be coming face to face with Keane again, you can be sure that Keane feels that too.

It's complicated. Since Saipan, since long before that, it has never been black and white. Nobody has had a monopoly of right. Nobody has been completely wrong. There's a thousand nuanced things which we don't know about grouting the few things we do know about in this story.

Roy Keane, for a start. None of us knows him, the troubles he's had, the troubles he's seen. Many of us have accepted modest fees to pretend we know him, to let on that we understand what makes him tick, but essentially none of us knows him. This entire argument and the convulsive national response to it has been about the shifting paradigms of what we do know. It's been kneejerk and reactionary and excessive.

Roy walks out. Ergo he was a bastard. Moscow, Lansdowne Road and Genesis happen. Ergo Roy was a visionary saint. By Glasgow this week he had become a 'wanker'.

It's useful maybe to stop reacting and to begin just putting it into perspective. Try being Roy Keane for a while. See what it's like living in that head.

Be him. Leave aside your views on whether he was right or wrong. Don't even ponder what other demons eat at Roy Keane. Don't ask yourself whether he overreacted or crusaded.

Just be Roy Keane. Thirty years old. A million miles from home on 24 May 2002.

Be Roy Keane in Saipan on the morning after the famous row. Don't assume the position you've taken in the pub every time the argument has come up since then.

Just be Roy Keane. Nobody else.

In your home you've spoken to Mick McCarthy about your views on the preparation of the team. You thought you were consulting. You know now he was hearing 'Yada yada yada, blah blah blah…'

You've been seething. You have the sense that the manager would be more than half glad to see you go home, you've been longing for this World Cup and instead it's National Lampoon's Footie Vacation. You have been confronted in front of the team and the staff over an interview you have given as captain of the Irish team. You have exploded. The three most senior players on the team, the boys you have known the longest, have gone to a press conference to denounce you.

Now you are alone in your room. It's morning time. 24 May. You can hear the lads you've played with for ten years moving about outside, getting ready to go to the World Cup.

Nobody knocks.

Nobody calls in begging you to give it one last go.

Nobody says, c'mon, we've all done things we regret, but we've been through a lot together.

Nobody says goodbye.

You get nothing from them. You're shaking. Sure, sure, sure, you're spiky, narky sometimes. You are temperamental and you are a loner, but you have contributed to this team. You contributed hugely. You played your guts out, you wanted everyone around you to do the same. And isn't that what teams are about? Accommodating the loners and the roustabout guys together?

But nobody knocks. Nobody says the World Cup is bigger than this. Nobody says that they know you've been having a hard time. If anyone stops to think about it, they must realise that you're going through your own personal hell behind the door there. Anger. Regret. Loneliness. Just as a human being. You are flawed like the rest of them.

You go home alone. To a media siege. To months of controversy. Riding the borders of nervous breakdown country. Everyone with a half-baked opinion is an expert on you. The noise never stops.

Have you had enough of being Roy Keane now? Have you felt the hurt? Okay, switch to being any other Irish World Cup player on the morning of 24 May in Saipan. You've either liked Keane, idolised Keane, or just plain respected him.

Now he's in his room and you have your navy-blue Umbro bag in your fist and you're off to Izumo. You glance at his room, the door closed as always, this guy you've played with for ten years, nine years, whatever. You walk on by.

Have you felt that hurt? Keane's hurt? The players' hurt? McCarthy's hurt?

In Saipan, the genie got out of the bottle and the professional relationship which underpins a team and which we pretend amounts to a willingness to die for one another, that professional relationship vanished and was replaced by something raw. The genie was never going back into the bottle.

Last week is easier to understand now. The explanations make a little more sense. It's only flesh-and-blood people we are talking about.

Sure, Manchester United probably informed Roy Keane in plenty of time about what a resumption of his international career would mean, medically. Yet when Brian Kerr came calling it must have been possible for Roy to be impressed first by the man's meticulousness and by his innate ability with people. If Kerr thought that he could facilitate a return to the way things once were between Keane and the Irish panel, well, then it's easy to see how Keane would be enthusiastic, too. Easy to see how he felt that perhaps a few words in front of the players in another hotel room somewhere would somehow erase everything that had gone before. After all, he's had a thousand football rows and forgotten them all himself.

It would be perfect. This guy Brian Kerr sitting in front of you impresses you more than you ever imagined he would, you will come back into the warm centre of Irish life and every good moment you had in a green jersey would be a voodoo stab in the heart of Mick McCarthy. When Brian Kerr gets up to leave, you ask him when you can start.

But on Friday, Alex Ferguson, the one man you trust above all others in your game and in your life, calls and explains that, yes, maybe United left the question of a continued international career at your discretion, but that was on the assumption that you would say no.

He gives it to you on a plate. He, Sir Alex Ferguson, does not want you playing for Ireland. He, Sir Alex, thought you shared the dream of a Champions League win this year. Do you not? Sir Alex thought that, instead of trudging around Tbilisi and Tirana with those people to whom you owe nothing, this spring you'd want to be resting up for the latter stages of the Champions League.

It wouldn't have to be said aloud that this is the Sir Alex Ferguson who stood by you come hell or high water for the last ten years. He wouldn't have to remind you of the morning he came to get you out of a Manchester police cell.

Nor how it never leaked from his lips that you were going to quit the game after your fight with Alan Shearer. He wouldn't have to talk about standing by you when you criticised the corporate sector of the club. He wouldn't mention that Jaap Stam left when he wrote a slightly controversial autobiography, but that you, Roy Keane, stayed when you wrote an extremely controversial one.

He wouldn't need to explain that in the relationship you have with him every tackle is defensible, every lapse is forgivable, every sin is absolvable. That when it comes to Manchester United he has always assumed that you and he shared precisely the same myopic passion.

It's Alex Ferguson asking you to do this one thing. Not even asking, just explaining. You owe him big. And Brian Kerr has gone away now and, in the cold light of day, part of your brain suspects that things might never be the same again between yourself and the players. You were thinking wishfully yesterday.

You were charmed.

And you think of the money Manchester United pay you. You think of how long you want to postpone the lonely day when you wake up and aren't a footballer any more. You think of the hassle. The media circus. The expectation. Vacillation is the human response.

Finally, you pick the phone up and call Brian Kerr and explain you are sorry but...

Roy Keane's decision not to return to the Irish jersey was more complicated than it needed to be, but it was not necessarily a bad decision and not a treacherous one. The world is still turning.

The timing of Keane's announcement on Tuesday was awkward and the nature of Manchester United's statement on Wednesday gave an insight into how unwilling either the PLC or the manager were to take the heat on such an emotional issue.

Those things are disappointments, but they are just sideshows.

It can be argued, of course, by those of us who hoped to see him play for Ireland again, that all Keane had to do was to give six more games to the jersey. 6 x 90. That's all the country asked.

It is naive, however, not to concede that the decision was about more than that, about more than 540 minutes spent on the pitch. It was about the emotional derailment which the player risked by coming back. It was about the investment of energy in training, playing and travelling as opposed to long periods of rest. It was about the impact on the entire squad.

It has been pointed out that Keane has played FA Cup and League Cup games since his comeback this season. There is a difference, though, between games played as Manchester United strive to get a player back to match fitness and international games at the end of long journeys to uncomfortable places.

Keane has lost the PR war, but, in time, he will reflect ruefully on the strange fickleness of all that.

Just imagine. Keane and Steve Staunton, old friends, fresh enemies, ran into each other in a village square in Portugal during the summer and coldly ignored each other. Staunton is retired from the international game, preserving himself for a prolonged club career. He is still loved and respected. Keane has opted for the same route. He is despised and pilloried. Keane has always known that his is a lonely walk. He has been hero-worshipped, stitched-up, horse-flogged, lionised, canonised, betrayed. At the end, it's little wonder that he did what was best for Roy Keane.

As for Brian Kerr, he has lost a Grade A footballer but dodged a bullet. The only way it could have worked out better was if Keane came back to play and all concerned were afflicted with selective amnesia about the summer war.

Kerr gave it a shot. He persuaded Keane to come back and then somehow he, Kerr, got shafted by events. Keane's reputation takes the heat there though. Kerr is spared the tricky business of beginning a process of laying the seeds for the rehabilitation of Keane and stepping back to let the team awkwardly embrace their old captain.

Keane and Kerr may both have felt that re-introducing Keane to the society of old friends was ultimately worthwhile, but being spared the task of integration has its benefits, too.

This season, the Premiership has seen plenty of the residual spite from Saipan being traded between Keane and Irish players who were there. Insults have been traded in more cases than just the celebrated Jason McAteer book-review incident. Feelings still run high. The books and the newspaper columns haven't helped. Keane has had to be paid a share of the players' pool from the World Cup. They paid him so that he would have nothing to grumble about. Some players feel that McCarthy was sacrificed so that Keane could be rehabilitated. They resent his iconoclasm, his lone-wolf routine.

It was never going to be easy. Those close to the squad feel that one or two players would have been unlikely to continue if Keane were welcomed back into the fold. If that were to happen, or even if they were to remain on in a state of aggravation, the entire chemistry which the Irish team has thrived on would be altered.

Kerr played a blinder this week, his shrewdness never more in evidence than immediately after he got the news that Keane was breaking the news blackout on his future. Kerr took the players into the Hampden dressing room and issued a passionate rallying call about moving on, about everything now being about the future. On the bus journey back from Glasgow to the team hotel in Kilmarnock he took another decision when the FAI spin doctors called.

Rather than use the Park Hotel's press-conferencing facilities, he would speak informally with his back to the wall. At once he presented himself as a man to whom this was happening rather than a player in the whole thing. He made less of it all than might have been made. He avoided questions, spoke briefly and well and just moved on. Everyone, even those of us who questioned the wisdom of having a press conference against a wall in a hotel lobby, were impressed.

And on Thursday morning, in Dublin Airport, Kerr put everything in context, he squared the thing off, trimming the emotional reactions and the hyperbole. Yes, he'd heard his own name chanted in Hampden the previous night. Yes, he'd heard the same people chanting that 'Roy Keane Is A Wanker'. And yes, he knew straight away that the names are interchangeable. Mick McCarthy was chaired from Suwon but hung as a goat before Christmas. Keane was pilloried, then deified, and now pilloried again. Who can blame any one of them for ultimately suiting themselves?

On Wednesday, under the first game of a new Irish manager, Keane was denounced from the terraces as being a wanker. At the end of the last game of the previous Irish manager, his name was chanted reverentially. 'Keano! Keano! Keano!' A funeral rite for

Mick McCarthy's management career. Kerr knows a little of what Keane knows. The songs, the adulation, the hype.

All bollox. Ultimately in football you'll always walk alone. That's the lesson of the last nine months.

Maybe the reasons for Roy Keane's decision last week weren't the ones we wanted to hear, maybe the manner of it left something to be desired, but, in such a fickle world, can he be blamed for preserving himself, for not trusting the baying mob? He has given us lots, including our qualification for the last World Cup and the millions of conversations it spawned.

The easiest, most selfish thing would have been to come back and paper over the cracks and to absorb the national sense of pleasure. Keane bit the bullet instead. It was an ugly, jagged and poorly explained way of doing things, but as such the ending fitted the story.

Drink sponsorship isn't black and white

10 March 2003

Really, you'd think that the guys with the keys to the executive washroom over at Catholic Church plc would have more than enough to be doing just keeping their own show on the road. Not so. Bishop Dermot Clifford finds time every now and then to pull hard across the back of the legs of the GAA. The bishop is a patron of the association and, when he pulls hard with the old crozier, it stings. Rule 21? Swoosh! Féile? Smack! And again and again swinging hard on alcohol and the GAA. The Croke Park nabobs must wonder why they need enemies when they have patrons like Dr Clifford.

He's well-intentioned, I'm sure, but it seems to me that the bishop's urge to ban and prohibit and abstain and repress and censor is just the flipside of the national immaturity about drink.

Most of us live in this big and complex world. Our government has no real regional sports policy. Catholic Church plc has mightily betrayed its stockholders. Sport is one of the few good, reliable things that is left to us.

If they could tax it or ban it or make it a sin, they probably would. Sport isn't like that. Drink isn't black and sport isn't white. Sport is not a goody-goody, squeaky clean, all-sins-absolved-while-you-wait deal. It's part of mainstream community life. Like drink is. If Guinness were to stop sponsoring the All-Ireland hurling championships tomorrow, hurling would be the poorer, the GAA would be the poorer.

The cleverest drink ads would still appear during *Friends*. The pub would still be the only place to go to watch big-time sport on the television. There'd still be rock 'n' roll and Witness. Temple Bar would still be a year-round version of the Munich beer festival. A visit from an American president still wouldn't be complete without the Taoiseach bringing him to his local.

We'd still drink for all the usual reasons: hereditary factors, cultural factors, poverty, affluence, availability, tradition, depression, elation, the fact that the skies are never blue or You're a Star never bloody ends. A percentage of us would still drink too much.

And what would happen next? The puritans would move on. Drink licences for sporting clubs would be the next target. And soon it would be the 1950s again with no places to go other than the saloon bar or the boys' sodality. No thanks.

I'd feel happier sending the kids to the bar.

Drinking did not start in this country when Guinness began sponsoring the All-Ireland hurling championships in 1995. Nobody came rushing out of their house and said that, bejaysus, the scales had just fallen from their eyes, all that stood between them and an All-Ireland medal was a good feed of stout. And drinking won't end when we have the Eat Your Greens All-Ireland Hurling Championship.

Alcohol sponsorship of sport is a trade-off. To me it seems worth it, not just in terms of the hurls and helmets or whatever the money buys, but in terms of placing drink in a context for kids. In the real world, drink doesn't exist in a reservation over here while sport proceeds in a separate territory over there.

If we are going to meddle, well, let's meddle with the culture first. We are up to our beer bellies in deterrents. We have an advertising standards authority whose rules state that drinks advertising cannot suggest that consumption of alcohol even contributes to social success. We have temporarily closed over 100 bars so far for serving underage drinkers. We have our Rules of the Road.

Good. Good. Good. We still drink, though. Where are the positive reinforcements? The sustained alcohol education campaigns? What are we doing when kids find out anecdotally and empirically that alcohol is a social lubricant? The Guinness All Ireland? Get over it.

My kids play in a GAA club that has a fine bar. The adult teams there are sponsored by a brewery. If in a few years they start coming home spancilled by alcopops, it won't be the GAA's fault. It will be mine. I'll want to know who sold them the stuff and why they felt they needed it and if the need for it is big and dangerous or if it's nothing more than what we all went through.

To fend that day off I'd be happier if their social life mingled with their sporting life; if meeting people in a sporting environment where drink is present just became natural to them, if they drank primarily around people who know them and will look out for them. I'd prefer if drinking is to be a phase that sport was a constant all through it.

Prohibition never worked. You'll never divide the world into the good children who play sports and the evil youths who drink. You'll never close off the influences which make people drink or banish the troubles which make them drink too much.

A moderate consumption of alcohol and regular sporting activity isn't a decadent lifestyle. It beats getting scuttered in the park. The problem, it seems to me, lies with shutting 'youth' off to socialise and drink in their own ghettoes, in disengaging from their lives and always blaming someone else when they become adults with adult problems.

From when I was a kid I remember an awful accident when some kids from nearby were drinking cider or something on the railtracks near Fairview and a night train ran over them. Back then, kids drank in parks and down laneways and in the dark corners at discos, and they threw up copiously before going home. It seemed glamourous and fun. It was never advertised as such. We were never educated otherwise. Nobody told us to recognise the role of alcohol or identify the warning flags when it comes to our own consumption. We never drank in adult company and it took the longest time for us to become mature about drinking.

If we have a huge cultural weakness when it comes to drink, well sport should be part of the solution, not part of the problem. Sport can be part of a healthy approach to drink. It's not an either/or situation.

Two million times when we were young we were told simply that drink was bad. It didn't work. We drank anyway. Most of us went through a phase of drinking more than was good for us. Some of us didn't pull out of it. I think we'd have had a better chance if we were introduced to drink in a different way, rather than all together left to our own devices, furtively puking and giggling down laneways after discos.

Some brands become cooler than others through advertising, but I've never met anyone who drank because of ads they've seen and I have yet to attend a sports event sponsored by Vodka Mules or whatever. Nor have I ever met anyone who killed lots of people because they saw Bruce Willis do it in a cool movie. Kids understand media and advertising instinctively. Peer pressure and cultural conditioning is different.

You can mount a thousand pulpits and tell kids that drinking isn't 'cool'.

You can shine a saintly light on the front pews where all the lads with neat partings and pioneer pins are kneeling and you can play celestial music and get those lads to thoughtfully rest their chins on the tops of their hurleys and then you can say 'Gosh, kids, now that's God's kind of cool', but you'll be drowned out by laughter. Being an outlaw is always cooler and experimenting will always be cooler. And thinking that your generation is the first to drink like hogs? Excellent!

So do we ban alcohol-related sports sponsorships and happily stick our heads back in the sand, or do we do these things: monitor ads and sponsorships; put a fixed percentage of all alcohol-related sports sponsorships into sport for kids (with no branding opportunities involved); take a chunk of the tax take on drink and divert it to coaching and pitches and educational campaigns; introduce kids to drink in a rounded, healthy, adult context?

I suspect it's a battle the GAA hasn't much appetite for. The arguments against are too pat and shrill. Pity. How do you get to be a patron anyway? Do they have their own bar? Free drink?

Salute the beloved monument that was Lar Foley

5 May 2003

News of the death of Lar Foley swung like a wrecking ball into a gentle Sunday morning.

Just this day last week Lar was made a patron of the Friends of Dublin Hurling. We awaited his arrival in the Gresham that day and when he walked in he lit the place up with his enthusiasm.

One minute we were men in a room telling Lar Foley stories. The next minute he'd arrived and we were his audience gathered around him as he told yarns, took us each down a few pegs, rubbed his hands together in that way of his and punctuated everything he was telling you with a sharp punch to your upper arm.

And yesterday there was a minute of silence for Lar in Croke Park.

You couldn't begin to catalogue the stories that men will tell about Lar this week. They belong in a book or in the living folklore of the GAA. You could spend this week in the bar in St Vincent's clubhouse and another seven days out in Lar's beloved north county and you could just listen to people talking about the man. You'll not hear the same Lar Foley story told twice.

Old games. Old rows. Old half-time speeches. Quotes from the lines that ran off his wonderfully salty tongue. Last week I heard him collar an alarmed county-board official. 'D'ya know what. If you were a duck, I wouldn't shoot ya.' Why not Lar? 'I wouldn't like my dog to pick ya up.'

It seemed to me that everywhere we walked as kids we had the giant footprints of Lar Foley ahead of us. In St Joseph's of Fairview, in St Vincent's, and, for those who were lucky enough and good enough, in Croke Park. People took the same path but nobody ever filled the space like Lar did.

He won minor county titles with St Vincent's in '55 and '56, All-Ireland minor medals with Dublin the same years and a Leinster schools title with 'Joey's' in '56. He played in senior hurling and football All Irelands and was winning championships with the club into the '70s.

And he was elder brother, of course, to Des Foley, who won a minor All-Ireland medal in 1958 on the day Lar won his first senior All Ireland. Des, whose reputation began as a Railway Cup player while he was still a schoolboy, enjoyed a reputation which was burnished faithfully by Lar, who would claim no special sporting abilities for himself but in a row might ask you earnestly if you'd ever seen Desser play and, if you hadn't, to go home and ask someone who had. On the pitch he protected Des like a lion protects his young; off the field he deprecated himself constantly to explain his brother's skills. When Des's heart gave up a few years ago, it shook a lot of the zest out of Lar for quite some time. His return to his usual ebullient self was slow but welcome. For everyone who ever came under his influence on a pitch or in a dressing room he left some part of his great passion in their heart. Personally, I was lucky. He trained the very first St Vincent's team I ever played on and we were all mesmerised by him from the moment he presented himself to us on the field beside the O'Brien Institute, his fingers thick as telephone directories.

He'd wrap his hand around a football so that it looked like a baseball and hurl it towards our chests. 'Watch for the O'Neill's sign, boys.' We were kids and not too talented either, but he stuck with us, loading us and driving us in his station wagon around the back lanes of Dublin, hauling us after him on one especially memorable trip to Coventry. Sometimes himself, Tom Walsh and Mark Wilson looked like men trying to mind mice at a crossroads, but they coached us patiently and we went from being awkward boys to being gawky teens and finally gawky, awkward men.

My regret is that I never had him as an adult mentor; never saw the true, almost frightening, passion he brought to a senior dressing room. I know men who say that it was easier to stick your head into the spot where the hurls were flying than it was to face Lar in the dressing room afterwards if he thought you'd chickened out.

He once arrived into Croke Park with a bag of new hurleys for a big game. 'Forty-five sticks in there, lads. At the end of the day I just want to be left with kindling.'

He had a highly pragmatic view of the games he played. You gave as good as you got and, if you couldn't give it, then if your team-mates were worth a lick they'd give it on your behalf.

A county final in the early '80s against O'Toole's and Lar enraged on the sideline and beyond it, persuaded to sit down only by the thought ingeniously suggested to him that O'Toole's had planned to wind him up and get him disciplined. Lar planted himself on the bench and stayed there defiantly.

There were a couple of infamous days. An afternoon in Portlaoise which he never quite lived down. And the All-Ireland hurling final of 1961, an immense regret of his. Typically, he was acting on behalf of others. Des Ferguson took a knock while lifting a ball. Lar went to deal with the transgressor, Tom Ryan.

Lar and Tom Ryan got sent off. Dublin lost by a point. It was a harsh sending off and cost Dublin the game. Lar had been performing brilliantly, outshone only perhaps by his brother at midfield.

Hurling remained his great love, though. With the St Vincent's seniors and with Dublin, his coaching was passionate and often improvised. Lads still talk about the evenings out in the north county when they'd hurl on a pitch Lar had mowed and work out in a gym he had created himself in his barn.

He nearly made the breakthrough, reaching two Leinster finals in the early '90s, losing by just two points to Kilkenny on the second occasion.

He loved it, the life, the company of GAA people, the argument and the sentiment, the possibilities. Meeting him last week was an all-too-rare treat.

He was in fine form though. Being a Patron of the Friends of Dublin Hurling seemed a fitting task for him. He was a one-man Mount Rushmore to the game in Dublin and his presence as patriarch was just right.

When I was leaving the Gresham, he administered the customary friendly thump to the arm and said with a big grin, 'Hey, don't you write bad things about me when I'm gone.' 'No true stories then, Lar?' I said. He was delighted.

Truth is, he was the toughest and the greatest, a beloved monument of a man. No one ever filled his footprints and nobody will ever repair the hole in the landscape that his parting leaves. Those easy Gaelic words were never more fitting: *Ní bheidh a leithéid ann arís.*

All aboard for the 'Chicks with Sticks!' revolution

12 May 2003

In America, when they think of sunsets and Mom's apple pie and things which America as a nation deems to be incontestably good, they often talk about fathers playing catch with sons. A baseball, an old catcher's mitt, a napkin of green grass and a father telling himself that, hey, the kid's got a good arm, just like the old man.

Where are the girls in this picture? Learning to make Mom's apple pie? Ironing the baseball uniforms? Pressing their noses up against the window thinking they could do that? Only better. Who knows? Who's ever known? Sport, the great metaphor for life, traditionally excluded girls and women as squarely as life.

What do girls do? When I was young I knew what they did. They played intricate games that involved various ways of bouncing rubber balls off brick walls while singing lyrical little songs. 'Plainy the marmalade. Plainy the marmalade.' Bounce. Catch. Bounce. Catch. Bounce. Catch. They would stand around in groups and watch each other do this from dawn to dusk. They seemed happy.

Girls had evolved, indeed, to the extent where they could also perform complicated skipping manoeuvres while singing these type of songs. 'In and out goes Saucy Bluebells, in and out goes Saucy Bluebells', and two of them would twirl the rope while a third, playing, I imagine, the role of the indecisive Saucy Bluebells, would literally jump in and out.

There was no end of real-life situations in which this skill would be useful. Perhaps it would be televised live and they would all become millionaires.

They could do these things and they could play chasing, pull hair and learn to knit. That's as far as I understood their remit, anyway. Later, they disappeared from view, only to re-emerge as fully-formed young women who were smarter than us and knew it.

I don't know for sure what changed and when it changed, but everywhere I go now I see hordes of kids carrying hurleys. Girls as often as boys. From Cabra to Donnycarney to Marino to Ballyboden to Kilmacud, girls are doing unbelievable things, they are moulding themselves into teams, expressing themselves, challenging themselves, pushing themselves. I see fathers out pucking *sliotars* around with their daughters until the girls give permission to head for home. I see girls fighting over whose sideline cut it is, arguing with refs, soloing forty yards, executing perfect blocks. Just enjoying the best sport in the world.

And it has a coolness to it. When we were kids, getting on a bus with a hurley meant hearing none-too-subtle remarks about 'boggers' and 'rednecks' and 'gahmen'. The games have a different cachet now, for some reason we can't understand but have to welcome.

Camogie, despite itself perhaps, has undergone a huge change. In those estates which teem with kids, GAA clubs and soccer clubs have always thrived, while sport for girls has always been something of an afterthought, if even that. Now, perhaps because of a change in the safety of the environment and a change in the expectation levels of girls and their parents, camogie has been in there competing for customers. Girls still play basketball and soccer and Gaelic football, but more and more of them walk around with hurleys in their hands.

Some clubs just can't get enough coaches for their mini leagues. It's intriguing and thrilling to watch. Girls are as different from boys in team situations as cats are from dogs. A dog will fetch sticks without thinking about it. A dog will pull a sled through snow without question. Just happy to be there. That's boys, the incessant tail-waggers of the sporting world. Girls have to see the point of everything.

'You're going to run out there, jab-pick the ball and solo back and handpass,' says the coach.

'Yeah? Why?' comes the answer.

But they love it. Their play is an extension of their personality, their intensity, and the will to win is sometimes frightening.

And camogie was there all along? How did they keep it a secret from the Saucy Bluebells crowd? I asked three twelve-year-olds this week what they were going to be when they got older. One surgeon (Clare), two professional hurlers (Fionnuala and Carol).

Camogie has problems, though. It's a competitive world out there and the game has more skills to be learned than any other you can think of. Takes time. Needs money. Requires patience. Gaelic football has gobbled up the imagination of much of its natural constituency. Soccer too. Fixture lists are often chaotic, with not enough games being played in summer, while minor grade is at under-16 so the sport haemorrhages good kids too early. And the game needs, not to be gender specific about it, a make-over, not to make it look like something it isn't, but for its image to begin to reflect what it has become.

Next year is the centenary of the association, and camogie is looking to put as much life into its image as it has into its game. To that end, the association has formed a committee, the average age of which is twenty-seven and which will be electrifying the sport's image over the next year or so.

This isn't unusual. Sports market themselves all the time for the better.

It's a world full of sharks out there, and the tragedy of camogie is that it has suffered for too long from its image of being something for big girls with fat ankles to do between Macra dances. It has no face, no stars, no real impact on those who don't play it or know it.

How radical are they going to be? Well, try 'Chicks with Sticks!' as a slogan. The working group (I repeat, average age twenty-seven, not a Macra dance between them) will be moving at last towards a stronger GAA/camogie alliance, with all the benefits that would bring. That alliance on a national level will change both the GAA and camogie forever.

Tests have shown that, once you've tried a GAA club with a thriving and vibrant camogie section, you'll never go back to the old 'men stewing in their own bitterness' model. The GAA club at its best is part of the community, not a men's retreat house.

Having a camogie section means the club represents the community better and opens itself up to new perspectives and new ways of thinking. We have a strange way of thinking about sport in this country. Largely, we view it the wrong way around. A Sonia O'Sullivan happens despite ourselves, really. Then we start rewarding elite athletes to make up for our earlier negligence. We don't target girls for sporting development and we don't reward them. We don't cover enough girls' sports on Monday mornings. Oddly, we don't view women as a market for sport.

It's shocking that, despite the huge impact camogie has on ordinary, day-to-day life in Ireland, the senior inter-county leagues and championships in the sport are still available for sponsorship, and no one has taken those competitions by the neck, tagged their name to them and committed the rest of their spend to telling the stories and revealing the personalities.

Girls don't stand up laneways and throw rubber balls against walls anymore. You hardly ever see them skipping. They are housebound and baby-sat by the Gameboy and the TV. But, let loose, the chicks with sticks get to play on teams and grow and express themselves strenuously.

Girls have discovered camogie for themselves. They are waiting now for the rest of the world to discover them.

Life begins at 100.

The Dub prepares for attack
on Clones

23 June 2003

Not many of you will have been to Ushuaia on the island of Tierra del Fuego, the southernmost tip of the Americas. Fewer still will have made the journey by road from there to Prudhoe Bay in Alaska, the northernmost tip of the Americas.

Many of you will travel from Dublin to Clones next Saturday, however, and, for the true Dub, it's pretty much the same thing.

It's never easy being a Dub. It's an endless cycle of worries and duties.

PAYE (or FarmAid, as heroic metropolitans call it) and filling the coffers of the GAA are but two of The Dub's quotidian tasks. For thanks, The Dub is constantly depicted as an irascible fool in radio and TV ads, and right now the GAA wants to partition the city.

The Dub has only his county's GAA prowess and laughing at Enda Kenny to lighten his burden. Occasionally The Dub must set out on knightly quests such as this coming one to Clones. It goes hard on The Dub, but it must be done, this questing.

People don't understand. The Dub is a hibernator by creature. There may be just 5,000 Dubs visible at a winter league match in

Donnycarney, but, in the summer, well over ten times that number need tickets to big matches. This is why being made to play in Clones is so unfair. Deliberately, Clones has refused to build a 100,000-seater stadium. It's further proof of the anti-Dublin bias which has always nourished the GAA hobgoblins.

The Dub heading off to Clones does so with trepidation. Many Dubs still wake up crying at night after finding out too late just how far away Thurles was a couple of years back. Arduous and heartbreaking was the questing back then. You still see younger Dubs out joyriding boyishly in T-shirts which say Hard Rock Café, Durrow or My Da Went Thru Urlingford and All I Got was This Lousy T-shirt.

The Dub had been promised that the questing would be as happy as that of 1983, when he overcame language and cultural hurdles and expeditioned to Cork. Not to be.

Clones is tricky. It could be in Ireland, it could be in the UK. Must The Dub cross borders? International datelines? Is there a chance of weightlessness?

What about the G-forces upon re-entry? Will there be arseboxing there? It's not that The Dub isn't better prepared than a paranoid boy scout. Typically, The Dub likes to leave his castle a full hour or so before a game. He does this in order to have a few social tinctures with the brethren along the way. Any questing requiring greater organisational skills than that is difficult, however.

If you've been in Clones on non-match days, it's a tidy enough little town, edgy though. Prim, with the streak of madness that Pat McCabe has tapped into. The Dub believes he travels with a mandate to brighten up such places, whether they want to be brightened up or not. Much as kids delight to hear the jingle jangle tune an approaching ice-cream van makes, so The Dub imagines that whole villages come alive when they hear a massed chorus of 'We Are Dubs, We Are Dubs. We Are, We Are, We Are Dubs.'

For its part, Clones will see the hordes of questing Dubs as pillaging aliens bent on the extermination of a way of life. It may be dour, but it is a way of life. They will heap abuse upon The Dubs and discourage The Dubs from lounging about in their gardens. This process is called having the crack with the locals.

The Dub has a medical condition which causes him to become easily waylaid by the need for gargle.

On longer trips this can cause difficulties, but the more sensible Dub operates a system of short stoppages when six of the seven occupants of a Cortina drink above the legal limit but the seventh abstains or limits his consumption to below the legal limit. This person is the designated driver and the duty rotates among the occupants of the car so that everybody arrives safely but also in high spirits.

This sensible approach to drinking is a necessary fortification. The Dub knows that the rest of the world is lying in wait in order to sandbag him. For instance, the unsatisfactory location of Clones will, by 4.15 on Saturday afternoon, be adequate proof to carlocked Dubs that the oul' Gah is creatively dastardly in the ways it devises to get up the nostril of The Dub.

My own grandfather had an especially developed view of this. He used tell me that there were three circles in the GAA and that no Dublin man would ever get near the innermost circle. It has yet to be proven to me this isn't the case.

From those of us who travel to Clones frequently, here are a few tips. If you are reading this and you haven't yet left Dublin, you will arrive sooner if you park in Finglas and walk the rest of the way.

Don't leave yourself time to see the museums. Despite Clones's aspirations to become European City of Culture, frankly, the museums aren't great.

Bring your own broccoli. People in Monaghan don't eat vegetables. That's why Paddy Kavanagh left. They won't grow in the stony grey soil apparently. Instead, a big game in Clones is seen as a festival of meat-eating. If on the way home you drop into the Four Seasons in Monaghan town and consume their entire mixed grill, you will have eaten more meat in one day than an adult lion consumes in a lifetime of dining on wildebeest.

In St Tiernach's Park, the side of the ground with the big steep hill on it is nearest the town. When lying down to sleep on the Hill, point your feet towards the field and your head towards the summit. Too many fans lying sideways has caused Grand Duke Lyons and his men to emerge from the other side of the ground.

The Hill is the best place from which to observe that juicy half-time tunnel action.

Remember, in Ulster they play by different rules. In Ulster, a tackle is legal up to the point wherein a tackling player may emerge with the gallstones of the man who was originally in possession. A tackle is only late if there is no hot water left in the showers at the time when the tackle takes place. Sutures are considered effete. Heading to casualty in an ambulance is an affectation likely to draw derision.

Finally, people outside Dublin often have difficulty seeing how a Dublin All Ireland would be 'good for the GAA'. Let it lie.

No time to draw breath

11 August 2003

In Wexford, when old grandfathers dandle little ones on their knees in forty years time, they'll talk about 1996 and how it was the Riverdance of sport and they'll talk about 2003 and how it was the summer of staying alive.

Between the yarns of glory and songs of survival they'll have imparted a good deal of what it's like to be a Wexford hurling person.

They'll talk about brave Larry Murphy and how he got his old hands to so many dropping balls in the dying minutes but couldn't set the net blazing. They'll talk about time trickling away. About Cork hitting four wides towards the death, about how they were so absorbed they never worried about traffic. And then Damien Fitzhenry's puck-out, Mitch Jordan's pass and Rory McCarthy's goal.

And forty years hence in Cork? Who knows what they'll be saying? This summer could end in glory or tragedy yet and neither is likely to dent the way future blood-and-bandage generations feel about themselves. Confidence is non-negotiable by the Lee.

They'll be playing this one again at Croke Park, on Saturday, the same day Ireland take on Wales in a World Cup warm-up over at Lansdowne Road.

Whichever way the replay of this All-Ireland semifinal goes, the game will be spoken about for generations. It was epic and beautiful and it conjured an ending to fit the whole. It was the latest instalment in a hurling relationship that stretches back almost fifty years to the days of Ring and Foley. It left our impressions of both teams vastly enhanced.

Of Wexford in particular. This season they have been like a car with a jumpy battery. Some days they purr. Some days they are flat. They have some venerable features but the restoration of various veterans to the side seemed only to highlight the inadequacies of youth. Until yesterday we'd seen the kids but we hadn't seen the whizz.

Together they hurled up a storm yesterday. If you ever doubted the influence of bloodlines and breeding, the pace and touch of the two Jacob brothers ended the argument. They had the touch of their father and the touch of Oulart men, as exemplified elsewhere by the peerless Liam Dunne. And Mitch Jordan, who seems to have spent a long time at the door clearing his throat, finally stepped into the parlour yesterday. He had 1–3 of his own and coolly set up that last goal.

Cork, perhaps because they were more highly rated yesterday morning, will have harder questions to ask today. They played superbly for patches, but, with a two-point lead heading towards the death, they came over all prodigal and squandered four point chances just for the hell of it.

Their half-back line didn't do what it says on the tin and the successful restoration of Diarmuid O'Sullivan to the full-back position wasn't enough to banish the concerns about Pat Mulcahy, the incumbent.

Yet it would be churlish to pick over the entrails so soon. Mostly, this game was filled with good things. The coltish brilliance of Setanta Ó hAilpín was rewarded with 1–3. His brother, Sean Óg, came into the game as it grew and hit such a plenitude of long, raking diagonal passes to his brother, he is in danger of becoming known as Setanta's Little Helper.

John Gardiner had a difficult time from placed balls with the new *sliotar* but his four points from play were all exceptional. And Joe Deane? It's not that Daragh Ryan had a bad day – he didn't, he picked plenty of high ones and swept away lots of balls with rare style and confidence – but Joe Deane ended up with 1–7, all but four points of it from play. And O'Sullivan got through a mountain of work in the second half, even late on when Murphy, working himself into the ground, managed to get his hand to a few clearances which came down snow-tipped and dangerous.

Both sides went away with their regrets and their sweet memories. Almost 60,000 people left with the intention of begging, stealing or borrowing to get to the replay.

'It was a game we could have won and a game we could have lost,' mused Cork's Donal O'Grady. 'It was a fair result. If they'd have had a bit of luck they could have won. Yet we were three points up, having said that, and our shooting was a bit wayward. Maybe if we'd have carried it on the stick and got a handy little free…'

And his thoughts drifted off to the vast continent of what might have been and what could have been. John Conran was in slightly more chipper form down the corridor. Underdog's privilege.

'My heart specialist is being paid overtime,' he smiled. 'The lads are well used to being down. Every game we've played we've been down four or five points. We just took longer than usual to come back!'

Managers aren't permitted smiles before their work is fully done and he soon sobered up with memories of 2001. 'We were in this position before, though. We did this against Tipp two years ago and lost in the replay. We have no intention of doing that again.'

Indeed the echoes of two years ago are interesting. Rory McCarthy goaled that day as well. And Wexford were five points down late on before they pulled it back. Six days later, it rained and Wexford were ragged. They lost two players to red cards, lost all composure and lost the game by eleven points.

That's not a story grandfathers will recite, but it's one Conran will be telling over and over this week.

Family affair that breaks into the world of the mythical

13 September 2003

In Semple they were never boys. Always giants. Hurling and flaking. Driving and shouting. Striding the world. Every sweet day the same. Ignoring all injunctions to go handy, to rest up, to take care. Obeying only the sun, its morning call, its evening farewell. Dinner in between. The posts were steel with a wooden crossbar. Still are. Sometimes their mother, Emeli, would stand underneath them goaltending, refereeing, threatening the sanction of 'No Dinner' for anyone who flaked too hard or tried too little. Five of them on summer days in Blarney, roaring in Fijian in a garden called Semple.

And the *sliotars* would escape. Fugitives from the Ó hAilpín fury. Off with them, scarpering into the long grass of the Osborne farm beyond, where they would be munched eventually by agricultural machinery. Within the jurisdiction the boys had an ingenious *sliotar*-recovery system.

Goats. They'd tether one of their two goats near where a *sliotar* was last seen and, in half a day, the animal would have eaten all the grass around the ball. Hey presto! 'They're gone about a year now,' says Setanta of the goats. 'Passed away. You'd miss them around.'

'They saved us a few bob alright,' says Sean Óg. 'Arrah, most of the balls would have been compliments of Pairc Uí Chaoimh anyway,' says Setanta with a huge impulsive laugh. 'Myself and Theu, we had a thing going when I was young and he was playing. He'd hit all the balls out to me behind the goals.' As long they are hurling they reckon the goalposts will always be there. Emeli christened it Semple long ago and it became the field where their dreams took wings.

This summer, Sean Óg and Setanta have outgrown boyhood dreams. Tomorrow they will have seventy minutes of outsized reality. Sean Óg, the swashbuckling wing back. Setanta, the lightning rod of the Cork attack, the hand that reaches, the legs that dance. 'In the dressing room we say I take the flakes and Joe [Deane] takes the scores!' says Setanta. 'That's what Semple out there is for,' says Sean. 'Mum would go in goal. She's no Brendan Cummins, but she'd get something to it. Too many goals and it's no dinner. So we'd go for points. There's no flaking like what we did to each other out there.'

The teams were always the same; eldest and youngest vs the middle pair. Sean Óg and Aisaki vs Theu and Setanta. If somebody was missing, it was every man for himself. Once, years ago, Sean Óg threw up the ball and Aisaki came in and blocked early. The ball was gone. Sean Óg's swing unhindered. 'I split him. Huge gash above the eye.'

'You split him that day,' says Setanta. 'And about two years later I split him on the other eye. We still laugh about it. I whipped on the ball, he slid in and I missed him. Next we went again. He slid; I pulled. I hit him a flake. The blood started gushing. We rushed him to hospital.' Rushed is a qualified term.

Their Dad was working. Emeli doesn't drive. The boys were too young to steer a car, so they improvised a Bobby Ryan bandage, wrapped it on Aisaki's head and walked the couple of miles into Blarney, then caught the bus to Mercy Hospital.

Sean Óg was fifteen at the time. He was in charge of the expedition. By the time they got to Mercy, Aisaki looked as if he'd laid his head down on a landmine.

Blood everywhere. Only a family could enjoy telling that story as much as the Ó hAilpíns do.

If Semple doesn't tell you enough about what kind of family Sean Ó hAilpín dreamed of having when he was labouring in Australia and Fiji, then two minutes in the homestead will. None of the homogenised units and surfaces that make every house look the same as every other house.

This is a home. Faded cuttings concerning Fermanagh football and its readiness hang on the walls. Old All-Star selections. Fijian souvenirs. Outside in the shed there are a million hurleys. Three million *sliotars*. Jerseys flap on the line. Mantelpieces groan with medals and trophies. Sean met Emeli while he was working on the small island of Rotuma back in the 1980s. They married. They moved to Sydney.

Finally one rainy winter they moved to Ireland and Fairhill in North Cork. Sean Óg was eleven or so at the time. He joined Na Piarsaigh. Went to North Mon. His three brothers followed. The girls, Soroti and Etain, went similar paths. Now the house is a babel of language: Irish, Fijian, and English for the visitors. Everyone speaks with passion and enthususiasm. GAA is the common language. They could never have known what they would become. Two of the sons are superstars. Another lives in America. The last, the hapless Aisaki, played in Croke Park twice this summer for Cork minor sides.

When they came to Cork first, it wasn't the dreamland that had been promised them. Sean still gets asked how he met Emeli, how she came to be here. He likes to amuse himself with stories about how he had to go to meet the tribal chief and he was set several challenges and conquests. Sounds better than saying that she was behind the reception desk in the place he was working on.

In Cork, Sean Óg played rugby league. Nobody else in Cork did. Sean Óg spoke with a thick Sydney accent. Nobody else in Cork did. Other stuff too. Not that they consider it worth speaking about now.

'Arrah, we would have got a bit but not much,' Says Sean. 'In fairness, even Dad knew the scenario. "Take it," he said. "You'll be subject to it." He said to take it and get on with it.

'Living up Fairhill at the start you'd get a few comments. Ye're only black cunts or whatever. We just went on. Because to be honest there was another twenty hanging behind if we didn't. Then, since we started hurling with Na Piarsaigh, it just dwindled away.'

'A fella once told me,' says Setanta, 'that if someone is bothered going out of his way to call you something, it's a compliment in a way. I used smile at them!' And on the pitch they thrived to the extent that they just got hurling abuse. "I'll take you're head off, if you do that again." More compliments. The strangeness of the world they left behind, the strangeness of their lives now, these things seldom occur to them. Last summer Emeli went home to Rotuma for the first time in fourteen years.

There are about two and a half thousand people on the island and they live with sand between their toes and the sun on their backs. Emeli brought a video of Sean Óg playing in an All-Ireland final. They found a machine to put the video in. All of Rotuma was shocked. Not by the stickwork. By the crowd. 'Are those all really people?' they asked.

'It was a good summer for Mum to go,' says Sean Óg laughing. 'Cork were beaten early. She didn't have championship work.' Championship work. Emeli is about it now. She asks if you'll have pasta. Her boys say no, you'll have dinner. She's lifting big steaks from the cooker to the plates. Each steak weighs as much as a small child. Then suddenly there is a range of vegetables on the table, a mountain range. The potatoes at the top of the pile are cooling at altitude.

The pasta is there too, but, just in case that's not enough, Emeli produces a large colander filled with roast chicken. Every time the Ó hAilpíns sit at table, it's a holocaust in the chicken world. 'The day we quit hurling is the day we all become forty stone,' says Setanta. 'Just eat,' says Emeli.

The house is filled with food and with hurling and with talk and with love. Setanta is hunched over his steak. The kid is something new to hurling.

Something luminous and effervescent. Good-looking beyond reason, talented beyond fairness and unpredictable with it. They'll love him or they'll hate him, but they'll never have to use his surname.

There was Sean Óg. There is Setanta. John Allen, the Cork selector, reckons Setanta will have his own cult at the end of the year. He'll certainly have his imitators. Back in Blarney, he takes the longest in the bathroom in the morning because of the Del Piero, the pencil-thin beard that delineates his jaw. Much eye-rolling around the table. 'Ah, the Del Piero. It's only a five-minute job once you have the gimmicks.' 'Every morning, though?' 'Sure it keeps me busy. That's why I'm late for work.' 'He has to get it right,' says Sean Óg. 'He has to get an examiner to look at it. Usually Aisaki. He's The Examiner.' 'That's because Aisaki is the real Don Juan in our family,' says Setanta.

Sean remembers days long ago and not so long ago training with the club, flat out and earnest as ever and Setanta would be hanging off the goalposts upside down. Abie Allen, the coach, would be driven to dementia.

'Setanta, stop hanging off the goalposts! Get down, ya divil!' He was well known always. He was the fella who'd get the *sliotars* behind the goal and hit them back out. At the end of the night they'd throw him a ball for his troubles.

That and the couple he had in his pocket would make it worthwhile.

Setanta was always the wildest. For everything. For hurling, for women, for the *craic*. 'I'm a person who keeps driving on,' he says, elaborating on the hurling part. 'I've lost a few county medals and a few other medals. You think life is over. It's the fella who goes back the next day and keeps practising that gets there. Once you learn from it as a person, you'll grow and winning will be sweeter.' In the meantime, it's hard being young and devoted to the monastery of Cork hurling. The vows chafe against a young man's instincts. Evenings driving through the village of Blarney, Sean Óg and Setanta have the windows rolled down and there are fellas of their own age loitering at the bus stop. The hurlers can smell them. They can inhale the fragrance of whatever has been slapped on all over.

Some days the brothers will drive on and say nothing. Other days one will turn to the other and say: 'Fuck it, boy, what are we at this for? Is it worth it?'

'To be honest it is,' says Sean Óg. 'You've got to make a difference in this life. Being involved in sport has made a difference for us compared to the fella standing at the bus stop on a Saturday night going into town. A night before the Munster final we're worrying and not sleeping and we're looking at the fella who's just worrying if he'll pull somebody. You'd wish it was you sometimes.'

'But listen,' says Setanta. 'As Donal Óg Cusack says, it's memories of matches and fellas you played with that you'll bring to your grave. He's right. That's Donal Óg's famous quote.' Has Setanta got a famous quote yet? 'Give the ball to me!' says Sean Óg.

Setanta has always been, and still is, a work in progress. In Na Piarsaigh, in Cork underage teams, in college. Always developing. At the time when Sean Óg went to North Mon, it was a bona fide fame academy for hurling. Times are harder there now. It took Setanta four or five years to win a Harty match. Just one. 'A great game. We beat Limerick CBS in the first round. Donal O'Grady was manager. Stop boy! Waterford Institute of Technology made me feel like a better player again. What brought me on was going down to IT hurling with Tipp, Kilkenny, Wexford people. The amount of hurling you do. Hurling with Henry Shefflin, Brian Dowling, J.J. Delaney. Great hurlers. You look at them on telly and think you actually played with them and fought for a cause with them. To be meeting them in a final is sweet.'

In WIT, he became 'Santy'. Too many players couldn't get their tongue around his name when he was in possesion and they wanted to stress how urgently they required a pass. Santy he was and Santy he is to much of the hurling world he has been introduced to this year. A year late, according to Sean Óg. 'To be honest, he should have been on the team last year. There were trial games and Setanta would clean up, but he was never picked. Last year, when I think of it, for the Waterford match he was hurley carrier. And he was cleaning up in A vs B matches.

'I remember one match and all the players were saying he definitely has to play. They didn't bring him on the panel even. He was involved with the 21s and they got knocked out and they asked him would he do hurley carrier again for the Galway game.' And? 'First plane out of here,' says Setanta. He went to New York. Labouring on sites. Hurling with Limerick. Footballing with Kerry.

Living with Theu in the Bronx. Watched Cork and Galway on the telly in a pub. Came back with a huge hunger.

'I played the summer with Theu. I wanted to come back and play for Cork. Sean Óg has been my driving point. As a young fella I always looked up to him. Everyone loved him. He was the kiddie on the block when I was young, now he's telling me what to do, giving me great encouragement. I love going training with him. We've a bond between us, brothers. A bond that will never be broken.' They talk hurling all the time. It dominates the house. Not a day that goes by without training, matches, treatment, something. The replays are made over the kitchen table, then out on Semple. They talk about each other easily and with ferocious loyalty. Setanta remembers Sean Óg breaking through to stardom and the buzz of it, the added weight of all fraternal advice, the thrill of just standing behind the goals at Cork training, watching his brother.

Sean Óg thinks his own pre-eminence has made it harder for Setanta. 'People expect things from him too quickly. It's a burden, but he's carried it great. They think he should have something scored before he ties his laces.'

'The best advice I got was from Joe Deane,' says Setanta. 'Before my very first game, against Clare, we were on the bus. Joe said if you touch the ball today it's a bonus. That stuck. If I touch it. If I bring a man away. "It's up to the old fellas," he said. At the time I was thinking this fella now thinks I'm cat – I'll be doing well to touch a ball. He thinks O'Grady picked me because I went to the Mon and we bate his team in the Harty.

'After the game I realised what he meant though. That day I was head down and the sweat was dripping off me. I was scared, boy.' He was scared and the abiding memory of him that day is getting a massive dunt in the corner of the field early on and him leaping to his feet shaking his fists, suddenly energised beyond fear. Everything beyond that is legend.

'Listen,' says Sean, leaning across the table. 'In this house it's an undisputed fact that, pound for pound, Setanta is the best product of the family. We'd all have our own strengths but he has all those in the one.' He pauses. Takes a drink of milk. 'I can see why he was Dad's number one pet for years,' Emeli joins in. 'No doubt! The golden boy!' 'He got away with murder,' says Sean Óg. 'Too cute. He's a special kid like.' Now everywhere he goes people want a part of him. He loves it. Special upbringing. 'It's good,' he says. 'Nice that people have the bit of interest, in fairness. Memories like that are what you'll have when you are older. People took the time to talk to you and see how you were getting on once upon a time.' Once upon a time, right at the beginning.

'You know,' says Sean Óg, 'even when I was that age I wasn't as…' 'Wired to the moon?' says Setanta. 'No. Outgoing. He's like a stallion you can't keep on a rope.' Sean Óg. School. Club. Home. That's the radius of his life, he says.

It's a life that's reached the mid-point in hurling terms.

Once upon a time he was thrilled just to wear red. Thrilled for Abie Allen and Tom Walsh in the club. His glory was theirs. Now he's a lifer, a long-haul man. He's glad to see Na Piarsaigh men coming up behind him. Setanta keeps him fresh. The older he got the more cynical he got and then suddenly this summer he had this young fella beside him who had wide eyes and scarcely a worry in the world. He'd listen to his comments and say, Jesus Christ but it's good to be young like.

It's knocked a few years off him though.

He's protective but in a big picture way. He didn't keep Setanta out of the Paddy Power fiasco as was widely reported earlier in the year. It just happened that way.

The man came calling, collecting the hurleys of the relevant players. In Blarney that night Setanta was marked absent. He'd gone to play for the Cork under-21s against Tipperary. The sort of date upon which a man brings his best sticks.

Sean Óg gave the man a few planks from the shed, but when Setanta came in and learned that his inferior hurleys were up in Dublin for tattooing, he realised he had only one thing to do. Get Sean Óg to call. Paddy Power were good about it and it's small beer.

Sean Óg worries about other stuff. His own biggest mistake was not being careful. He had the arrogance of a kid when it came to his own body. Thought he was bulletproof. Invincible.

On the day he's thinking of, he drove to Dublin instead of taking the train.

'Dad told me that Thursday to get the train. To do the smart thing. Guinness were doing this promotion in Dublin. I said, "Arrah, I'll drive." It cost me two years. Before that I never had a hamstring, a groin. The last thing I thought was I'd be in a car crash.'

He was rushing home. He was near Copland, closing in on Templemore. Invincible and rash. He went to overtake a fella where he shouldn't have. Suddenly, there was a car coming the other way. Blue, with lights flashing.

Sean Óg couldn't tuck back in. He said the quickest prayer, hit the brake and braced himself. Serious pain suggested he was alive. He opened his eyes.

'Yeah. Fuck it, I'm alive. I was in shock. There was this excruciating pain in the right leg. I had chinos on. There was a lump near the pocket.'

His kneecap had shot, gone like a hockey puck inside his leg. His car was written off. The blue car was written off. Its five occupants poured out of its doors while Sean Óg was locating his patella.

'They came out safe and sound and I'm happy with that. If one of them had passed away, you couldn't live with it. You couldn't go on. I was conscious. Pain. Shock. The people I hit came over and tore down the door on my car. The car I was overtaking had zoomed off. There was just the two of us. Me and them.

They opened up the door. To be honest, they were in shock too. The driver had a face on him. He was going to kick the shit out of me and rightly so. What got me off was they recognised me. Tipp lads.'

'Fuck. You're not Sean Óg.'

'Yeah.'

'You got a match Sunday. Limerick. Don't think you'll make it.'

'Maybe.'

They pulled him out. He was screaming. His right leg buckled. They carried him to the ditch, sat him down and called 999 from his mobile. He never heard from them again.

'I got operated on. I'd ruptured the patella tendon. They had to get the kneecap back down and stitch the tendon.'

Cork were due to play Limerick on that Sunday. They lost by a point on the day when Diarmuid O'Sullivan scored that point from about 500 yards. Sean Óg watched from hospital. Brian Corcoran was missing too, finger broken in a match up in Enniscorthy. Sean Óg watched on telly and then faced defeat. Summer was empty.

'When the cast came off, my leg was wasted away. It was like an image from the Third World. I had to go through rehab. I got in touch with Ger Hartman. He was brilliant and he was realistic. I'd thought that if Cork got over Limerick I'd be back for the Munster final that year. When they said twelve months, the jaw dropped like a fella in the cartoons.'

He came back in 2002. He could run, but he couldn't get into games. His touch was red raw. No speed. No stick work. All gone. He'd thought to prove them all wrong, to show he could be as good again, but it was a disaster of a year.

'I'm only looking for the form now. The way I look at it, the old fella is done and dusted. I'm the new version now. With a rehab knee. I play the percentages. I loved covering for everyone, all over the place. Now I do my own patch. I do that and that's it. That's all I can hope for out of it. Days like we had this year made it worthwhile.

'I just wanted to get back to prove to myself that I could. This summer, the knee is as good as it ever will be. In the winter, with the cold, it hurts. I've changed my training habits, I warm up out in Semple here with Setanta before going in training. I use hot water bottles, the ice bath. The knee will never be the same, but I can run, turn and jump. It's enough.'

Growing up in this house, if they wanted a pair of boots Sean would reach into his pocket and find whatever it took. Fifty, sixty punts. Whatever. If they wanted Mars bars, there was no jingle forthcoming. No money for rubbish.

Sean had a dream of Ireland and Irishness. His family lived it with him. He drove his boys in and out to training, waiting in the car for them to finish. He'd often watch Cork training sessions rather than drive home and have to turn around and drive back to Cork almost immediately. It was the habit of a lifetime.

Most mornings he'd be out the gap and down the road at 8 am and he'd collect the boys in the evenings and bring them training and wait and watch because he'd no time to go home.

His boys each outgrew the other and all of them outgrew him. Sean Óg was surpassed by Theu who is overshadowed by Setanta who is just beginning to be eclipsed by Aisaki.

For years he brought his boys to games and afterwards shook his head and sang the same lament. 'I don't care if you have no ability, what I can't understand is a fella not going out and not giving one hundred per cent.'

They laugh at him now. His love for Fermanagh. His old-fashioned *grá* for the GAA. But he and Emeli are at the centre of their solar system.

'Dad always forgot to tell us we had some ability. That's what he always kept secret. Everything for us was just giving one hundred cent. It was kind of a surprise to grow up and find we had some ability as well. Dad gave us that work ethic.'

Hence they think Aisaki has great ability, but, being the youngest, growing up with stars, maybe the work ethic is slower.

How do you think you played? Setanta? Brilliant! Three goals. And Sean would be shaking his head slowly.

'Did you count the balls you wasted? You forgot what you were told the last game. Did you learn nothing?' And with talks like that and Emeli roaring in Fijian from the sideline, they grew up, grew towards this summer and tomorrow.

What a unique gift they are to the game. On semifinal day in Croke Park they were to be found last out of the Cork dressing room, two sublime contributions behind them, each wondering if the other had the hair gel. They wondered *as Gaeilge*, switching to English when approached.

Dinner is over now in their home of hurling. Language becomes fragmented as people rise. Fijian by the sink. Gaeilge trailing into the sitting room. They could play forever, they think, and not have another summer like this.

Donal O'Grady met their passion and matched it this summer. In the dressing room this afternoon, his words to them will be in Irish as always. They laugh when they think of him badgering them in training. A ball will be picked one-handed. '*Dhá laimh in ainm Dé,*' he will bellow.

On Sean Óg's first day back training this year, he forgot about Donal O'Grady, not having seen him since school days. He was ten minutes late.

'Ah, Donal, good to see ya,' I said, 'but he fecked me out of it.
Jimmy Barry, Tom Cash, anyone. There'd have been nothing said.
For Donal, training at seven means seven on the pitch. If you're late,
he'll warn you and he'll let you know he can get someone else
who'll come at seven. After the first incident you just tell yourself
you'll never be late again.

'With other managers it was always "Lads, you're good enough,
go out and do it". With Donal we analyse the opposition, what
they've got, what they do. This, that and the other. He runs the shop
like a school. Abide by the rules. If you don't like it, move to a new
school. This year, well it's hard for us older lads to grasp. We're not
used to it. We're used to taking it seriously on the pitch but being late
for training or having a bit of *craic*. If you're chatting when you are
stretching, it's "Lads, I hear you talking. You're not focused, lads." It
wouldn't be popular but it's gotten results.'

It pays off. O'Grady lives to see Cork doing well. Bottom line. He
told the squad early this year that Croke Park was built for Cork to be
playing there. That they should be there every year. They went home
and thought about it. If Kilkenny could do it, Cork could.

The Ó hAilpín boys list off the influences. O'Grady is high on the
list for both of them. Shared language. Shared love.

In Blarney, life is simple and life is Semple. Hurling is family and
hurling is oxygen.

'We live it,' says Sean Óg, 'twelve months of the year really.' 'But
winter is easier,' says Setanta. 'Winter is our summer time. We might
get to see Cork city on a Saturday night.'

'Yeah,' says Sean Óg softly, *'An rud is annamh is iontach.'*